SONG LYRICS AND POEMS

VOLUME III

HERTHEY HILL

authorHOUSE®

AuthorHouse™
1663 Liberty Drive
Bloomington, IN 47403
www.authorhouse.com
Phone: 1 (800) 839-8640

Published by AuthorHouse 03/03/2017

ISBN: 978-1-5246-2147-6 (sc)
ISBN: 978-1-5246-2146-9 (e)

CONTENTS

A BLIND DATE

VERSE ONE:
      ONE OF THE WORST TIMES ... I BELIEVE I EVER HAD ...
WAS GOING ON A BLIND DATE ... THAT REALLY TURNED OUT BAD.
      A FRIEND GOT IT FOR ME ... AND I JUST COULD'NT WAIT ...
      TO MEET A VERY SPECIAL GIRL ... ON MY FIRST BLIND DATE.

VERSE TWO:
      WHEN I GOT TO WHERE ... WE WERE SUPPOSED TO MEET ..
IT WAS HARD TO BELIEVE ... AND MY HEART FELL TO MY FEET.
      SHE HAD REAL SHORT HAIR ... AND BIG BUCK TEETH ...
SHE LOOKED LIKE SOMETHING ... THAT WAS DRUG IN OFF THE
STREET.

VERSE THREE:
      YOU COULD'NT KISS HER LIPS ... HER TEETH WAS IN THE WAY ...
AND HER HAIR LOOKED LIKE ... A PILE OF STACKED UP HAY.
      AND THEN WHEN SHE TRIED TO SMILE ... SHE BIT HER
      BOTTOM LIP ...
AND I KNEW RIGHT THEN IT WAS TIME ... FOR ME TO TAKE A TRIP.

VERSE FOUR:
      IT DID'NT TAKE VERY LONG ... FOR ME TO COME UP WITH A
      LIE ...
I SAID I HAD TO GET BACK HOME ... ONE OF MY FAMILY IS ABOUT
TO DIE.
      SHE SAID SHE UNDERSTOOD ...AND THEN SHE SHE WALKED
      AWAY ...
AND I NARROWLY ESCAPED ... THAT BLIND DATE THAT DAY.

VERSE FIVE:
      THAT BUCK TEETH BLIND DATE ... NEARLY TOOK MY LIFE THAT
      DAY ...
I TOLD MYSELF RIGHT THEN ... THAT I'LL FIND ANOTHER WAY.
      I DID'NT KNOW WHAT WAS IN STORE ... AND THE PRICE I
      HAD PAY ...
BUT THAT MEMORY WILL STICK WITH ME ... UNTIL MY DYING DAY.

CHORUS:

      THERE WILL BE NO MORE ... BLIND DATES FOR ME ...

MY FIRST AND LAST BLIND DATE ... WENT DOWN IN HISTORY.

      I WILL NEVER FORGET THAT DAY ... MY HEAD WENT SPINNING
      AROUND ...

THAT BLIND DATE NEARLY TURNED ... MY WHOLE WORLD UPSIDE
DOWN.

A BORNED AGAIN BELIEVER

VERSE ONE:

    HE ALWAYS DID WHATEVER ... AND ANYTHING HE WANTED TO ...

NOBODY WOULD STAND UP ... AND TELL HIM WHAT TO DO.

    SAY SOMETHING TO HIM ... AND HE WAS READY TO FIGHT.

AND HE REALLY DID'NT CARE ... IF IT WAS WRONG OR RIGHT.

VERSE TWO:

    BUT IN HIS HEART HE BELIEVED ... THERE WAS A BETTER WAY..

HE KNEW THE LIFE HE LIVED... WOULD HAVE TO CHANGE SOMEDAY.

    HE PLAYED AROUND WITH THE DEVIL ... THEN HE BEGAN TO SWAY...

HE TOLD THE DEVIL HE WAS TIRED... OF LIVING FOR HIM THAT WAY.

CHORUS:

    FOR THE FIRST TIME IN HIS LIFE ... HE MADE THE DEVIL MAD ...

AND FOR THE NEW LIFE HE FOUND ... HE WAS REALLY GLAD.

    GOD GAVE HIM SOMETHING ... TO LIVE AND DIE FOR ...

AND WHEN HE LEAVES THIS LIFE ... HE'LL BE ON HEAVEN'S SHORE.

VERSE THREE:

    HE HAD HEARD OF A MAN ... THAT THEY CALLED JESUS ...

WHO HAD LIVED AND DIED ... AND SHED HIS BLOOD FOR US.

    JESUS TOLD US OF A PLAN ... OF A MUCH BETTER LIFE ...

YOU MUST BE A BORNED AGAIN BELIEVER ... TO RECIEVE THE PRIZE.

VERSE FOUR:

    HE READ HIS WORDS ... AND HE TOOK THEM TO HIS HEART ...

GOD SAID IF YOU LET HIM COME IN ... HE WILL NEVER EVER PART.

    SO HE FELL DOWN ON MY KNEES ... AND REPENTED OF HIS SIN ...

AND THEN HE FOUND A NEW LIFE ... WHEN HE INVITED JESUS IN.

CHORUS:

FOR THE FIRST TIME IN HIS LIFE ... HE MADE THE DEVIL MAD ...

AND FOR THE NEW LIFE HE FOUND ... HE WAS REALLY GLAD.

GOD GAVE HIM SOMETHING ... TO LIVE AND DIE FOR ...

AND WHEN HE LEAVES THIS LIFE ... HE'LL BE ON HEAVEN'S SHORE.

A CALF ROPIN' COWBOY

VERSE ONE:

A MAN FROM NORTH CAROLINA ... ALWAYS HAD DREAMS ...
HE WANTED TO BE A COWBOY ... AND LET OFF SOME STEAM.
SO HE WENT OUT TO TEXAS ... AND JOINED THE RODEO ...
HE BECAME A CALF ROPIN' COWBOY ... THAT EVERYBODY KNOWED.

VERSE TWO:

IN THE OUTSIDE WORLD ... HE WAS JUST A LITTLE MAN ...
BUT IN THE RODEO HE WAS A GIANT ... WITH A ROPE IN HIS HAND.
WHEN THEY LET THE CALVES LOOSE ... HE WOULD ROPE AND
THROW ...
HE BECAME THE FAVORITE CALF ROPIN' COWBOY ... IN THE RODEO.

CHORUS:

HE WAS A CALF ROPIN' COWBOY ... WORKING AT THE RODEO ...
IT WAS HIS WAY OF LIFE ... AND THE ONLY LIFE HE KNOWED.
HE FOLLOWED HIS LIFE'S DREAMS ... WITH HIS WIFE BY HIS
SIDE ...
HE WAS A CALF ROPIN' COWBOY ... UNTIL THE DAY THAT HE DIED.

VERSE THREE:

     HE WAS A GOOD CHRISTIAN MAN ... AND HE LOVED HIS WORK ...

BUT EVERY SUNDAY YOU COULD FIND HIM ... AND HIS WIFE IN CHURCH.

     HE WOULD NEVER WORK ON SUNDAY ... THAT WAS HIS DAY OF REST ...

HE WAS A CALF ROPIN' COWBOY ... THAT WAS KNOWN AS THE BEST.

VERSE FOUR:

     SOME PEOPLE HAVE DREAMS ... THAT THEY NEVER PURSUE ...

BECAUSE THEY DON'T KNOW WHAT ... THEY REALLY WANT TO DO.

     BUT RON DAVIS KNEW ... WHAT HE WAS GOING TO DO ...

HE WOULD BE A CALF ROPIN'COWBOY ...AND MAKE HIS DREAMS COME TRUE.

CHORUS:

     HE WAS A CALF ROPIN' COWBOY ... WORKING AT THE RODEO ...

IT WAS HIS WAY OF LIFE ... AND THE ONLY LIFE HE KNOWED.

     HE FOLLOWED HIS LIFE'S DREAMS ... WITH HIS WIFE BY HIS SIDE ...

HE WAS A CALF ROPIN' COWBOY ... UNTIL THE DAY THAT HE DIED.

A COWBOYS SONG

CHORUS:
      A COWBOY SINGS ... A COWBOYS SONG ...
AS HE SITS IN THE SADDLE ... ALL THE NIGHT LONG.
      HE MAY BE SMALL ... BUT HIS VOICE IS STRONG ...
WHEN A COWBOY SINGS ... A COWBOYS SONG.

VERSE ONE:
      THEY ALWAYS RIDE ... FROM SUNDOWN TO DAWN ...
AS THEY WEAR A COWBOYS HAT ... AND A SIX GUN ...
      THEY HAVE A JOB TO DO ... AND IT'S GOT TO BE DONE ...
AS A COWBOY SINGS ... A COWBOYS SONG.

VERSE TWO:
      SINGING WHILE WATCHING ... OVER THEIR HERDS ...
AND THE COWS ARE LISTENING ... TO EVERY WORD.
      THEY REMAIN CALM ... ALL THE NIGHT LONG ...
AND THEY SEEM TO LOVE ... A COWBOYS SONG.

CHORUS:
      A COWBOY SINGS ... A COWBOYS SONG ...
AS HE SITS IN THE SADDLE ... ALL THE NIGHT LONG.
      HE MAY BE SMALL ... BUT HIS VOICE IS STRONG ...
WHEN A COWBOY SINGS ... A COWBOYS SONG.

VERSE THREE:
      WHEN THE SUN GOES DOWN ... OVER ON THE HORIZON ...
SOMETIMES THE WOLVES ... STARTS TO A HOWLING.
      THE CATTLE GETS NERVOUS ... WHEN THEY HEAR THE SOUND ...
BUT A COWBOYS SONG ... SEEMS TO SETTLE THEM DOWN.

CHORUS:
      A COWBOY SINGS ... A COWBOYS SONG ...
AS HE SITS IN THE SADDLE ... ALL THE NIGHT LONG.
      HE MAY BE SMALL ... BUT HIS VOICE IS STRONG ...
WHEN A COWBOY SINGS ... A COWBOYS SONG.

A FALLING IN LOVE

VERSE ONE:

    YOU MAY NOT REMEMBER ... WHEN WE WAS FALLING IN LOVE ... WE WOULD FEEL LIKE ... WE WAS UP IN HEAVEN ABOVE.
    BUT WE HAD TO COME DOWN ... GET OUR FEET ON THE GROUND ...
AND THAT'S WHEN WE HEARD ... THAT WEDDING BELL SOUND.

VERSE TWO:

    WE WOULD HAVE A PICNIC ... DOWN AT THE OLD MILL STREAM ... WE WOULD ALWAYS HAVE FUN ... JUST TALKING OF OUR DREAMS.
    WE WOULD GET OUR LUNCH OUT ... LAY A BLANKET ON THE GROUND ...
AFTER LUNCH WE WOULD LAY AROUND ... UNTIL THE SUN WENT DOWN.

CHORUS:

    BUT SOMEHOW WE MADE IT ... LONG ENOUGH TO GET OLD ... AND NOW WE CAN LOOK BACK ... AT THE DAYS OF LONG AGO.
    WE THINK OF WHEN ... WE WERE YOUNG AND GROWING UP ... WE WERE JUST TWO YOUNG PEOPLE ... A FALLING IN LOVE.

VERSE THREE:

    WE WERE JUST TWO YOUNG PEOPLE ... A FALLING IN LOVE ... WE WERE'NT WORRIED ABOUT TOMORROW ... OR ANY OF THAT STUFF.
    WE WERE JUST ENJOYING LIVING ... IF ONLY FOR THAT DAY ... AND WISHING THAT EVERYTHING ... WOULD JUST STAY THAT WAY.

VERSE FOUR:

    AFTER WE WERE MARRIED ... WE BOUGHT US A HOME ... THEN SOON AFTER THAT ... THE KIDS CAME ALONG.
    WE ALWAYS TRIED TO BE ... JUST ONE BIG HAPPY FAMILY ... BUT TIMES WERE A LOT HARDER ... THAT WE THOUGHT IT WOULD BE ...

CHORUS:

    BUT SOMEHOW WE MADE IT ... LONG ENOUGH TO GET OLD ...
AND NOW WE CAN LOOK BACK ... AT THE DAYS OF LONG AGO.

    WE THINK OF WHEN ... WE WERE YOUNG AND GROWING UP ...
WE WERE JUST TWO YOUNG PEOPLE ... A FALLING IN LOVE.

A FAMILY OF MANY COLORS

HE WAS A LOVING FATHER ...THOUGH DADDY'S HAIR WAS WHITE...
BUT SOMETIMES HE FELT BLUE ... WHEN THINGS DID'NT GO RIGHT.
AND HIS HEART WAS AS GOOD ... AS IF IT WAS SOLID GOLD ...
AND MY MOMMA'S HAIR WAS GRAY ... BEFORE SHE GOT OLD.

WHEN THEY WERE YOUNG ...THEY PLANNED A FUTURE SO BRIGHT...
AND THE FAMILY SEEMED TO GROW ... WITH THE SPEED OF LIGHT.
THE KIDS ALWAYS DRESSED ... IN MANY DIFFERENT COLORS ...
IT WOULD BE IN BLACK ... SOMETIMES IN BLUE AND YELLOW.

MY DADDY WAS A FARMER ... AND HE HAD REAL BIG DREAMS ...
HE PLOWED UP THE FIELDS ... AND RAISED LOTS OF GREENS.
WE EVEN HAD A DOG ... THAT WAS ALMOST SOLID BLACK ...
BUT IT HAD A TAN STREAK ... DOWN THE MIDDLE OF IT'S BACK.

WHEN MY MOTHER SMILED ... SOMETIMES SHE WOULD BLINK ...
AND HER FAVORITE COLOR WAS ...AN AFRICAN VIOLET PINK.
SHE TAUGHT HER CHILDREN ... TO BE HONEST AND RIGHT ...
AND TAUGHT US ALL TO BE PROUD ... THAT WE WERE ALL WHITE.

ALL OF US KIDS WOULD HELP OUT ... UNTIL AFTER SUNDOWN ...
THEN MOMMA WOULD FRY UP A CHICKEN ... UNTIL IT WAS REAL BROWN.
OUR TRUE COLORS STILL SHINE ... EVEN WHEN CLOUDS ARE GRAY ...
AND THOSE COLORFUL MEMORIES ... ARE STILL WITH US TODAY.

A GOOD TRUCK DRIVIN' MAN

CHORUS:
 IF YOU THINK TRUCK DRIVING IS EASY ...
YOU BETTER MAKE ANOTHER TURN.
 BECAUSE EVERY DOLLAR THEY MAKE ...
YOU CAN BET THEY REALLY EARN.

VERSE ONE:
 WHEN IT COMES TO GOOD TRUCK DRIVING ...
THEY NEVER DO GIVE UP.
 IT'S ONE STOP AFTER ANOTHER ...
CLIMBING IN AND OUT OF THEIR TRUCK.

VERSE TWO:
 EVEN WHEN THEY DON'T FEEL LIKE IT ...
THAT LOAD HAS GOT TO GO.
 SO THEY GET IN AND START THE ENGINE ...
AND GET MOVING ON DOWN THE ROAD.

VERSE THREE:
 ALWAYS TRYING TO DODGE THE SMOKIES ...
AND TRYING TO MISS ALL THE SCALES.
 A GOOD TRUCK DRIVER STAYS ALERT ...
WHEN HE IS DRIVING BEHIND THE WHEEL.

VERSE FOUR:
 IF THEY SEE A CAR THAT IS STRANDED ...
THEY STOP TO OFFER A HAND.
 IF ANYONE EVER ASK WHO HELPED YOU ...
JUST TELL THEM A GOOD TRUCK DRIVIN' MAN.

A HICK TOWN WOMAN

VERSE ONE:

    SHE WAS A HICK TOWN WOMAN ... A LOOKING FOR SOME LOVIN' ...
WHEN SHE SAW ME ... A LOOKING HER WAY.
    SHE WAS A REAL BEAUTY ... WHEN SHE CAME TO ME ...
AND I DON'T NEVER WANT ... TO FORGET THAT DAY.

VERSE TWO:

    WHENEVER SHE SMILED ... IT NEARLY DROVE ME INSANE ...
I FORGOT TO EVEN ASK HER ... WHAT IS HER NAME.
    SHE REACHED OUT HER HAND ... AS IF TO SAY ...
I HOPE EVERYTHING HAS ... BEEN GOING YOUR WAY.

CHORUS:

    SHE WAS A HICK TOWN WOMAN ... IN A SMALL HOMETOWN ...
AND EVERYONE KNEW HER ... FOR MILES AROUND.
    SHE HAD A EASY GOING WAY ... TO GET TO YOUR HEART ...
SHE WAS A HICK TOWN WOMAN ... IN THE SHADOWS OF THE DARK.

VERSE THREE:

    SHE WAS A HICK TOWN WOMAN ... JUST MESSING AROUND ...
YOU COULD TELL SHE CAME FROM ... A VERY SMALL TOWN.
    I WILL HAVE TO SAY ... THAT I HAVE NEVER FELT BETTER ...
AND I'LL NEVER FORGET ... THE DAY THAT I MET HER.

VERSE FOUR:

    SHE WAS A HICK TOWN WOMAN ... WITH A SILVER SPOON ...
AND HOPING SOMEDAY ... SHE COULD CLIMB TO THE MOON.
    DREAMING THAT MAYBE ... SHE WOULD MEET A MOVIE SCOUT ...
AND HE WOULD LIKE WHAT HE SAW ... AND INVITE HER OUT.

CHORUS:

    SHE WAS A HICK TOWN WOMAN ... IN A SMALL HOMETOWN ...
AND EVERYONE KNEW HER ... FOR MILES AROUND.
    SHE HAD A EASY GOING WAY ... TO GET TO YOUR HEART ...
SHE WAS A HICK TOWN WOMAN ... IN THE SHADOWS OF THE DARK.

A KID LOOKING FOR SOME FUN

CHORUS:

    I WAS IN JAIL IN PRISON ...
FOR SOMETHING I HAD'NT DONE.
    THEY LOCKED ME UP ... FOR NO REASON.
BUT THEY HAD TO BLAME SOMEONE.

VERSE ONE:

    THEY SAID I HAD SHOT SOMEONE ...
AND I HAVE NEVER EVEN FIRED A GUN.
    I HAD BEEN INVITED TO A PARTY ...
JUST A KID LOOKING FOR SOME FUN.

VERSE TWO:

    THE JUDGE SAID I WAS GUILTY ...
AND THEN HE SENTENCED ME.
    HE WAS IN COMPLETE CONTROL ...
WHEN HE GAVE ME LIFE WITHOUT PAROLE.

VERSE THREE:

    I PULLED THREE YEARS AND A DAY ...
WHEN A CHANCE CAME TO MAKE AN ESCAPE.
    I MADE IT PAST ALL THE GUARDS ...
UNTIL I WAS PLUM OUT OF THE YARD.

VERSE FOUR:

    BUT I WILL NEVER REALLY BE FREE ...
BECAUSE THEY WILL ALWAYS BE AFTER ME.
    AND I'LL ALWAYS BE ON THE RUN ...
BECAUSE I WAS A KID LOOKING FOR SOME FUN.

A MAN WITH NO DREAM

VERSE ONE :

    MOST OF MY FAMILY ... DRIVES A BRAND NEW AUTOMOBILE ... SOMETIMES I WONDER IF MINE ... WILL MAKE IT OVER THE NEXT HILL.

    I HAVE NEVER WENT IN DEBT ... TO BUY A BRAND NEW CAR ... NOW I'M RUNNING ON THREADS ... I CAN'T EVEN BUY A NEW TIRE.

VERSE TWO :

    THINGS HAVE NOT ALWAYS BEEN ... AS BAD AS THEY SEEM ... BUT I JUST DON'T SEEM TO CARE ... I'M A MAN WITH NO DREAM.

    I HAVE WORKED VERY HARD ... JUST TRYING TO SURVIVE ... BUT ALL I EVER WANTED OUT OF LIFE ... WAS JUST TO STAY ALIVE.

CHORUS :

    I'M A MAN WITH NO DREAM ... I'VE NEVER WANTED FANCY THINGS ...
AND PEOPLE CAN'T UNDERSTAND ... WHY I DON'T HAVE BIG DREAMS.

    I HAVE ALWAYS HAD AT LEAST... A DOLLAR IN MY JEANS ... I FELT THAT'S ALL THAT I NEEDED ... I'M A MAN WITH NO DREAM.

VERSE THREE :

    SOME PEOPLE LIKES BIG HOUSES ... AND FANCY CARS TO DRIVE ... BUT I JUST WANTED QUITING TIME ... TO HURRY UP AND ARRIVE.

    THEN I WOULD GO SOMEWHERE ... AND LET OFF SOME STEAM ... AND I ALWAYS FELT CONTENT ... I'M A MAN WITH NO DREAM.

VERSE FOUR :

    WHEN PEOPLE ASK WHAT I DO THAT FOR ... I CAN'T TELL THEM WHY ...
I SAY IT'S JUST MY WAY OF LIVING ... AND IT WILL BE UNTIL I DIE.

    I DON'T LOOK FOR TOMORROW ... OR WHAT IT MIGHT BRING ... I JUST LIVE FOR TODAY ... BECAUSE I'M A MAN WITH NO DREAM.

CHORUS :

I'M A MAN WITH NO DREAM ... I'VE NEVER WANTED FANCY
THINGS ...
AND PEOPLE CAN'T UNDERSTAND ... WHY I DON'T HAVE BIG
DREAMS.
I HAVE ALWAYS HAD AT LEAST... A DOLLAR IN MY JEANS ...
I FELT THAT'S ALL THAT I NEEDED ... I'M A MAN WITH NO DREAM.

A MOTHER'S WORK IS NEVER DONE

VERSE ONE _
    MY DADDY DIED ... WHEN I WAS JUST ONE ...
AND MY MOTHER'S WORK ... WAS NEVER DONE.
    SHE WAS TIED DOWN ... WITH A HOUSE FULL OF KIDS ...
SHE HAD NEVER THOUGHT ... IT WOULD BE LIKE THIS.

VERSE TWO:
    SHE WOULD GO TO BED ... EACH NIGHT AND PRAY ...
THAT GOD WOULD HELP HER ... AND SHOW HER THE WAY.
    SHE'D WORK ALL DAY ... UNTIL AFTER NIGHT TIME COMES ...
A GOOD MOTHER'S WORK ... IS NEVER DONE.

VERSE THREE:
    SHE WOULD RAKE AND SCRAPE ... IN EVERY WAY SHE COULD ...
TO SEE THAT HER KIDS ... WAS ALL BROUGHT UP GOOD.
    SHE NEVER HAD TIME ... TO GO OUT AND HAVE ANY FUN ...
BECAUSE A MOTHER'S WORK ... IS NEVER DONE.

VERSE FOUR:
    SHE PUT CLOTHES ON OUR BACK ... AND SHOES ON OUR FEET ...
SHE KEPT FOOD ON THE TABLE ... AND ANYTHING ELSE WE NEED.
    A GOOD MOTHER'S LOVE ... GOES ON AND ON ...
AND A MOTHER'S WORK ... IS NEVER DONE.

VERSE FIVE:
    SHE SHOWED HER RESPECT ... TO EVERYONE AROUND ...
SHE HAD THE GREATEST LOVE ... THAT COULD EVER BE FOUND.
    SHE WOULD CHECK ON US KIDS ... ALL NIGHT UNTIL DAWN ...
A MOTHER'S WORK ... IS NEVER DONE.

CHORUS:
    I FEEL SO PROUD ... OF THE MOTHER THAT I HAD ...
AND THE WAY THAT I WAS RAISED ... I WAS REALLY GLAD.
    SHE WAS THE GREATEST MOTHER ... UNDER THE SUN ...
AND A MOTHER'S WORK ... IS NEVER DONE.

A REAL GOOD PAYDAY

VERSE ONE:

I HAVE ALWAYS THOUGHT ... PEOPLE SHOULD TRY TO HAVE SOMETHING ...
BUT FOR ALL OF MY LIFE ... I HAVE NEVER HAD NOTHING.
I DON'T KNOW KNOW WHY ... LIFE HAS TREATED ME THIS WAY ...
BUT I STILL HAVE SOME HOPE ... I WILL GET A REAL GOOD PAYDAY.

VERSE TWO:

I WENT AND MORGAGED MY HOME ... WITH A TWENTY YEAR LOAN ...
I SURE WILL BE GLAD ... WHEN THOSE TWENTY YEARS ARE GONE.
NOW I'M SURE NOT TRYING TO WISH ... MY WHOLE MY LIFE AWAY ...
BUT WHEN THAT LOAN IS PAID ... IT WILL BE A REAL GOOD PAYDAY.

CHORUS:

A REAL GOOD PAYDAY ... WILL SOON BE COMING MY WAY ...
IT WON'T BE TO LONG BECAUSE ... I'M STANDING AT THE BAY.
I BELIEVE IT'S GOING TO HAPPEN ... THAT'S ALL THAT I CAN SAY ...
I KNOW IT WON'T BE LONG UNTIL ... I GET A REAL GOOD PAYDAY.

VERSE THREE:

I HAVE NEVER HAD MUCH MONEY ... SINCE LIVING AROUND HERE ...
BUT I'VE BEEN LAYING UP TREASURES ... FOR WHEN I GET UP THERE.
I HAVE A HOME IN HEAVEN ... PAID FOR BY GOD'S SON ...
AND I'M GONNA MOVE IN ... WHEN MY LIFE HERE IS DONE.

VERSE FOUR:

I HAVE NEVER HAD MUCH MONEY ... TO AMOUNT TO ANYTHING ...
BUT I'VE FOUND OUT THAT MONEY ... CAN'T BUY YOU EVERYTHING.

BUT THAT WILL ALL BE DIFFERANT ... WHEN I GET MY BACK
PAY ...
AND I KNOW THAT IT WILL BE ... A REAL GOOD PAYDAY.

CHORUS:
A REAL GOOD PAYDAY ... WILL SOON BE COMING MY WAY ...
IT WON'T BE TO LONG BECAUSE ... I'M STANDING AT THE BAY.
I BELIEVE IT'S GOING TO HAPPEN ... THAT'S ALL THAT I CAN
SAY ...
I KNOW IT WON'T BE LONG UNTIL ... I GET A REAL GOOD PAYDAY.

A SWEET LOVE SONG

CHORUS:

      EVERYONE KEEPS SAYING ... TO WRITE A SWEET LOVE SONG ...
ABOUT A LOVE THAT LASTED ... AND WILL LAST FROM NOW ON.
      IT WILL DO MANY WONDERS ... UNTIL THIS LIFE IS GONE ...
AD ALL BECAUSE SOMEONE WROTE ... A SWEET LOVE SONG.

VERSE ONE:

      LOVE CAN MAKE YOU HAPPY ... AND CHASE THE BLUES AWAY ...
THERE WILL ALWAYS BE SUNSHINE ... IN YOUR LIFE EVERYDAY.
      IT WILL BRIGHTEN UP YOUR LIFE ... TO SEE YOUR LOVER SMILE ...
AND A SWEET LOVE SONG ... CAN LAST A LONG LONG WHILE.

VERSE TWO:

      A FAMILY WITH SOME CHILDREN ... IS EVERYONE'S DREAM ...
WHEN THEY MIX IT WITH LOVE ... THEN THEY HAVE EVERYTHING.
      SOMEDAY YOU MAY WONDER ... WHAT BROUGHT IT ALL ON ...
THEN YOU'LL KNOW IT STARTED ... WITH A SWEET LOVE SONG.

CHORUS:

      EVERYONE KEEPS SAYING ... TO WRITE A SWEET LOVE SONG ...
ABOUT A LOVE THAT LASTED ... AND WILL LAST FROM NOW ON.
      IT WILL DO MANY WONDERS ... UNTIL THIS LIFE IS GONE ...
AD ALL BECAUSE SOMEONE WROTE ... A SWEET LOVE SONG.

VERSE THREE:

      THOUGH YOU HAVE NO MONEY ... YOU CAN LIVE ON LOVE ...
THAT'S THE MOST IMPORTANT THING ... THEY ARE THINKING OF
      JUST KEEP LOVE IN YOUR HEART ... AND SOMEONE TO
      LEAN ON ...
AND ALWAYS KEEP ON A SINGING ... A SWEET LOVE SONG.

CHORUS:

      EVERYONE KEEPS SAYING ... TO WRITE A SWEET LOVE SONG ...
ABOUT A LOVE THAT LASTED ... AND WILL LAST FROM NOW ON.
      IT WILL DO MANY WONDERS ... UNTIL THIS LIFE IS GONE ...
AD ALL BECAUSE SOMEONE WROTE ... A SWEET LOVE SONG.

AFRAID OF THE DARKNESS

VERSE ONE:

    I JUST SIT HERE A LOOKIN' ... OUT OF MY WINDOW ...
I'M WATCHING THE LATE EVENING ... SUN GO DOWN.
    AS I STARE INTO THE DARKNESS ... I WONDER WHAT ...
COULD BE WAITING OUT THERE ... IN THE SHADOWS OF THE DARK.

VERSE TWO:

    THINGS ARE CHANGING SO FAST ...I CAN'T KEEP UP WITH IT...
SOMETIMES I JUST WANT TO ... THROW UP MY HANDS AND QUIT IT.
    I DON'T KNOW WHAT'S AHEAD ... I'M AFRAID OF THE SORROW.
I'M AFRAID OF THE DARKNESS... IF THERE IS A TOMORROW.

CHORUS:

    I'M AFRAID OF THE DARKNESS ... IT'S A VERY SCARY THING ...
AND I'M AFRAID OF TOMORROW ... AND WHAT IT MIGHT BRING.
    SO PUT ME IN THE LIGHT ... AND THERE LET ME STAY ...
LET ME WALK IN SUNSHINE ... AND KEEP THE DARKNESS AWAY.

VERSE THREE:

    THERE'S LIGHTS IN THE HOUSE ... BUT IT'S DARK ON THE
OUTSIDE ...
I CAN SEE IN THE LIGHT ... BUT I'M AFRAID OF WHAT'S OUT THERE.
    I CAN'T SEE INTO THE FUTURE ... OR WHAT'S IN IT FOR ME ...
AND I'M AFRAID OF THE DARKNESS ... FARTHER THAN I CAN SEE.

VERSE FOUR

    I CAN'T THINK OF THE FUTURE ... WITH ALL OF IT'S SORROW ...
I CAN'T SEE NO FARTHER THAN TODAY ... WITH NO HOPE OF
TOMORROW.
    TODAY IS THE PRESENT ... AND THE PAST IS SOMEWHERE
BEHIND ...
I'M NOT LOOKING FOR TOMORROW ... I'M AFRAID OF WHAT I MIGHT
FIND.

CHORUS:

    I'M AFRAID OF THE DARKNESS ... IT'S A VERY SCAREY THING ...
AND I'M AFRAID OF TOMORROW ... AND WHAT IT MIGHT BRING.
    SO PUT ME IN THE LIGHT ... AND THERE LET ME STAY ...
LET ME WALK IN SUNSHINE ... AND KEEP THE DARKNESS AWAY.

ALL ACROSS AMERICA

CHORUS:

     ALL ACROSS AMERICA ... YOU CAN HEAR THE PEOPLE CRY ...
STOP THOSE HIGH PRICES ... BECAUSE THE PRICES ARE TOO HIGH.
     I CAN'T BUY THE THINGS I WANT ... AND PEOPLE ASK ME
     WHY ...
BUT THAT'S VERY PLAIN TO SEE BECAUSE ... PRICES ARE TOO HIGH.

VERSE ONE:

     I AM JUST AN ORDINARY ... EVERYDAY WORKING MAN ...
I TRY TO MAKE A LIVING ... THE BEST WAY THAT I CAN.
     WHEN I GO TO BUY THE THINGS ... THAT I NEED TO GET BY ...
I ALWAYS FIND OUT THAT ... ALL THE PRICES ARE TOO HIGH.

VERSE TWO:

     I GO TO THE GROCERY STORE ... TO GET SOME CHICKEN TO
     FRY ...
WHEN I COME HOME EMPTY HANDED ... THEN MY WIFE ASK
ME WHY.
     I TELL HER THAT IT'S NOT BECAUSE ... THAT I DID NOT TRY ...
BUT MY FUNDS WERE TOO LOW ... AND THE GROCERIES WERE TOO
HIGH.

CHORUS:

     ALL ACROSS AMERICA ... YOU CAN HEAR THE PEOPLE CRY ...
STOP THOSE HIGH PRICES ... BECAUSE THE PRICES ARE TOO HIGH.
     I CAN'T BUY THE THINGS I WANT ... AND PEOPLE ASK ME
     WHY ...
BUT THAT'S VERY PLAIN TO SEE BECAUSE ... PRICES ARE TOO HIGH.

VERSE THREE:

     EVERYTIME I BUY GROCERIES ... THE PRICES SEEM TO RISE ...
EVEN A CAN OF PORK AND BEANS ... SOMETIMES IS WAY TOO HIGH.
     NOW WHEN I GET MY LIGHT BILL ... I CAN'T BELIEVE MY
     EYES ...
BUT CONGRESS DON'T UNDERSTAND ... THAT PRICES ARE TOO
HIGH.

VERSE FOUR:

     NOW WHEN YOU STOP FOR GASOLINE ... BE PREPARED TO CRY ...

IF YOU FILL YOUR GAS TANK UP ... IT WILL DRAIN YOUR POCKETS DRY.

     A POOR MAN JUST CAN'T WIN ... NO MATTER HOW HARD HE TRYS ...

BECAUSE ALL ACROSS AMERICA ... THE PRICES ARE TOO HIGH.

ALL OVER AGAIN

CHORUS:
> THINGS ARE NO DIFFERANT ... THAN IT WAS THEN ...
WHY MUST I GO BACK ... TO WHERE I'VE ALREADY BEEN .
> WHY DO I GET UP ... AND THINK THAT I CAN ...
DO THE SAME OLD THING ... ALL OVER AGAIN.

VERSE ONE:
> EACH TIME I WAKE UP ... A LITTLE CONFUSED ...
AND THEN I REALIZE ... THAT I'VE BEEN USED.
> THOUGH I AM HURT ... I DON'T UNDERSTAND ...
WHY DID I HAVE TO DO IT ... ALL OVER AGAIN.

VERSE TWO:
> I HAD TO GO AND DO IT ... ALL OVER AGAIN ...
WHEN I KNEW THAT ... I JUST COULD'NT WIN.
> I KNOW THAT IT'S OVER ... I'VE LOST THE FIGHT ...
BUT I'LL TRY IT AGAIN ... TOMORROW NIGHT.

CHORUS:
> THINGS ARE NO DIFFERANT ... THAN IT WAS THEN ...
WHY MUST I GO BACK ... TO WHERE I'VE ALREADY BEEN .
> WHY DO I GET UP ... AND THINK THAT I CAN ...
DO THE SAME OLD THING ... ALL OVER AGAIN.

VERSE THREE:
> YESTERDAY WAS ... THE BEST DAY OF MY LIFE ...
EVERYTHING WENT MY WAY ... THINGS SURE WENT RIGHT.
> IF I COULD TURN BACK TIME ... AND NEVER LET IT END ...
I'D PLAY IT OVER AND OVER AND OVER ... ALL OVER AGAIN.

CHORUS:
> THINGS ARE NO DIFFERANT ... THAN IT WAS THEN ...
WHY MUST I GO BACK IN TIME ... TO WHERE I'VE ALREADY BEEN .
> WHY DO I GET UP ... AND THINK THAT I CAN ...
DO THE SAME OLD THING ... ALL OVER AGAIN.

ALWAYS BELIEVE

VERSE ONE:

A FRIEND OF MINE ... AND I WERE TALKING ONE DAY ...
ABOUT HOW BAD THE WORLD ... HAD GONE ASTRAY.
I SAID IT WON'T BE LONG ... AND I CAN BE FREE ...
THAT'S WHAT BELIEVING IN JESUS ... MEANS TO ME.

VERSE TWO:

I WON'T ALWAYS WORRY ... ABOUT GETTING THRU THE DAY...
BECAUSE GOD HAS SHOWN ME ... THERE'S A BETTER WAY.
THAT BY LIVING BY WORKS ... AND NOT BY FAITH ALONE ...
AND BELIEVING IN JESUS ... I WILL SOON BE GONE.

VERSE THREE:

I'LL LEAVE THIS WORLD ... FRIENDS AND FAMILY BEHIND ...
I'VE BEEN BELIEVING IN JESUS ... FOR A LONG LONG TIME.
IN MY HEART I CAN SEE ... A PICTURE OF THE GOLDEN GATE ...
AND FOR ME TO PASS THRU ... I CAN HARDLY WAIT.

CHORUS:

JESUS SAID HE IS COMING BACK ... TO EARTH SOMEDAY ...
TO GET ALL HIS BELIEVERS ... AND TAKE THEM AWAY.
THE BIBLE ALWAYS SAID TO ME ... TO ALWAYS BELIEVE ...
WHEN HE COMES BACK BE PACKED ... AND READY TO LEAVE.

VERSE FOUR:

I'LL ALWAYS BELIEVE ... THAT HE IS COMING BACK ...
AND HE WILL WEAR A WHITE ROBE ... UPON HIS BACK
JUST ONE BEAUTIFUL DAY ... NO SUCH THING AS TIME ...
AND HE WILL REIGN OVER DEATH ... WITH NO MORE DYING.

ALWAYS HELP SOMEONE

HE WAS NEVER KNOWN ... AS SOMEONE WHO WAS GREAT ...
HE NEVER HAD NO MONEY ... NOR DID HE HAVE ANY HATE.
HE WILL ALWAYS BE REMEMBERED ... AFTER HE IS GONE ...
AS ONE THAT UNHAPPY ... UNLESS HE HELPED SOMEONE.

HE WILL BE REMEMBERED ... BY ALWAYS DOING GOOD DEEDS ...
LIKE WHEN HE HELPED THE BLIND MAN ... TO CROSS THE STREET.
OR WHEN HE SAW A BEGGAR MAN ... DOWN ON HIS KNEE'S...
AND HE HELPED HIM UP ... AND GAVE HIM SOMETHING TO EAT.

OR WHEN HE SAW A CHILD ... WALKING DOWN THE STREET ...
WITH RAGGED CLOTHES ON ... AND NO SHOES ON HIS FEET .
HE WENT TO THE GOODWILL STORE ... AND DRESSED HIM UP...
AND TO THINK IT ONLY COST HIM ... A COUPLE OF BUCKS.

ONCE HE GAVE HIS PAYCHECK ... JUST TO HELP SOMEONE ...
WHO WAS BEHIND ON THEIR MORGAGE ... LOSING THEIR HOME.
HE WOULD GIVE ALL HE HAD ... TIL THERE WAS NOTHING
LEFT...
HE ALWAYS THOUGHT OF OTHERS ... MORE THAN HIMSELF.

IF THE WHOLE WORLD ... WAS WILLING TO SHARE AND GIVE ...
IT WOULD BE A MUCH BETTER PLACE ... FOR US TO LIVE.
SO BEFORE YOU BUY SOMETHING ... THAT YOU DON'T NEED ...
ALWAYS HELP SOMEONE ELSE ... AND DO A GOOD DEED.

AN EXHAUSTED NOBODY

CHORUS:

HE HAS ALWAYS FELT LIKE HE WAS ... AN EXHAUSTED NOBODY ...
BUT HE ALWAYS TRIED TO DO GOOD ... JUST LIKE EVERYBODY.
AND I GUESS LIKE ANYBODY ... HE WANTED TO BE SOMEBODY ...
BUT ALL HE EVER WAS ... IS JUST AN EXHAUSTED NOBODY.

VERSE ONE:

THE MORE HE WOULD TRY ... THE WORSE IT WOULD GET ...
BUT HE WANTED TO BE SOMEONE ... HE HAD NEVER MET.
SO HE MADE UP HIS MIND ... HE WAS GOING TO BE SOMEBODY ...
BUT ALL HE CAME UP WITH ... WAS AN OLD EXHAUSTED NOBODY.

VERSE TWO:

HE TRIED AND KEPT TRYING ... UNTIL HE WORE HIMSELF OUT ...
WHEN ALL HIS MONEY WAS GONE ... HE STARTED LIVING WITHOUT.
BUT HE DID'NT GIVE UP ... HE WAS GOING TO BE SOMEBODY ...
BUT THERE HE STILL WAS ... JUST AN EXHAUSTED NOBODY.

VERSE THREE:

WITH LIFE IT ALWAYS SEEMS ... THAT'S THE WAY IT GOES ...
AFTER YOU LOSE EVERYTHING ... ALL YOU OWN IS YOUR CLOTHES.
DON'T TRY TO LIVE TOO HIGH ... JUST LIVE WITHIN YOUR
MEANS ...
BECAUSE BEING AN EXHAUSTED NOBODY ... IS NOBODY'S DREAM.

VERSE FOUR:

FINALLY THE OLD DIED ... AND THERE NO ONE WHO CRIED ...
BUT THERE WAS SOMEONE ... WHO KNEW HOW HARD HE HAD TRYED.
AND NOW HE GONE ON ... TO A MUCH BETTER LAND ...
JUST AN OLD EXHAUSTED NOBODY ... BY THE MASTERS HAND.

CHORUS:

HE HAS ALWAYS FELT LIKE ... HE WAS AN EXHAUSTED
NOBODY ...
BUT HE ALWAYS TRIED TO DO GOOD ... JUST LIKE EVERYBODY.
AND I GUESS LIKE ANYBODY ... HE WANTED TO BE SOMEBODY ...
BUT ALL HE EVER WAS ... IS JUST AN EXHAUSTED NOBODY.

AN OLD FASHIONED FAMILY

VERSE ONE:

    I WOULD LIKE TO TELL YOU ... A TRUE STORY ...
ABOUT A LITTLE BAREFOOT ... COUNTRY BOY.
    IT WAS MANY YEARS AGO ...OUT IN THE COUNTRY...
ALL HE HAD WAS ... WAS AN OLD FASHIONED FAMILY.

VERSE TWO:

    HIS FAMILY WAS SO POOR ... THEY HAD NO LIGHTS ...
ONLY USED CANDLES ...TIL THEY WENT TO BED AT NIGHT.
    IT WAS A LONG TIME AGO... DURING THE DEPRESSION ...
THE TURMOILS OF LIFE ... LEFT HIM BAD IMPRESSIONS.

VERSE THREE:

    THEY FACED THE WORLD ... THE OLD FASHIONED WAY...
JUST DO WHATEVER YOU CAN ... BUT DO IT TODAY.
    TOMORROW MAY NOT GET HERE... THE PAST IS GONE.
AND ALL THEY HAD ... WAS AN OLD FASHIONED HOME.

VERSE FOUR:

    THEY LOVED EACH OTHER ... MORE THAN THEY COULD SAY...
AND THEIR LOVE KEPT GROWING ... DAY AFTER DAY..
    THE LITTLE BOY GREW UP... AND IS STILL ALIVE TODAY ...
BECAUSE HIS PARENTS LOVED HIM ...THE OLD FASHIONED WAY.

AN OLD POCKET KNIFE

VERSE ONE:

I ONCE KNEW A MAN ... WHO LED A LONELY LIFE ...
AND HE WOULD RUN AROUND ... ALMOST EVERY NIGHT.
SOMETIMES HE WOULD ALWAYS ... GET INTO A FIGHT.
HE WOULD ALWAYS USE ... AN OLD POCKET KNIFE.

VERSE TWO:

HE KEPT AN OLD POCKET KNIFE ... SHARP AND SLICK ...
AND HE COULD PULL IT OUT ... OF HIS POCKET REAL QUICK.
SOON THE NEWS GOT OUT ... ALL OVER TOWN ...
THE MAN WITH AN OLD POCKET KNIFE ... DID'NT PLAY AROUND.

VERSE THREE:

HE WOULD CUT YOU BEFORE ... YOU COULD BAT AN EYE ...
AND HE WOULD'NT STOP ... UNTIL HE MADE THE BLOOD FLY.
HE WOULD START AT YOUR BELLY ... AND RIP YOUR INSIDES...
YOU MIGHT GET BLOOD POISON ... FROM AN OLD POCKET KNIFE.

VERSE FOUR:

HE WAS FAST AND QUICK ... AND MEAN AS HE COULD BE ...
AND HE HAD NO FRIENDS ... BECAUSE HE WAS CRAZY.
HE WOULD NEVER SMILE ... SOMETIMES HE WOULD CRY ...
THE ONLY FRIEND HE HAD... WAS AN OLD POCKET KNIFE.

CHORUS:

DON'T LET YOUR REPUTATION ... TAKE YOU TO THE GRAVE ...
ALWAYS MAKE FRIENDS ... AND DON'T TRY TO BE BRAVE.
ALWAYS TREAT OTHERS ... AS YOU WANT THEM TO TREAT
YOU ...
AND LEAVE A GOOD MEMORY ... WHEN YOUR LIFE IS THROUGH.

VERSE FIVE:

HE DID'NT DIE A LONER ... HE FOUND A NEW LIFE ...
WHEN HE HEARD ABOUT JESUS... HE WAS FULL OF DELIGHT.
AND WHEN THEY PASSED THE PLATE ... THAT SUNDAY NIGHT ...
ALL HE HAD TO OFFER ... WAS AN OLD POCKT KNIFE.

AND THEN ONE DAY

VERSE ONE:
     WE WERE IN LOVE ... OUR HEARTS BEAT AS ONE ...
WE WOULD GO EVERYWHERE ... AND HAVE LOTS OF FUN.
     WE SAID OUR LIVES TOGETHER ... WOULD NEVER END ...
BUT THIS IS NOW ... AND THAT WAS THEN.

VERSE TWO:
     THEN ONE DAY HER PARENTS ... TOOK HER AWAY ...
SAID THEY WOULD BE GONE ... ONLY A COUPLE OF DAYS.
     I WAITED AND I WAITED ... MY HEART FULL OF SCREAMS ...
WHEN HER PARENTS LEFT ... THEY TOOK ALL MY DREAMS.

VERSE THREE:
     AND THEN ONE DAY ... I NO LONGER WANTED TO LIVE ...
I FELT THAT MY LIFE NO LONGER ... HAD NOTHING TO GIVE.
     I DROVE UP ON A MOUNTAIN ... LOOKED DOWN BELOW ...
WONDERING WHERE ON EARTH ... DID SHE GO.

VERSE FOUR:
     I COULD'NT FIND THE ANSWERS ... I WAS LOOKING FOR ...
SO I STARTED DOWN THE MOUNTAIN ... WORSE THAN BEFORE.
     WITH TEARS IN MY EYES ... AND LUMPS IN MY THROAT ...
I DID'NT SEE THE CURVE ... AND I WENT OFF OF THE ROAD.

VERSE FIVE:
     WHEN MY CAR STOPPED ... I WAS IN TOP OF A TREE ...
UPSIDE DOWN ... LIKE THE DREAMS SHE LEFT ME.
     I CLIMBED OUT OF THE TREE ... GOT BACK ON GROUND...
THAT ACCIDENT MADE MY WORLD... STOP SPINNIMG AROUND.

CHORUS:
     NOW THAT WAS WHEN ... AN ANGEL CAME MY WAY ...
AND SAID DON'T GIVE UP ... THERE'S A BRIGHTER DAY.
     FORGET ABOUT THE PAST ... AND THINK ABOUT NOW ...
THEN ONE DAY YOUR DREAMS ... WILL COME TRUE SOMEHOW.

ANOTHER BAD DAY

I WOKE UP THIS MORNING ... IT LOOKED LIKE A GOOD DAY ...
SO I WALKED OUT MY DOOR ... AND STARTED ON MY WAY.
I GOT ME A NEWSPAPER ... TO SEE WHAT IT HAD TO SAY ...
BUT THE THINGS I READ ... TURNED MY BLUE SKY TO GRAY.

THE FRONT HEADLINES READ ... TERROR IN BOSTON ...
THIS IS BEGINNING TO HAPPEN ... MUCH TOO OFTEN.
THE PRESIDENT VOWS JUSTICE ...THEY WON'T GET BY WITH IT...
THEY WILL BE PUNISHED ... TO THE FULLEST EXTENT.

THE SUN WAS A SHINING ... ALL OF A SUDDEN IT TURNED
GRAY ...
I KNEW I HAD BETTER GET READY ... FOR ANOTHER BAD DAY.
DARK CLOUDS WAS ARISING ... AND FORMING ALL AROUND ...
IT WAS GETTING READY ... FOR THE RAIN TO COME DOWN.

EVERYTHING WAS SO LOVELY... UNTIL IT TURNED DEADLY...
AND THE PEOPLE IN BOSTON ... JUST WAS'NT READY.
BOMBS WENT OFF ... AND PEOPLE STARTED CRYING...
MANY WERE IN PAIN ... THEY FELT LIKE THEY WERE DYING.

WHEN THEY CATCH THE GUILTY... PUT THEM BY THEMSELVES ...
THEN BLOW THEM UP ... LIKE THEY DO EVERYONE ELSE.
DON'T PUT THEM IN PRISON ... SO THAT THEY CAN ESCAPE ...
THEY WOULD ONLY MAKE PLANS ... TO MAKE ANOTHER BAD DAY.

ANOTHER GAME

VERSE ONE:

    WHEN I STARTED TO SCHOOL ... I WAS SCARED TO DEATH ...
IT WAS SOMETHING NEW ... I COULD'NT HELP BUT TO FRET.
    I REALLY MISSED MY FAMILY ... AND I FELT SO ASHAMED ...
WHEN THE TEACHER SCOLDED ME ... IT WAS ANOTHER GAME.

VERSE TWO:

    I GREW UP FAST ... AND NOW MY SCHOOL DAYS ARE GONE ...
NOW I'VE GOT TO USE WHAT I LEARNED ... SINCE I LEFT HOME.
    I'M A GROWN MAN NOW ... AND NOTHING IS THE SAME ...
I LEARNED A LOT OF THINGS ... SO I PLAYED ANOTHER GAME.

CHORUS:

    SOMETIMES LIFE ... CAN ALMOST DRIVE YOU INSANE ...
BUT I'M A GONNA LIVE BETTER ... AND AS LONG AS I CAN.
    WHEN IT COMES TO DYING ... I'LL GO THE WAY I CAME ...
TO PLAY ANOTHER GAME ... WOULD BE A ROTTEN SHAME.

VERSE THREE:

    GOOD OLD NORTH CAROLINA .. IS WHERE I COME FROM ...
BACK WHERE I WAS KNOWN ... AS THE TOWNS BEST BUM.
    THEN I WENT OUT WEST ... TO SEEK FORTUNE AND FAME ...
NOW I'M GOING BACK HOME ... TO PLAY ANOTHER GAME.

VERSE FOUR:

    I ALWAYS WORKED HARD ... BUT PEOPLE COULD'NT SEE
    THAT ...
SO I HAD TO GET AWAY ... LIKE A LONG GONE CAT.
    I STRUCK IT RICH ... IN THE CALIFORNIA LOTTERY GAMES ...
AND NOW I'M GOING BACK HOME ... TO SHARE MY FAME.

CHORUS:

    SOMETIMES LIFE ... CAN ALMOST DRIVE YOU INSANE ...
BUT I'M A GONNA LIVE AS GOOD...AND AS LONG AS I CAN.
    WHEN IT COMES TO DYING ... I'LL GO THE WAY I CAME ...
TO PLAY ANOTHER GAME ... WOULD BE A ROTTEN SHAME.

AROUND CHRISTMAS TIME

CHORUS :

      WE LOVED THE CHRISTMAS SPIRIT ... AROUND CHRISTMAS
      TIME ...

WE HAD LOVE IN OUR FAMILY ... EVEN IF THE SUN DID'NT SHINE.

      IN A TOWN CALLED HIGH POINT ... IN THE MIDDLE OF THE
      PIEDMONT ...

EVERYONE WAS NIEGHBORS ... NO MATTER WHERE THEY CAME
FROM.

VERSE ONE :

      I WAS ALWAYS THE HAPPIEST ... AROUND CHRISTMAS TIME ...

WHEN I SAW ALL THE LIGHTS ... AND HEARD THE CHRISTMAS BELLS
CHIME.

      I LIVED IN NORTH CAROLINA ... SOMETIMES THE SNOW
      WOULD FALL ...

IN THE MIDDLE OF THE PIEDMONT ... THE MOST BEAUTIFUL PLACE
OF ALL.

VERSE TWO :

      WATCHING LITTLE CHILDREN ... AS THEY'RE PLAYING IN THE
      SNOW ...

BUILDING THIER SNOW MEN ... THROWING SNOW BALLS TO
AND FRO.

      I CAN'T TELL YOU HOW I FELT ... ALWAYS AROUND CHRISTMAS
      TIME ...

THOSE MEMORIES WILL ALWAYS BE THERE ... IN THE BACK OF MY
MIND.

CHORUS :

      WE LOVED THE CHRISTMAS SPIRIT ... AROUND CHRISTMAS
      TIME ...

WE HAD LOVE IN OUR FAMILY ... EVEN IF THE SUN DID'NT SHINE.

      IN A TOWN CALLED HIGH POINT ... IN THE MIDDLE OF THE
      PIEDMONT ...

EVERYONE WAS NIEGHBORS ... NO MATTER WHERE THEY CAME
FROM.

VERSE THREE :

     NOW WHEN I TAKE TIME OUT ... TO WATCH THE CHILDREN PLAY ...

MY MIND GOES BACK IN TIME ... TO THOSE GOOD OLD DAYS.

     BACK WHEN I WAS YOUNG ... AND YOUTH WAS ALL MINE ...

AND ALL THE FUN I HAD ... AROUND CHRISTMAS TIME.

CHORUS :

     WE LOVED THE CHRISTMAS SPIRIT ... AROUND CHRISTMAS TIME ...

WE HAD LOVE IN OUR FAMILY ... EVEN IF THE SUN DID'NT SHINE.

     IN A TOWN CALLED HIGH POINT ... IN THE MIDDLE OF THE PIEDMONT ...

EVERYONE WAS NIEGHBORS ... NO MATTER WHERE THEY CAME FROM.

AS I START TO THINK

VERSE ONE:
 SITTING IN MY FRONT YARD ... IN MY SWING ...
WITH NOTHING ELSE TO DO .. I JUST START TO THINK.
 I THINK OF THE GOOD TIMES ... THAT I HAVE HAD ...
THEN AS I START TO THINK ... OF SOME OF THE BAD.

VERSE TWO:
 HOW I MADE IT THROUGH ... I'LL NEVER KNOW ...
BUT I COULD'NT HAVE DONE IT ... WITHOUT YOU THOUGH.
 YOU MADE ALL THE BAD TIMES ... TURN INTO GOOD ...
AND THE MORE I START TO THINK ... I KNEW YOU WOULD.

CHORUS:
 THANK YOU LORD FOR GIVING ME ... A NEW LIFE AND NEW START ...
AND FOR TAKING AWAY ... THAT OLD COLD COLD HEART.
 AND AS I START TO THINK ... I WOULD'NT BE HERE NOW ...
BUT WITHOUT YOUR LOVE ... IT WOULD'NT MATTER NO HOW.

VERSE THREE:
 I START TO THINK OF WHEN ... I ASK YOU TO HELP ME ...
I DID'NT KNOW THEN ... ALL THE PROBLEMS THERE WOULD BE.
 THE MORE I START TO THINK NOW ... THE MORE I KNOW ...
IF HAD'NT BEEN FOR YOU ... IT WOULD HAVE BEEN OVER LONG AGO.

VERSE FOUR:
 IN MY COLD HARD HEART ... OF LONLINESS AND SADDNESS ...
YOU FILLED IT WITH YOUR LOVE ... AND GAVE ME HAPPINESS.
 NOW AS I LOOK BACK ... I START TO THINK ABOUT IT AGAIN ...
AND I JUST THANK GOD MY LIFE ... AIN'T LIKE IT WAS BACK THEN.

CHORUS:
 THANK YOU LORD FOR GIVING ME ... A NEW LIFE AND NEW START ...
AND FOR TAKING AWAY ... THAT OLD COLD COLD HEART.
 AND AS I START TO THINK ... I WOULD'NT BE HERE NOW ...
BUT WITHOUT YOUR LOVE ... IT WOULD'NT MATTER NO HOW.

BACK TO THE BEGINNIN'

CHORUS:

LET'S GO BACK TO THE BEGINNIN' ... WHERE IT ALL GOT STARTED ...

BACK TO THE BEGINNIN' ... WHEN WE FIRST BECAME DISHEARTED. DON'T EVER CARRY YOUR PROBLEMS ... YOUR WHOLE LIFE THROUGH ...

GO BACK TO THE BEGINNIN' ... FIND OUT WHAT'S BOTHERING YOU.

VERSE ONE:

WHENEVER YOU HAVE PROBLEMS ... DON'T BLAME SOMEONE ELSE ...

YOU WERE THE REASON FOR THEM ... YOU STARTED THEM YOURSELF.

GO BACK TO THE BEGINNIN' ... AND REMEMBER WHAT YOU DID ...

THE THINGS THAT YOU WERE DOING ... COULD NEVER HAVE STAYED HID.

VERSE TWO:

IF YOU DON'T STOP AND THINK ... OF SOME OF THE THINGS YOU DO ...

SOMETIMES THEY HURT OTHERS ... MUCH MORE THAN THEY DO YOU.

IF THINGS ARE'NT WORKING OUT FOR YOU ...THEN STOP THAT GRINNIN' ...

JUST TRY TO FIGURE IT OUT ... AND GO BACK TO THE BEGINNIN'.

CHORUS:

LET'S GO BACK TO THE BEGINNIN' ... WHERE IT ALL GOT STARTED ...

BACK TO THE BEGINNIN' ... WHEN WE FIRST BECAME DISHEARTED. DON'T EVER CARRY YOUR PROBLEMS ... YOUR WHOLE LIFE THROUGH ...

GO BACK TO THE BEGINNIN' ... FIND OUT WHAT'S BOTHERING YOU.

VERSE THREE:

THERE'S ALWAYS A STARTING POINT ... FOR EVERYTHING THAT WE DO ...

SOMETIMES WE PUSH THEM ASIDE ... AND DON'T CARRY THEM THROUGH.

SO WHEN THINGS DON'T ALWAYS GO ... THE WAY THAT WE PLANNED ...

JUST GO BACK TO THE BEGINNIN' ... AND MAYBE WE CAN UNDERSTAND.

VERSE FOUR:

DON'T EVER THINK THAT THINGS ... JUST HAPPENS THAT WAY ...

IF YOU DO THERE WILL HARD TIMES ... THAT YOU WILL HAVE TO PAY.

YOU HAVE TO MAKE THEM HAPPEN ... AND NOT AS THEY MAY ...

GO BACK TO THE BEGINNIN' ... START HAVING SOME HAPPY DAYS.

BEHIND THE SCENES

VERSE ONE:

I WENT HOME TODAY ... AND TURNED MY TELEVISION ON ...
AND THE THINGS THAT I SAW ... SURE CUT ME TO THE BONE.
PEOPLE WAS TALKING VULGAR ... ABOUT UNCLEAN THINGS ...
ABOUT NEWS OF WHAT WAS HAPPENING ... BEHIND THE SCENES.

VERSE TWO:

IT WAS KIDS KILLING KIDS ... ACROSS THE NATION IN SCHOOLS...
AND SHOWING PEOPLE BROUGHT UP ... WITH NO FAMILY RULES.
BUT STILL PEOPLE WONDERS ... WHAT MAKES PEOPLE SO MEAN ...
AND WHAT ON EARTH IS GOING ON ... BEHIND THE SCENES.

CHORUS:

SOMEDAY WE'LL WAKE UP ... AND FIND OUR WORLD ALL GONE ...
AND THEN WE'LL WONDER ... WHAT ON EARTH IS GOING ON.
WE WOULD'NT CHANGE OUR WAYS ... FOR A HILL OF BEANS ...
WE WAS TO SCARED TO EVEN LOOK ... BEHIND THE SCENES.

VERSE THREE:

FOLKS KILLING ONE ANOTHER ... FOR NO REASON AT ALL ...
PEOPLE ROBBING THE CUSTOMERS ... IN THE SHOPPING MALLS.
DRUG DEALERS SELLING DOPE ... TO MOST OF OUR TEENS ...
AND PEOPLE DON'T EVEN LOOK AT ... WHAT'S BEHIND THE SCENES.

VERSE FOUR:

WHAT'S BEHIND THE SCENES ... OF BROKEN UP HEARTS ...
DESTROYING OUR LIVES ... AND TEARING OUR WORLD APART.
MOST PEOPLE'S DAILY LIVES ... ARE SO BUSY IT SEEMS ...
THEY DON'T EVEN CARE WHAT'S HAPPENING ... BEHIND THE
SCENES.

CHORUS:

SOMEDAY WE'LL WAKE UP ... AND FIND OUR WORLD ALL
GONE ...
AND THEN WE'LL WONDER ... WHAT ON EARTH IS GOING ON.
WE WOULD'NT CHANGE OUR WAYS ... FOR A HILL OF BEANS ...
WE WAS TO SCARED TO EVEN LOOK ... BEHIND THE SCENES.

BELIEVE IN THE BIBLE

I BELIEVE IN THE BIBLE ... AND WHAT IT TELLS ME ...
THAT GOD'S SON LIVED ... AND HE DIED ON CALVARY.
HE GAVE HIS LIFE ON EARTH ... FOR ALL WHO BELIEVE,,,
SO I BELIEVE IN THE BIBLE ... AND WHAT IT DOES FOR ME.

IT GIVES ME MORE REASON ... TO KEEP ON GOING ...
AND LET THE BLESSINGS OF GOD ... JUST KEEP ON FLOWING.
I BELIEVE THAT SOMEDAY ... I WILL MEET HIM FACE TO FACE ...
AND I BELIEVE THAT THE BIBLE ... HAS PREPARED ME THE WAY.

GOD LET HIS SON DIE ... FOR OUR UNWORTHY SOULS ...
SO THAT THRU HIS BLOOD ... WE COULD BE MADE WHOLE.
HE DID'NT HAVE TO ... BUT HE DIED ON THE CROSS ...
SO THAT IF YOU BELIEVE IN THE BIBLE ... YOU WON'T BE LOST.

IF YOU DON'T MAKE IT TO HEAVEN ... IT IS YOUR OWN FAULT ...
JUST BELIEVE IN THE BIBLE ... YOUR TICKETS BEEN BOUGHT.
JUST BE READY TO LEAVE ... WHEN HE CALLS YOUR NAME ...
HE HAS GIVEN US DIRECTIONS,,, THEY ARE VERY PLAIN.

BELIEVE IN THE BIBLE ... IT WILL TAKE US THERE SOMEDAY...
KEEP LISTENING READING AND DOING ... IT'S THE ONLY WAY.
ALWAYS BE A BLESSING ... TO THOSE AROUND YOU ...
YOU WILL HAVE TREASURES ... WHEN YOUR JOURNEY IS THROUGH.

BOJANGLE'S FIRST CLASS BUM

VERSE ONE:

I JUST LOVED LOW PRICES ... IT WAS ALL I COULD AFFORD ...
THEY KNEW WHAT I WANTED ... AS SOON AS I CAME THRU THE
DOOR.

THEY NEVER DID ASK ME ... WHERE DID I COME FROM ...
THEY JUST ALWAYS CALLED ME ... BOGANGLE'S FIRST CLASS BUM.

VERSE TWO:

I ALWAYS THOUGHT BOJANGLE'S ... WAS REALLY GOOD ...
BUT I WOULD ALWAYS BUY ... THE LOWEST PRICED FOOD.

WHEN I WALKED IN ... THEY WOULD SAY HERE HE COMES ...
THEY THOUGHT OF ME AS ... BOJANGLE'S FIRST CLASS BUM.

CHORUS:

YOU DON'T HAVE TO BE RICH ... TO EAT MEALS THAT'S
HEALTHY ...
BECAUSE I ALWAYS EAT GOOD ... AND I SURE AIN'T WEALTHY.

BUT I WANT YOU TO UNDERSTAND ... JUST HOW IT IS DONE ...
IF YOU LISTEN AND LEARN FROM ... BOJANGLE'S FIRST CLASS BUM.

VERSE THREE:

YOU'LL GET MEALS SO GOOD ... YOU WILL SAY UH ... UM ...
AND THAT'S GREAT COMING FROM ... BOJANGLE'S FIRST CLASS BUM.

BOJANGLE'S SERVE FOOD ... THAT IS GOOD FOR THE SOUL ...
AND THE WORKERS THAT WORKS THERE ... ARE AS GOOD AS GOLD.

VERSE FOUR:

I ALWAYS GET A GLASS OF WATER ... TO DRINK WITH MY
MEAL ...
AND BEFORE I FINISH EATING ... I GET A FREE REFILL.

I HAVE TO STAY ON A BUDGET ... THAT I AM WORKING ON ...
BECAUSE AFTER ALL I AM ... THE BOJANGLE'S FIRST CLASS BUM.

CHORUS:

    YOU DON'T HAVE TO BE RICH ... TO EAT MEALS THAT'S HEALTHY ...

BECAUSE I ALWAYS EAT GOOD ... AND I SURE AIN'T WEALTHY.

    BUT I WANT YOU TO UNDERSTAND ... JUST HOW IT IS DONE ...

IF YOU LISTEN AND LEARN FROM ... BOJANGLE'S FIRST CLASS BUM.

BORN TO BE A LEGEND

CHORUS:
    HE HAD BLACK HAIR ... AND HE WORE BLACK SHOES,,,
HE WORE A BLACK SHIRT ... AND BLACK PANTS TOO.
    HE PLAYED A BLACK GUITAR ... THAT SOUNDED SWEET ...
AND HE WORE BLACK SOCKS ... TO COVER HIS FEET.

VERSE ONE:
    HE WOULD WALK OUT ON STAGE ... DRESSED IN BLACK ...
AND PEOPLE WOULD SCREAM ... GLAD TO HAVE HIM BACK.
    HE WOULD SING SONGS ... THAT WOULD MAKE YOU TINGLE ...
IT MIGHT BE A LOVE SONG ... OR JUST A FUNNY JINGLE.

VERSE TWO:
    HIS REPUTATION GREW ... LARGER THAN A LUMBER JACK ...
AND HE WAS SIMPLY KNOWN ... AS THE MAN IN BLACK.
    HE WROTE SOME SAD SONGS ... AND FUNNY SONGS TOO ...
HE WAS BORN TO BE A LEGEND ... BEFORE HE WAS THROUGH.

VERSE THREE:
    THERE WAS TIMES IN HIS LIFE ...THINGS GOT OUT OF HAND...
BUT THE PEOPLE OF THIS WORLD ... STILL LOVED THIS MAN.
    THEY PRAYED AND PRAYED ... UNTIL THINGS CHANGED ...
AND NOW THE WHOLE WORLD ... WILL NEVER FORGET HIS NAME.

VERSE FOUR:
    MANY YEARS WENT BY... BEFORE HIS TIME TO DIE CAME ...
EVERYONE KNOWS JOHNNY CASH ... WAS THIS MAN'S NAME.
    HE WILL NEVER BE FORGOTTEN ... THOUGH HE IS GONE ...
BECAUSE HE BUILT A LEGEND ...THAT WILL FOREVER LIVE ON.

BOTTOM OF THE BARRELL

THEY SAY THERE'S A BAD APPLE ... IN EVERY BARRELL ...
A BAD APPLE IS AS USELESS ... AS A BOW WITHOUT AN ARROW.
AND I WAS THE BAD APPLE ... OF MY WHOLE FAMILY.
IT SEEMED THAT EVERYTHING ... WAS ALWAYS BLAMED ON ME.

SO I WOULD ALWAYS DO ... WHATEVER I WANTED TO ...
AND THERE WAS NOT ANYTHING ... THAT I DID'NT DO.
I WAS ABOUT AS LOW ... AS ANYONE COULD EVER GET ...
AT THE BOTTOM OF THE BARRELL ... SCRUBBING THE BOTTOM
OF IT.

THEN I STARTED LOOKING ... FOR A WAY TO GET OUT ...
BUT I DID'NT EVEN KNOW ... WHAT LIFE WAS REALLY ABOUT.
THEN ONE DAY I MET SOMEONE ... THAT WAS SMARTER
THAN ME ...
AND HE TOLD ME THAT THE TRUTH ... WOULD SET ME FREE.

HE PULLED ME UP FROM ... THE BOTTOM OF THE BARRELL ...
AND SET ME ON A PINNACLE ... ON TOP OF THE WORLD.
IT WAS GOD THE FATHER ... MAKER OF ALL MANKIND ...
AND HE WRAPPED ME IN HIS LOVE ... JUST IN TIME.

NOW I HAVE SO MUCH FOR ME ... TO LIVE AND DIE FOR ...
THAT YOU'LL NEVER CATCH ME ... ON THE BOTTOM ANYMORE.
BUT WHEN I DIE ... AND THEY LAY ME DOWN TO REST ...
I HOPE THE PEOPLE WILL SAY ... HE DID HIS BEST.

BURGER KING IS

VERSE ONE:
    BURGER KING IS ... WHERE THE TASTE TELLS THE TALE ...
THEY SAY WHAT YOU EAT ... IS HOW YOU FEEL.
    YOU WILL LEAVE HAPPY ... THERE IS NO DOUBT ...
CAUSE THIS MESSAGE IS WHAT ... IT'S ALL ABOUT.

CHORUS:
    IF YOU WANT TO GO OUT ... AND HAVE A GOOD MEAL ...
COME TO BURGER KING ... YOU WILL FIND OUR SERVICE IS REAL.
    YOU WILL FIND OUT ... WE'RE NOT HERE FOR THE SALE...
BECAUSE BURGER KING IS ... WHERE THE TASTE TELLS THE TALE.

VERSE TWO:
    BURGER KING IS ... WHERE THE TASTE TELLS THE TALE ...
SO USE THE COUPONS ... THAT YOU RECIEVE IN THE MAIL.
    YOU CAN GO TO TOWN ... LOOKING ALL AROUND ...
AND STILL NOT BE HAPPY... AT WHAT YOU HAVE FOUND.

VERSE THREE:
    WHEN YOU EAT HERE ...YOU WILL WANT TO SHOUT ...
BECAUSE THE MEALS ARE SO GOOD ... LIKE RIDING ON A CLOUD.
    BURGER KING IS ... WHERE THE TASTE TELLS THE TALE ...
AND YOU WILL KNOW ... THAT YOUR MEAL WAS SWELL.

CHORUS:
    IF YOU WANT TO GO OUT ... AND HAVE A GOOD MEAL ...
COME TO BURGER KING ... YOU WILL FIND OUR SERVICE IS REAL.
    YOU WILL FIND OUT ... WE ARE NOT HERE FOR THE SALE...
BECAUSE BURGER KING IS ... WHERE THE TASTE TELLS THE TALE.

BUY FROM US

THERE WILL BE ... NO BIG FUSS ...
IF YOU COME ... AND BUY FROM US.
YOU WILL HAVE ... ONLY TRUST ...
WHEN YOU BUY ... STRAIGHT FROM US.

WE WILL TREAT ... YOU ALL RIGHT ...
AND PUT YOU IN ... SHINING LIGHTS.
HERE YOU WILL ... FIND NO RUST ...
IF YOU BUY ... STRAIGHT FROM US.

IF YOU' BUY ... FROM SOMEWHERE ...
WHY NOT BUY ... FROM US HERE.
HERE WE HAVE ... THE BEST DEALS ...
SO BUY FROM US ... SEE HOW IT FEELS.

BUY FROM US ... AND SAVE SOME BUCKS...
WE'LL NEVER PUT YOU ... IN A CRUTCH ..
HERE YOU WON'T ... PAY TOO MUCH ...
YOU'LL BE GLAD ... YOU BOUGHT FROM US.

COLORFUL CAROLINA CHRISTMAS

VERSE ONE:

    WE HAVE GREEN GRASS GROWING ... IN NORTH CAROLINA ...

AND THE LAND LOOKS BETTER ... WHERE THE GRASS IS GREENER.

    WE PUT UP GREEN CHRISTMAS TREE'S ... WITH LIGHTS ALL AROUND ...

GREEN IS ONE OF THE PRETTIEST COLORS ... THAT CAN BE FOUND.

VERSE TWO:

    THEN THERE'S RED ... IN THE LIGHTS ON THE CHRISTMAS TREE ...

AND THEY SURE DO STAND OUT ... JUST LIKE YOU DO FOR ME.

    WITH A PRETTY RED RIBBON ... IN YOUR GOLDEN HAIR ...

AND A SMILE ON YOUR FACE ... THAT SHOWED THAT YOU CARE.

CHORUS:

   LET'S STOP FOR A MOMENT ... AND THINK ABOUT THE BLUE ...
THAT'S THE WAY THAT I FEEL ... WHEN I AM NOT WITH YOU.
   A COLORFUL CAROLINA CHRISTMAS ... YOU CAN MAKE RIGHT ...
IF YOU PUT BEAUTIFUL COLORS ... IN MY DREAMS TONIGHT.

VERSE THREE:

   LOOK AT THOSE YELLOW LIGHTS ... THAT SHINES LIKE THE
   SUN ...
THEY'RE BEAUTIFUL AT CHRISTMAS ... WHEN EVERYONE HAS FUN.
   YELLOW BOWS ON THE PRESENTS ... THAT GIFTS ARE
   WRAPPED IN ...
AND THEY'RE SEALED WITH LOVE ... FROM A VERY CLOSE FRIEND.

VERSE FOUR:

   THEN COMES THE SNOW FLAKES ... WITH SNOW SO WHITE ...
WHITE IS A NUTURAL COLOR ... BUT IT STANDS OUT SO BRIGHT.
   LIGHTS ON THE CHRISTMAS TREE ... RED YELLOW BLUE ABD
   WHITE ...
ALL THOSE BEAUTIFUL COLOLS ... JUST LIGHTS UP THE NIGHT.

CHORUS:

   LET'S STOP FOR A MOMENT ... AND THINK ABOUT THE BLUE ...
THAT'S THE WAY THAT I FEEL ... WHEN I AM NOT WITH YOU.
   A COLORFUL CAROLINA CHRISTMAS ... YOU CAN MAKE RIGHT ...
IF YOU PUT BEAUTIFUL COLORS ... IN MY DREAMS TONIGHT.

CHASING AFTER YOUR DREAMS

VERSE ONE:
> DID YOU EVER WONDER HOW ... TO SETTLE SOMETHING THAT MATTERED ..

WHEN YOU THOUGHT YOU HAD IT DONE ... ALL YOUR DREAMS SHATTERED.
> SOMETIMES YOU FEEL LIKE ... YOU WANT TO JUST LAY DOWN AND DIE ...

BUT YOU CAN'T JUST GIVE UP ... YOU CAN'T JUST LET IT LIE.

VERSE TWO:
> YOU DON'T WANT TO LET YOUR DREAMS ... ALL JUST FADE AWAY ...

SO YOU GET UP AGAIN ... BELIEVING THEY'LL COME TRUE SOMEDAY.
> YOU KEEP GOING FORWARD ... CHASING AFTER YOUR DREAMS ...

AND WHEN THEY DO COME TRUE ... YOU REALLY WANT TO SCREAM.

CHORUS:
> KEEP CHASING AFTER YOUR DREAMS ... UNTIL THEY COME TRUE ...

AND THEN YOU WILL FIND ... THAT YOU ARE A MUCH BETTER YOU.
> AS LONG AS YOU KEEP TRYING ... THERE'S NO WAY YOU CAN LOSE ...

KEEP CHASING AFTER YOUR DREAMS ... YOU'LL ALWAYS WIN IF YOU DO.

VERSE THREE:
> SO DON'T EVER GIVE UP ... BECAUSE THAT'S THE WORSE THING ...

SOMEDAY YOU WILL REACH YOUR GOAL ... SO KEEP CHASING YOUR DREAM.
> THE HARDEST PART OF ANY JOB ... IS TO GET THE NERVE TO START IT ...

REMEMBER TO THROW ENOUGH DARTS ... SOMEDAY YOU'LL HIT THE TARGET.

VERSE FOUR:

     KEEP CHASING AFTER YOUR DREAMS ... AND KEEP UP YOUR
     FAITH ...

AND DON'T LET THE CHALLENGE ... NEVER EVER TURN INTO HATE.
     BECAUSE FAITH IS THE SUBSTANCE ... OF THINGS THAT YOU
     HOPE FOR ...

AND THE EVIDENCE OF THINGS YOU RECIEVE ... IS YOUR BIG
REWARD.

CHORUS:

     KEEP CHASING AFTER YOUR DREAMS ... UNTIL THEY COME
     TRUE ...

AND THEN YOU WILL FIND ... THAT YOU'RE A MUCH DIFFERANT YOU.
     AS LONG AS YOU KEEP TRYING ... THERE'S NO WAY YOU CAN
     LOSE ...

KEEP CHASING AFTER YOUR DREAMS ... YOU'LL ALWAYS WIN IF
YOU DO.

CHRISTMAS DAY WAS MADE

CHORUS:

CHRISTMAS DAY WAS MADE ... JUST FOR ME ...
I'M A SINNER SAVED BY GRACE ... I HAVE BEEN SET FREE.
JESUS CHRIST WAS BORN ... ON EARTH AND I BELIEVE ...
THAT CHRISTMAS DAY WAS MADE ... JUST FOR ME.

VERSE ONE:

GOD SENT DOWN HIS SON ... HIS NAME WAS JESUS ...
SINCE THE DAY THAT HE WAS BORN ... WE CALL IT CHRISTMAS .
HE CAME SO THAT THE LOST ... COULD BE SET FREE ...
CHRISTMAS DAY WAS MADE ... JUST FOR ME.

VERSE TWO:

I WAS LOST IN SIN ... WITH NO HOPE FOR TOMORROW ...
UNTIL JESUS CAME TO EARTH ... AND TOOK AWAY MY SORROW.
AND NOW I HAVE HOPE ... FOR ALL OF ETERNITY ...
AND THAT'S WHY CHRISTMAS WAS MADE ... JUSR FOR ME.

HORUS:

CHRISTMAS DAY WAS MADE ... JUST FOR ME ...
I'M A SINNER SAVED BY GRACE ... I HAVE BEEN SET FREE.
JESUS CHRIST WAS BORN ... ON EARTH AND I BELIEVE ...
THAT CHRISTMAS DAY WAS MADE ... JUST FOR ME.

VERSE THREE:

SOMEDAY I'LL GO TO HEAVEN ... AND THEN I WILL SEE ...
WHY CHRISTMAS DAY WAS MADE ... JUST FOR ME.
THERE I'LL MEET JESUS CHRIST ... GOD'S OWN SON ...
AND I'LL PRAISE HIM FOREVER ... FOR WHAT HE HAS DONE.

VERSE FOUR:

HE GAVE ME A NEW LIFE ... AND TOOK AWAY MY SIN ...
I'LL NEVER LIVE AGAIN ... LIKE I DID BACK THEN.
HE CAME DOWN FROM GLORY ... GOT NAILED TO A TREE ...
AND THAT'S WHY CHRISTMAS DAY WAS MADE ... JUST FOR ME.

CHRISTMAS LIKE IT USED TO BE

CHORUS:
>IT JUST WON'T SEEM ... LIKE CHRISTMAS ...
WITH NO SNOW ... ON CHRISTMAS DAY.
>BUT MAYBE SANTA CLAUS ... WILL BRING ME ...
A BRAND NEW ... CHEVROLET.
>AFTER ALL ... WE ONLY HAVE CHRISTMAS ...
ONCE A YEAR ... SO COME WHAT MAY.
>BE THANKFUL ... AND COUNT YOUR BLESSINGS...
ON THIS JOLLY ... CHRISTMAS DAY.

VERSE:
>WE LIKE TO DECORATE ... OUR CHRISTMAS TREES...
WITH ORNAMENTS ... AND SHINING LIGHTS.
>THEN HOPE SOMEONE ... WILL PUT A PRESENT ...
UNDER THE TREE ... ON CHRISTMAS EVE.
>CHRISTMAS ... IS NOT CELEBRATED ...
THE WAY ... IT USED TO BE.
>WHEN WE WOULD CUT DOWN ... REAL LIVE TREES ...
FROM WAY DOWN IN ... THE COUNTRY.

CHORUS:
>IT JUST WON'T SEEM ... LIKE CHRISTMAS ...
WITH NO SNOW ... ON CHRISTMAS DAY.
>BUT MAYBE SANTA CLAUS ... WILL BRING ME ...
A BRAND NEW ... CHEVROLET.
>AFTER ALL ... WE ONLY HAVE CHRISTMAS ...
ONCE A YEAR ... SO COME WHAT MAY.
>BE THANKFUL ... AND COUNT YOUR BLESSINGS...
ON THIS JOLLY ... CHRISTMAS DAY.

CHRISTMAS LOVE

VERSE ONE:
    IF CHRISTMAS WAS LIKE ... IT USED TO BE ...
WHAT I REALLY WANT ... YOU CAN'T GET UNDER THE TREE ...
    I WILL STILL BE LOOKING FOR IT ... THIS CHRISTMAS DAY .
IF YOU WILL ONLY LISTEN ... TO WHAT I HAVE TO SAY.

VERSE TWO:
    I WANT YOUR LOVE...COMPLETELY WRAPPED IN MY ARMS ...
AND IN MY HEART ... WITH ALL OF YOUR CHARMS.
    BUT FIRST PUT YOUR HEART ... IN WHAT CHRISTMAS MEANS ...
AND THEN ALLTHE REST ... YOU CAN GIVE TO ME.

VERSE THREE:
    YOU BRIGHTEN UP THINGS ... WITH LOVE AT CHRISTMAS TIME ...
AND YOU PUT JOY IN MY HEART ... ALL OF THE TIME.
    YOU MAKE ME SMILE ... BOTH DAY AND NIGHT ...
AS LONG AS WE ARE TOGETHER ... MY FUTURE LOOKS BRIGHT.

VERSE FOUR:
    CHRISTMAS TIME IS THE HAPPIEST TIME ... OF THE YEAR ...
AND MY LIFE IS MUCH BRIGHTER ... WHEN YOU ARE HERE.
    SO STAY CLOSE BY ME ... BECAUSE I NEED YOU ...
AND DON'T MAKE MY CHRISTMAS CHEER ... TURN INTO BLUE.

VERSE FIVE:
    LET'S SING CHRISTMAS SONGS ... IN A MERRY WAY ...
BECAUSE CHRIST WAS BORN ... ON CHRISTMAS DAY.
    LET THE FEELING COME FROM... WITHIN OUR HEARTS ...
BECAUSE THAT IS WHERE ... OUR SALVATION STARTS.

CHORUS:
    SING SING SING ... THOSE HAPPY CHRISTMAS SONGS ...
AND LET'S ALL REJOICE ... AS WE RIDE ALONG.
    KEEP THE JOY OF CHRISTMAS ... IN OUR HEARTS AND MINDS ...
AND PRAISE JESUS CHRIST ... FOREVER AND ALL THE TIME

CHRISTMAS TIME'S A' COMIN'

CHORUS:
CHRISTMAS TIME'S A'COMIN'... IT'S THAT TIME OF THE YEAR...
EVERYONE'S A'FILLIN' ... CHRISTMAS STOCKINGS WITH CHEER.
SANTA CLAUS IS BUSY... WITH HIS SLED AND REINDEER...
CHRISTMAS TIME'S A'COMING ... IT'S THAT TIME OF THE YEAR.

VERSE ONE:
I HOPE THIS FINDS YOU HAPPY ... AND VERY HEALTHY TOO...
MAY THIS CHRISTMAS SEASON BE ..THE BEST YOU EVER KNEW.
EAT.. DRINK .. AND BE MERRY... AND FULL OF CHRISTMAS CHEER...
CHRISTMAS TIME'S A'COMIN' ... IT'S THAT TIME OF THE YEAR.

CHAPTER TWO:
HO...HO...HO...CAN'T YOU HEAR IT... ECHO'S EVERYWHERE...
OLD SAINT NICK'S AWAITING...TO BRING US CHRISTMAS CHEER.
HE LIKES TO KEEP HIS PROMISE ... AND HE WILL IF HE CAN ...
BUT TIMES ARE GETTING HARDER ... AND HE HOPES YOU
UNDERSTAND.

CHORUS:
CHRISTMAS TIME'S A'COMIN'... IT'S THAT TIME OF THE YEAR...
EVERYONE'S A'FILLIN' ... CHRISTMAS STOCKINGS WITH CHEER.
SANTA CLAUS IS BUSY... WITH HIS SLED AND REINDEER...
CHRISTMAS TIME'S A'COMING ... IT'S THAT TIME OF THE YEAR.

VERSE THREE:
WE MAY NOT GET A PRESENT... WE STILL EXPECT ONE THOUGH...
THE KIDS ARE WANTING TO BUILD ... A SNOWMAN IN THE SNOW.
THE CHRISTMAS LIGHTS A'GLEAMING... LIT UP EVERYWHERE ...
CHRISTMAS TIME'S A'COMIN' ... IT'S THAT TIME OF THE YEAR.

CHORUS:
CHRISTMAS TIME'S A'COMIN'... IT'S THAT TIME OF THE YEAR...
EVERYONE'S A'FILLIN' ... CHRISTMAS STOCKINGS WITH CHEER.
SANTA CLAUS IS BUSY... WITH HIS SLED AND REINDEER...
CHRISTMAS TIME'S A'COMING ... IT'S THAT TIME OF THE YEAR.

COLD COFFEE AND HOT BEER

CHORUS:
   THEY HAD COLD COFFEE ... AND HOT BEER ...
IT DON'T PAY TO BE BROKE ... AND LIVE AROUND HERE.
   I SURE WISH I COULD ... FIND ME SOME WORK ...
I'M SO TIRED OF BEING ... AS POOR AS DIRT.

VERSE ONE:
   WHERE I COME FROM ... IS THE POOR SIDE OF TOWN ...
I'VE NEVER HAD ANYTHING ... A' BUMMING AROUND.
   EVERYTHING I HAVE ... WAS GIVEN TO ME ...
OTHERWISE I WOULD'NT HAVE IT ... IF IT WAS'NT FREE.

VERSE TWO:
   I WENT TO A PARTY ... I WAS INVITED TO ...
BUT WHEN I GOT THERE ... THE PARTY WAS THROUGH.
   ALL THEY HAD LEFT ... WAS COLD COFFEE AND HOT BEER ...
I WONDERED WHAT ON EARTH ... WAS I DOING DOWN THERE.

CHORUS:
   THEY HAD COLD COFFEE ... AND HOT BEER ...
IT DON'T PAY TO BE BROKE ... AND LIVE AROUND HERE.
   I SURE WISH I COULD ... FIND ME SOME WORK ...
I'M SO TIRED OF BEING ... AS POOR AS DIRT.

VERSE THREE:
   ANYTHING IS BETTER ... THAN I HAVE DOWN HERE ...
EVEN IF IT IS COLD COFFEE ... AND HOT BEER.
   SOMEDAY I'LL FIND ME ... A MUCH BETTER WAY ...
I'LL HAVE HOT COFFEE ... AND COLD BEER SOMEDAY.

CORNER OF THE STREET

VERSE ONE:

    I WAS STANDING ... ON THE CORNER OF THE STREET ...
WHEN A GIRL DROVE BY ... AND BLOWED HER HORN AT ME.
    SHE THROWED UP HER HAND ... AND WAVED SO SWEET ...
AND LEFT ME STANDING ... ON THE CORNER OF THE STREET.

VERSE TWO:

    WHEN SHE PASSED ON BY ... SHE LOOKED BACK AT ME ...
MY HEART STOPPED PUMPING ... AS SHE WAS LEAVING ME.
    I SAW HER TURN AROUND... AND CAME BACK MY WAY ...
I WAS GLAD I WAS STANDING ...ON THE CORNER THAT DAY.

VERSE THREE:

    SHE STOPPED AND ASK ME ... IF I WANTED TO GO FOR A SPIN ...
I OPENED THE CAR DOOR ... AND JUMPED RIGHT IN.
    SHE TOLD ME HER NAME ... AND I TOLD HER MINE ...
AND MY HEART WAS BEATING FASTER ... ALL OF THE TIME.

VERSE FOUR:

    SHE WHAT I WAS LOOKING FOR ... STANDING ON THE STREET...
I SAID I WAS LOOKING FOR LOVE ... AND ASK COULD SHE HELP ME.
    SHE ASK WOULD I LIKE TO STOP ... AND HAVE AN ICE CREAM ...
NOT KNOWING I WAS EXPLORING ... MY WILDEST DREAM.

VERSE FIVE:

    WE STOPPED AT A SODA SHOP ... ON THE CORNER OF A STREET...
AND THE LOVE I FOUND THAT DAY ... HAS NEVER LEFT ME.
    I FOUND THE ONE THING I NEEDED ... TO MAKE NY LIFE
    COMPLETE...
WHILE STANDING ON THE CORNER ... OF A LONELY STREET.

CRUISING MAIN STREET

VERSE ONE:

    I CAN STILL REMEMBER ... MY FONDEST MEMORIES ...
WHEN I HAD A HOT ROD CAR ... AND CRUISING MAIN STREET.
    I WOULD LOOK FOR THE GIRLS ... ALL OVER TOWN ...
AND JUST CRUISE MAIN STREET ... UP AND DOWN.

VERSE TWO:

    SOMETIMES I WOULD HAVE TO STOP ... AT A RED LIGHT ...
IF I DID'NT SEE ANY GIRLS ... I'D SHOW OFF THAT NIGHT.
    IF THERE WAS A CAR BESIDE ME ... I'D RAISE THE ENGINE ...
WHEN THE LIGHT CHANGED ... MY WHEELS WOULD START
SPINNING.

CHORUS:

    JUST CRUISING MAIN STREET ... FROM LIGHT TO LIGHT ...
WE WERE RACING EVERYTHING ... THAT CAME INTO SIGHT.
    SOMETIMES WE WOULD EVEN ... TRY TO OUTRUN THE LAW ...
JUST CRUISIN' MAIN STREET ... AND REALLY HAVING A BALL.

VERSE THREE:

    WE'D TAKE OFF IN A DRAG ... TRYING TO OUTRUN THE OTHER ...
WE WOULD GET A REAL THRILL ... RACING ONE ANOTHER.
    SOMETIMES WE'D GET CAUGHT ... AND WOULD GET A TICKET ...
THEN WHEN WE WENT TO COURT ... WE'D HAVE TO PAY FOR IT.

VERSE FOUR:

    WHEN YOU GET A LITTLE AGE ON YOU ... YOU LOOK BACK ON
    LIFE ...
AND YOU SEE HOW WRECKLESS YOU WAS ... JUST FOR A LAUGH.
    I GUESS THAT WENT ALONG ... WITH GROWING UP TO BE A MAN ...
JUST CRUISING MAIN STREET ... WITH A BEER IN OUR HAND/

CHORUS:

    JUST CRUISING MAIN STREET ... FROM LIGHT TO LIGHT ...
WE WERE RACING EVERYTHING ... THAT CAME INTO SIGHT.
    SOMETIMES WE WOULD EVEN ... TRY TO OUTRUN THE LAW ...
JUST CRUISING MAIN STREET ... AND REALLY HAVING A BALL.

DADDY GET READY

CHORUS:

    THERE WAS ONCE A MAN ... WHO WAS ALWAYS READY ...
AND THIS MAN WAS NONE OTHER ... THAN MY DADDY.
    HE COULD HANDLE ANYTHING ... THAT WOULD COME HIS WAY ...
NOW DADDY GET READY ... I WOULD HEAR MY MOMMA SAY.

VERSE ONE:

    DADDY GET READY ... WE GOT COMPANY COMING TODAY ...
MY MOMMA ALWAYS WANTED ... EVERYTHING TO LOOK OKAY.
    DADDY WOULD GO OUT TO THE BARN ... AND GET A BIG OLD HAM ...
MOMMA WOULD COOK SUPPER ... BEFORE THEY CAME FROM TOWN.

VERSE TWO:

    AFTER THEY ATE SUPPER ... MOMMA WOULD WASH THE DISHES ...
DADDY WOULD SAT AROUND ... AND REMINISE OF THINGS HE MISSES.
    THEN MOMMA WOULD SAY ... DADDY GET READY IT'S BEDTIME ...
OH WHAT I'D GIVE TO GO BACK ... TO THOSE CHILDHOOD DAYS OF MINE.

VERSE THREE:

    THEN ON SUNDAY MOMMA WOULD SAY ... DADDY GET READY ...
LET'S GO TO CHURCH TODAY ... AND THANK THE LORD FOR OUR BLESSIN'.
    MOMMA WOULD LOAD UP THE CHILDREN ... PUT'EM ON THE WAGON ...
AND WE'D HEAD FOR TOWN ... TO WHERE CHURCH BELLS WAS SOUNDIN'.

VERSE FOUR:

      THEN DADDY GOT SICK ... AND WAS IN THE BED FOR A
      WEEK ...

THINGS WAS'NT LOOKING GOOD ... HE COULD HARDLY SPEAK.

      THE DOCTOR TOLD MOMMA ... I'VE DONE ALL I CAN DO ...

THEN MOMMA SAID DADDY GET READY ... THE LORD IS CALLING YOU.

VERSE FIVE:

      WELL DADDY LEFT THIS LIFE ... TO GO ON TO HIS NEW
      HOME ...

I CAN STILL HEAR MOMMA ... DADDY GET READY I'LL SOON BE
ALONG.

      YEARS HAVE PASSED NOW ... BUT THOSE WORDS ARE STILL
      THERE ...

DADDY GET READY ... THAT SAYING STILL ECHOES THROUGH
THE AIR.

DEATH HAS BEEN DEFEATED

VERSE ONE:

I CAN'T WAIT TO SEE ... WHAT'S BEEN PROMISED TO ME ...
THERE'S A MANSION BEING BUILT ... UP IN G - L - O - R - Y.
IT WAS PAID FOR BY THE BLOOD ... OF JESUS CHRIST ...
IT WAS SIGNED AND SEALED ... WHEN HE GAVE HIS LIFE.

VERSE TWO:

THEY TORCHERED HIM WITH THORNS ... AND VINEGER ON SPONGE ...
THEY PIERCED HIM WITH A SWORD ... IN HIS SIDE THEY DID PLUNGE.
THEY THOUGHT IT WOULD BE OVER ... IF THEY TOOK HIS LIFE ...
BUT HE SAID TODAY YOU WILL BE ... WITH ME IN PARADISE.

VERSE THREE:

HE HUNG HIS HEAD AND CRIED ... FATHER FORGIVE THEM ...
FOR THEY KNOW NOT WHAT THEY DO ... THEIR EYES ARE SO DIM.
THEN HE BOWED HIS HEAD AND SAID ... NOW IT IS OVER ...
THEN HE GAVE UP THE SPIRIT ... AND THEY SAW GOD'S POWER.

CHORUS:

HE WANTED US TO KNOW ... WHEN WE DIED WE WOULD ARISE ...
AND HE HAS A MANSION BUILT ... FOR US UP IN THE SKY.
DEATH HAS BEEN DEFEATED ... WHERE THERE IS NO SIN ...
WHEN THEY PUT US IN THE GRAVE ... WE WILL RISE UP AGAIN.

VERSE FOUR:

THEY PLACED HIM IN A TOMB ... AND BOUND IT WITH A STONE ...
BUT IT WAS REMOVED ... AND IN THREE DAYS HE WAS GONE.
THE GRAVE COULD'NT HOLD HIM ... HE CAME BACK LIKE HE SAID ...
AND IN JUST THREE DAYS .... HE DEFEATED DEATH.

CHORUS:

      HE WANTED US TO KNOW ... WHEN WE DIED WE WOULD
      ARISE ...

AND HE HAS A MANSION BUILT ... FOR US UP IN THE SKY.

      DEATH HAS BEEN DEFEATED ... WHERE THERE IS NO SIN ...

WHEN THEY PUT US IN THE GRAVE ... WE WILL RISE UP AGAIN.

DID YOU EVER

VERSE ONE:

  DID YOU EVER ASK ... WHAT AM I GOING TO DO? ...
DID YOU EVER THINK ... YOUR LIFE WAS ALMOST THRU.
  DID YOU EVER FEEL ... THAT YOU HAD NO FRIENDS ...
OR DID YOU EVER WISH ... YOUR LIFE WOULD SOON END.

VERSE TWO:

  DID YOU EVER LOSE ... SOMEONE THAT YOU LOVED ...
OR DID YOU EVER ... GET PUSHED AROUND AND SHOVED.
  DID YOU EVER MAKE AN F ... WHILE GOING TO SCHOOL ...
OR DID YOU EVER FEEL LIKE ... YOU WAS JUST A FOOL.

VERSE THREE:

  DID YOU EVER GET BEHIND BARS ... LOCKED UP IN JAIL ...
DID YOU EVER HAVE TO CALL SOMEONE ... TO GO YOUR BAIL.
  DID YOU EVER THINK ... THAT YOUR LUCK WAS ALL BAD ...
DID YOU EVER WISH THAT ... YOU HAD MORE THAN YOU HAD.

VERSE FOUR:

  DID YOU EVER GO ... WHERE YOU SHOULD'NT HAVE GONE ...
DID YOU EVER SAY ... YOU SHOULD HAVE STAYED AT HOME.
  DID YOU EVER WONDER ... WHY YOU WAS ALWAYS SCORNED ...
DID YOU EVER WISH ... YOU HAD NEVER BEEN BORNED.

CHORUS:

  LIFE IS NOT ALWAYS AS BAD ... AS IT MAY SEEM ...
EVEN THROUGH HARD TIMES ... YOU CAN STILL HAVE DREAMS.
  SO TAKE SOME TIME OUT ... AND THINK THINGS OVER ...
AND STOP ASKING YOURSELF ... WHY DID YOU EVER.

DON'T CRITICIZE ME

CHORUS:

      DON'T CRITICIZE ME ... FOR THINGS THAT I DO ...
FOR YOU HAVE NEVER WALKED ... A MILE IN MY SHOES.
      YOU DON'T KNOW HOW MUCH ... MY POOR HEART CRIES ...
BECAUSE YOU AIN'T SEEN THINGS ... THROUGH MY SAD EYES.

VERSE ONE:

      I HAVE SEEN BABIES ... CRYING FOR FOOD ...
WITH NO WAY TO HELP ... EVEN THOUGH I WANTED TO.
      PEOPLE COMPLAINING ... ABOUT PAYING BILLS ...
KNOWING THERE'S NOTHING I CAN DO ... GIVES ME A CHILL.

VERSE TWO:

      DON'T CRITICIZE ME ... IF I JUST WALK ON BY ...
THERE'S NOTHING I CAN DO ... EVEN IF I TRY.
      I WISH I COULD HELP ... BUT I CAN'T HELP MYSELF ...
ALL I CAN DO IS WISH YOU LUCK ... IN HELPIMG YOURSELF.

VERSE THREE:

      I HAVE HAD TO TAKE LIFE ... AS IT WAS HANDED TO ME ...
AND I HAVE HAD TO STRUGGLE ... AND I HAVE HAD TO PLEA.
      SO YOU DO YOUR THING ... AND I'LL DO MINE ...
BUT DON'T CRITICIZE ME ... LIKE A BOTTLE OF SPILLED WINE.

VERSE FOUR:

      I KNOW YOU HAVE PROBLEMS ... EVERYONE DOES ...
DON'T BLAME ME ... BECAUSE THINGS AIN'T LIKE THEY WAS.
      FIGHT YOUR OWN BATTLES... AND LEAVE MINE ALONG ...
THINGS WILL BE BETTER ... IF YOU JUST MIND YOUR OWN.

CHORUS:

      DON'T CRITICIZE ME ... FOR THINGS THAT I DO ...
FOR YOU HAVE NEVER WALKED ... A MILE IN MY SHOES.
      YOU DON'T KNOW HOW MUCH ... MY POOR HEART CRIES ...
BECAUSE YOU AIN'T SEEN THINGS ... THROUGH MY SAD EYES.

`DON'T DOUBLE YOUR DEBT

VERSE ONE:

    IF YOU SEE SOMETHING ...YOU AIN'T GOT MONEY TO GET ...
DON'T JUST JUMP IN ... AND DON'T DOUBLE YOUR DEBT.
    GOING IN DEBT ... IS A HARD ROAD TO TRAVEL ...
SOMETIMES IT'S ROCKIER ... THAN A ROAD OF GRAVEL.

VERSE TWO:

    GOING INTO DEBT ... IS REALLY EASY TO DO ...
AND THE DEBT CAN TAKE ... COMPLETE CONTROL OF YOU.
    IT WILL LEAVE YOU HANGING ... IN DOUBTS OF RELIEF ...
AND IT WILL ONLY BRING YOU ... A LOT OF GRIEF.

VERSE THREE:

    DON'T DOUBLE YOUR DEBT...AND GO OVER YOUR HEAD...
YOU MIGHT THINK ...YOU'D BE BETTER OFF DEAD.
    SOON IT WILL CONSUME ... ALL THAT YOU SAVED ...
AND IT WILL LEAD YOU ... STRAIGHT TO YOUR GRAVE.

VERSE FOUR:

    DON'T DOUBLE YOUR DEBT ... AND RUIN YOUR CREDIT ...
EVEN IF YOU THINK ... IT'S THE ONLY WAY TO GET IT.
    YOU WILL FIND OUT LATER ... IT WILL BRING REGRET ...
SO TAKE SOME GOOD ADVICE ... DON'T DOUBLE YOUR DEBT.

DON'T THEY KNOW

VERSE ONE;

EVERYONE SAYS TO ME ... WHAT I'M DOING IS NOT RIGHT ...
I STILL LIVE IN THE PAST ... AND LAY AWAKE AND PRAY AT NIGHT.
AND EVEN THOUGH THEY SAY... SHE WAS MUCH OLDER THAN ME ...
BUT DON'T THEY KNOW ... THEY CAN'T TAKE HER FROM ME.

VERSE TWO:

I HAVE NEVER KNOWN ANYONE ... THAT TREATED ME LIKE SHE DID ...
SHE HAD A SPECIAL LOVE FOR ME ... THAT COULD'NT BE HID.
WHY DON'T THEY MIND THEIR OWN BUSINESS ... AND JUST LET IT BE ...
WHY CAN'T THEY REALIZE .. THEY CAN'T TAKE HER FROM ME.

CHORUS:

EVERYBODY JUST WANTS TO ... TEAR MY WORLD APART ...
BUT THEY DON'T KNOW ... THE FEELINGS OF MY HEART.
I WISH THAT THEY WOULD ... JUST LET ME BE ...
BECAUSE DON'T THEY KNOW ... THEY CAN'T TAKE HER FROM ME.

VERSE THREE:

WHEN SHE WAS ALIVE ... SHE ALWAYS LOVED ME ...
BUT NOW ALL THAT I HAVE ... IS HER LOVING MEMORY.
SHE WILL ALWAYS HAVE ... A SPECIA PLACE IN MY HEART ...
BUT DON'T THEY KNOW ... HER MEMORY IS STILL A PIECE OF ART.

VERSE FOUR:

THEY WILL NEVER BE ABLE ... TO TAKE OUR PAST AWAY ...
THE TIMES THAT WE HAD TOGETHER ... WILL FOREVER STAY.
ANYTIME I WANT HER LOVE ... I TURN MY MIND TO YESTERDAY ...
AND DON'T THEY KNOW ... THEY CAN'T TAKE THAT AWAY.

CHORUS:

  EVERYBODY JUST WANTS ... TO TEAR MY WORLD APART ...

 BUT THEY DON'T KNOW ... THE FEELINGS OF MY HEART.

  I WISH THAT THEY WOULD ... JUST LET ME BE ...

BECAUSE DON'T THEY KNOW ... THEY CAN'T TAKE HER FROM ME.

DOWN AT THE CORNER CAFE

CHORUS:
    I WILL NEVER FORGET ... THOSE OLD MEMORIES ...
DOWN AT THE CORNER CAFE ... WHERE WE USED TO MEET.
    I LOVE TO SIT AROUND ... AND TALK ABOUT THOSE DAYS.
AND ALL THE TIMES WE HAD ... DOWN AT THE CORNER CAFE.

VERSE ONE:
    ALL THE LAUGHS WE HAD ... AND THE TRICKS WE PLAYED ...
WILL STAY WITH ME ... ALL THE WAY TO THE GRAVE.
    WE DON'T HAVE GOOD TIMES ... LIKE IN THOSE DAYS ...
I WOULD LIKE TO GO BACK ... TO THE CORNER CAFE.

VERSE TWO:
    WE WOULD DRINK A SODA ... AND JUST LAUGH AND PLAY ...
WE MADE A LOT OF MEMORIES ... BACK IN THOSE DAYS.
    I'D LIKE TO TURN BACK TIME ... AND RELIVE YESTERDAY ...
IF I COULD GO BACK ... DOWN AT THE CORNER CAFE.

VERSE THREE:
    THEY BUILT A NEW SHOPPING CENTER ...THE CAFE IS GONE ...
BUT THEY CAN'T TAKE THOSE MEMORIES ... THEY LIVE ON.
    I STILL HEAR THE LAUGHTER... AND SEE THEIR FACES TODAY ...
I CAN'T FORGET THE TIMES ... DOWN AT THE CORNER CAFE ...

CHORUS:
    I WILL NEVER FORGET ... THOSE OLD MEMORIES ...
DOWN AT THE CORNER CAFE ... WHERE WE USED TO MEET.
    WE STILL SIT AROUND ... AND TALK ABOUT THOSE DAYS.
AND ALL THE TIMES WE HAD ... DOWN AT THE CORNER CAFE.

DOWN BY THE OLD CREEK

VERSE ONE:

    WE WERE ALL YOUNG ... AND SO FULL OF FUN ...
AND WE ENJOYED ABOUT EVERYTHING ... THAT WE DONE.
    SOMETIMES WE PUT BLANKETS ... DOWN ON THE GROUND ...
DOWN BY THE OLD CREEK ... AND JUST LAY AROUND.

VERSE TWO:

    WE WOULD TALK ABOUT THINGS ... WE WOULD LIKE TO DO ...
AND HOPE THAT SOMEDAY ... OUR DREAMS WOULD COME TRUE.
    THE MEMORIES WE MADE THEN ... WE WILL ALWAYS KEEP ...
OF THE THINGS THAT WE DID ... DOWN BY THE OLD CREEK.

CHORUS:

    IT WAS A BEAUTIFUL PLACE ... WHERE WE USED TO MEET ...
WHERE WE HAD A LOT OF FUN ... DOWN BY THE OLD CREEK.
    SOMETIMES WE WOULD TAKE US ... SOME FOOD TO EAT ...
AND SIT DOWN ON THE GROUND ... DOWN BY THE OLD CREEK.

VERSE THREE:

    WE DID'NT EVEN KNOW ... WHEN WE TALKED ABOUT LOVE ...
WHAT THE DREAMS OF LIFE ... WAS REALLY MADE OF.
    BUT WE DID THE THINGS THEN ...TO MAKE OUR LIVES
COMPLETE...
AND IT ALL GOT STARTED ... DOWN BY THE OLD CREEK.

VERSE FOUR:

    MANY YEARS HAVE PASSED ... NOW WE ARE ALL OLD ...
BUT THE THINGS WE DID THEN ... IS WORTH MORE THAN GOLD.
    THE LIVES THAT WE LIVED ... ARE MEMORIES SO SWEET ...
AND THE THINGS THAT WE DID ... DOWN BY THE OLD CREEK.

CHORUS:

    IT WAS A BEAUTIFUL PLACE ... WHERE WE USED TO MEET ...
WHERE WE HAD A LOT OF FUN ... DOWN BY THE OLD CREEK.
    SOMETIMES WE WOULD TAKE US ... SOME FOOD TO EAT ...
AND SIT DOWN ON THE GROUND ... DOWN BY THE OLD CREEK.

DRIVE ... TRUCKERS ... DRIVE

CHORUS:
DRIVE TRUCKERS DRIVE ... THE ROADS ARE OPEN WIDE ...
THERE'S SMOOTH SAILING TONIGHT ... THERE'S NO SMOKIES IN SIGHT.
SO GET ON THAT RADIO ... AND LET'S GET ON OVER THE ROAD ...
IT'S TIME TO COME ALIVE ... SO DRIVE TRUCKERS DRIVE.

VERSE ONE:
WE'VE DROVE OVER THE MOUNTAINS ... DOWN THRU THE CITIES ...
AND WE NEVER HAVE FORGOTTEN ... OUR RESPONSIBILITYS.
WE RESPECT THE PATROL MEN ... AND THE LAWS WE HAVE TO OBEY ...
BUT WE NEED NO ONE TO ESCORT US ... OVER THE HIGHWAY.

VERSE TWO:
WE HAVE A JOB TO DO ... AND WE DO IT THE BEST WE CAN ...
SO LET US DO OUR WORK ... AND SUPPLY GOODS ALL OVER THE LAND.
THE NATION NEEDS US ... AS MUCH AS THEY NEED YOU ...
SO STAY OUT OF OUR WAY ... AND LET THE TRUCKS GO THROUGH.

CHORUS:

DRIVE TRUCKERS DRIVE ... THE ROADS ARE OPEN WIDE ... THERE'S SMOOTH SAILING TONIGHT ... THERE'S NO SMOKIES IN SIGHT.

SO GET ON THAT RADIO ... AND LET'S GET ON OVER THE ROAD ... IT'S TIME TO COME ALIVE ... SO DRIVE TRUCKERS DRIVE.

VERSE THREE:

WE HAVE TO DELIVER OUR LOADS ... AS WE RUN THE ROADS ... AND WATCH OUT FOR OTHER DRIVERS ... AND REMEMBER THE CODES.

RESPECT THE OTHER PERSON ... LAW ENFORCEMENT OFFICERS TOO...

WE'RE TO LOVE ONE ANOTHER ... AND HOPE THEY RESPECT YOU ...

VERSE FOUR:

SOMETIMES WE HAVE TO STRIVE ... IT'S A BIG JOB TO DO ... WE MUST TRY TO STAY ALIVE ... AND IN GOOD HEALTH TOO.

LAY OFF THE PILLS ... WHILE YOU DELIVER YOUR LOAD ... THEN WE CAN GO HOME ... AND GET OFF OF THE ROAD.

CHORUS:

DRIVE TRUCKERS DRIVE ... THE ROADS ARE OPEN WIDE ... THERE'S SMOOTH SAILING TONIGHT ... THERE'S NO SMOKIES IN SIGHT.

SO GET ON THAT RADIO ... AND LET'S GET ON OVER THE ROAD ... IT'S TIME TO COME ALIVE ... SO DRIVE TRUCKERS DRIVE.

EVERYTHING THAT LIFE COULD BRING

VERSE ONE:

THERE WAS A TIME IN MY LIFE ... WHEN I SEEMED TO HAVE
EVERYTHING ...
I HAD MONEY IN THE BANK ... AND ALL THE HAPPINESS THAT LIFE
COULD BRING.
I HAD EVERYTHING THAT I WANTED ... AND I NEVER HAD TO
BORROW ...
THEN ALL THE THINGS THAT LIFE COULD GIVE ... ONLY BROUGHT
ME SORROW.

VERSE TWO:

I HAD TURNED AWAY FROM GOD ... I WAS WALKING ON THIN
ICE ...
I THOUGHT I WAS DOING PRETTY GOOD ... I DID'NT NEED NOBODY'S
ADVICE.
BUT WHEN THE ICE HAD BROKEN THRU ... THE WATER WAS
TOO DEEP ...
I WAS SO FAR IN OVER MY HEAD ... AND THE WAY BACK UP WAS TOO
STEEP.

VERSE THREE:

EVERYTHING THAT LIFE COULD BRING ... WAS MORE THAN I
COULD AFFORD...
THERE WAS BUT ONE WAY FOR ME TO GO ... SO I WENT BACK TO
THE LORD.
HE REACHED DOWN AND PICKED ME UP ... WHEN I WAS DOWN
AND OUT ...
AND HE TAUGHT ME A THING OR TWO ... OF WHAT LIFE IS ALL
ABOUT.

VERSE FOUR:

HE PUT A PRAISE ON MY LIPS ... AND A SONG IN MY HEART ...
AND THE JOY THAT HE GIVES ... WILL NEVER EVER PART.
HE GAVE ME WORDS TO A SONG ... AND HE TOLD ME TO SING ...
ABOUT WHAT LIFE IS ALL ABOUT ... AND EVERYTHING LIFE COULD
BRING.

CHORUS:

    ALWAYS KEEP A SONG IN YOUR HEART ... DON'T BE AFRAID
    TO SING ...

AND ALWAYS ENJOY ALL THE THINGS ... THAT LIFE HAS TO BRING.

    BUT NO MATTER HOW HIGH YOU GET ... OR THE THINGS
    THAT YOU DO ...

JUST ALWAYS REMEMBER ... THERE'S SOMEONE MUCH HIGHER
THAN YOU.

EVERYTIME I SING THIS SONG

CHORUS:
    EVERYTIME I SING THIS SONG ...
I REMEMBER WHERE I BELONG
        AND I WISH THAT I WAS GONE ...
EVERYTIME I SING THIS SONG.

VERSE ONE:
    MANY TIMES WHEN I WAS AT HOME ...
I REMEMBER BEING ON THE TELEPHONE.
        MEMORIES WON'T LEAVE ME ALONE ...
 EVERYTIME I SING THIS SONG.

VERSE TWO:
        I WOULD WALK IN THE MOONLIGHT ...
WHEN THE STARS SHINED SO BRIGHT.
        THE MEMORIES STILL TWINKLE ON ...
EVERYTIME I SING THIS SONG.

VERSE THREE:
        EVERYTIME I SING THIS SONG ...
OLD MEMORIES STILL COMES ALONG.
        I GET HOMESICK TO GO HOME ...
EVERYTIME I SING THIS SONG.

 CHORUS:
        EVERYTIME I SING THIS SONG ...
I REMEMBER WHERE I BELONG
        AND I WISH THAT I WAS GONE ...
EVERYTIME I SING THIS SONG.

FAYE MY DARLIN'

VERSE ONE:

FAYE MY DARLIN' ... MY DARLIN' I LOVE YOU ...
PROMISE ME THAT ... YOU WILL STOP WHAT YOU DO.
MY HEART JUST CAN'T TAKE IT ... IT WILL BREAK INTO ...
BECAUSE FAYE MY DARLIN' ... MY DARLIN' I LOVE YOU.

VERSE TWO:

I'VE TRIED TO PUT UP ... WITH THINGS THAT YOU DO ...
BUT WHY MUST YOU LIVE ... A LIFE THAT IS SO UNTRUE.
I'VE TRIED TO MAKE BRIGHTNESS ... SPARKLE LIKE NEW ...
BECAUSE FAYE MY DARLIN' ... MY DARLIN' I LOVE YOU.

CHORUS:

FAYE I STILL LOVE YOU ... NO MATTER WHAT YOU DO ...
AND YOU CAN STILL MAKE ... MY DREAMS TO COME TRUE.
WHAT DO YOU SAY DARLING ... LET'S GIVE IT A PLUG ...
COME ON LET'S GET STARTED ... WITH A GREAT BIG HUG.

VERSE THREE:

WE USED TO BE SO HAPPY ... BUT LOOK AT US NOW ...
BECAUSE OF YOUR WILD WAYS ... WE DRIFTED APART SOMEHOW.
WHY DON'T YOU GIVE IT ALL UP.. LET'S START ANEW ...
BECAUSE FAYE MY DARLING ... MY DARLING I STILL LOVE YOU.

VERSE FOUR:

THE SAME OL' THINGS ... HAS GOT TO CHANGE ...
ALL THOSE BAD TIMES ... PUTS ME TO SHAME.
I'M SO CONCERNED ABOUT THINGS ... THAT YOU DO ...
BECAUSE FAYE MY DARLIN' ... MY DARLIN' I LOVE YOU.

CHORUS:

FAYE I STILL LOVE YOU ... NO MATTER WHAT YOU DO ...
AND YOU CAN STILL MAKE ... MY DREAMS TO COME TRUE.
WHAT DO YOU SAY DARLING ... LET'S GIVE IT A PLUG ...
COME ON LET'S GET STARTED ... WITH A GREAT BIG HUG.

FLAMES OF LOVE

VERSE ONE:
OUR FLAMES OF LOVE ... USED TO BURN SO HIGH ...
BUT NOW THEY DON'T ... AND WE DON'T KNOW WHY.
ALL THE FLAMES THAT WAS THERE... HAS LOST IT'S GLOW ...
IT PUT DARKNESS ALL AROUND ... WHEN THE FIRE GOT LOW.

VERSE TWO:
THE FLAMES OF LOVE ... THAT WE ONCE HAD ...
HAS ALMOST BURNED OUT ... AND LEFT US SO SAD.
THEY WERE SO BRIGHT ... THEY PUT FIRE IN OUR EYES ...
AND WE THOUGHT OUR LOVE ... WOULD NEVER DIE.

VERSE THREE:
THE FLAMES OF LOVE ... THAT WE ONCE KNEW ...
HAS ALMOST BURNED OUT ... AND LEAVING US BLUE.
WE STOPPED ADDING FUEL ... A LONG TIME AGO ...
NOW WE'RE STIRRING UP THE ASHES ... AS THE FIRE GETS LOW.

VERSE FOUR:
THE FLAMES OF LOVE ... WILL START BURNING AGAIN ...
IF WE GO BACK IN TIME ... AND DO THE THINGS WE DID THEN.
WE MUST FORGIVE ONE ANOTHER ... FOR THE THINGS WE DO ...
AND HANG ONTO EACH OTHER ... UNTIL WE SEE IT THROUGH.

VERSE FIVE:
THE FLAMES OF LOVE ... USE TO LIGHTEN OUR LIFE ...
WHEN IT BURNED SO HIGH ... AND GLOWED SO BRIGHT.
WE MUST GO BACK ... AND FIND OUT WHAT WENT WRONG ...
AND SEARCH FOR THE LOVE ... THAT WE HAD FOR SO LONG.

GET ON GONE

VERSE ONE:

    I GOT UP THIS MORNING ... DID'NT WANT TO LEAVE HOME ...
I LOOKED IN THE MIRROR ... SAID I GOT TO GET ON GONE.

    I GRABBED A CUP OF COFFEE ... AND A BITE TO EAT ...
THEN I HEADED OUT THE DOOR ... OUT TO THE STREET.

VERSE TWO:

    I GOT IN MY CAR ... AND I CRANKED THE ENGINE ...
I THOUGHT TO MYSELF ... TODAY IS A NEW BEGINNING.

    I WAS IN SO BIG A HURRY ... I FORGOT MY CELL PHONE ...
I SAID I DON'T HAVE TIME TO GO BACK ... I GOT TO GET GONE.

VERSE THREE:

    I GOT TO MY JOB ... AND PUNCHED IN MY TIME CARD ...
I REMEMBERED I LEFT THE NEWSPAPER ... LAYING IN THE YARD.

    NOW WHAT AM I GONNA DO ... WHEN IT COMES BREAKTIME ...
I CAN'T READ THE PAPER ... OR CALL ANYONE ON MY PHONE LINE.

VERSE FOUR:

    I MADE IT TO BREAK TIME ... THEN MORE TROUBLES BEGIN ...
I HAD FORGOT MY LUNCH BOX ... I HAD TO GET ON GONE AGAIN.

    I WENT TO THE CATERING TRUCK ... GRABBED A BITE TO EAT...
THIS IS SURE ONE DAY ... I HOPE HISTORY DON'T REPEAT.

VERSE FIVE:

    I WENT BACK TO WORK ... AND YOU CAN GUESS THE REST ...
THIS DAY HAS SURE BEEN ... FAR FROM BEING MY BEST.

    I'LL BE GLAD TO SEE QUITTING TIME ... IT WON'T BE LONG ...
THEN I'LL BE HEADED HOME ... AND I'M GONNA GET ON GONE.

GOD IS RIGHT BESIDE YOU

VERSE ONE:
WHEN YOU GET INTO TROUBLE ... AND DON'T KNOW WHAT TO DO ...
YOU DON'T HAVE TO WORRY ... GOD IS RIGHT BESIDE YOU.
GOD IS HERE AND GOD IS THERE ... GOD IS EVERYWHERE ...
HE LIVES WITHIN OUR HEART ... AND WILL ALWAYS BE THERE.

VERSE TWO:
YOU CAN TRUST IN GOD ... IN EVERYTHING THAT YOU DO ...
GOD IS RIGHT BESIDE YOU ... AND HE WILL SEE YOU THROUGH
HE WILL ALWAYS BE THERE ... EVEN WHEN TIMES GET ROUGH ...
SO GIVE HIM ALL YOUR LOVE ... YOU CAN NEVER GIVE ENOUGH.

CHORUS:
GOD IS RIGHT BESIDE YOU ... AND HE WILL DO HIS PART ...
IF YOU WILL BELIEVE IN HIM ... AND GIVE HIM YOUR HEART.
DON'T EVER FEEL ALONE ... HE WILL NEVER LEAVE YOU BEHIND ...
YOU CAN ALWAYS TALK TO HIM ... HE IS THERE ALL THE TIME.

VERSE THREE:
HE WILL GIVE YOU HIS LOVE ... WHEN YOU NEED IT THE MOST ...
GOD IS RIGHT BESIDE YOU ... IN THE HOLY GHOST.
EVEN THOUGH YOU CAN'T SEE HIM ... HE IS STILL THERE ...
AND HE IS ALWAYS WILLING ... TO SHOW YOU THAT HE CARES.

CHORUS:
GOD IS RIGHT BESIDE YOU ... AND HE WILL DO HIS PART ...
IF YOU WILL BELIEVE IN HIM ... AND GIVE HIM YOUR HEART.
DON'T EVER FEEL ALONE ... HE WILL NEVER LEAVE YOU BEHIND ...
YOU CAN ALWAYS TALK TO HIM ... HE IS THERE ALL THE TIME.

GOLD COLORED CURLS

CHORUS:

HE WAS A SMALL TOWN BOY ... IN A BIG TIME WORLD ...
HE DID'NT KNOW WHAT HE WAS DOIN' ... HIS HEAD WAS IN A WHIRL.
HE GOT WIPED OFF HIS FEET ... HIS LIFE BEGAN TO SWIRL ...
WHEN HE SAW THOSE BLUE EYES ... WITH GOLD COLORED CURLS.

VERSE ONE:

HE WAS FALLING IN LOVE ... WITH A CUTE LITTLE GIRL ...
WHO HAD PRETTY BLUE EYES ... WITH GOLD COLORED CURLS.
HIS WORLD WAS SPINNING FAST ... HE COULD'NT EVEN EAT ...
BECAUSE HE COULD'NT CATCH UP ... WITH HIS HEARTS FAST BEAT.

VERSE TWO:

NOW ALL HE IS HEARING ... ARE THOSE WEDDING BELLS...
HE CAN'T THINK OF NOTHING ELSE ... OR AT LEAST HE WOULD'NT
TELL.
HIS MIND WAS MADE UP ... THERE WAS NOTHING ELSE TO DO ...
BLUE EYES AND GOLD COLORED CURLS ... MADE HIS DREAMS
COME TRUE.

CHORUS:

HE WAS A SMALL TOWN BOY ... IN A BIG TIME WORLD ...
HE DID'NT KNOW WHAT HE WAS DOIN' ... HIS HEAD WAS IN A WHIRL.
HE GOT WIPED OFF HIS FEET ... HIS LIFE BEGAN TO SWIRL ...
WHEN HE SAW THOSE BLUE EYES ... WITH GOLD COLORED CURLS.

VERSE THREE:

THEY GOT MARRIED AND SETTLED DOWN ... IN THAT SMALL
TOWN ...
THEY HAD A HAPPY LIFE ... WITH SMALL KIDS RUNNING AROUND.
SO HE HAD MADE UP THE BED ... HE HAD TO SLEEP IN ...
WITH BLUE EYES AND GOLD COLORED CURLS ... HE WOULD DO IT
AGAIN.

CHORUS:

    HE WAS A SMALL TOWN BOY ... IN A BIG TIME WORLD ...
HE DID'NT KNOW WHAT HE WAS DOIN' ... HIS HEAD WAS IN A WHIRL.
    HE GOT WIPED OFF HIS FEET ... HIS LIFE BEGAN TO SWIRL ...
WHEN HE SAW THOSE BLUE EYES ... WITH GOLD COLORED CURLS.

GOT TO COOL DOWN

VERSE ONE:

     I FOUND ME A JOB ... AND I GAVE IT ALL I'VE GOT ...
DOING SOME YARD WORK ... WHEN THE WEATHER WAS HOT.
     THEN I STARTED SWEATIN' ... SO I LOOKED AROUND ...
TO FIND A COOL SPOT ... BECAUSE I'VE GOT TO COOL DOWN.

VERSE TWO:

     I FOUND ME A PLACE ... UNDER A BIG OLD OAK TREE ...
I SAID THIS IS THE PLACE ... WHERE I NEED TO BE.
     I SQUATTED DOWN ... AND LEANED AGAINST THE TRUNK ...
AND I COULD'NT GET BACK UP ... AS IF I WAS DRUNK.

VERSE THREE:

     THEN I REALIZED ... I'M NOT AS YOUNG AS I USED TO BE ...
THEN I STARTED TO WORRY ... UNDER THAT BIG OAK TREE.
     I START TO TREMBLE ... AND BEGAN TO GET WEAK ...
I COULD'NT EVEN STAND ... ON MY OWN TWO FEET.

CHORUS:

     JUST COOLIN' IT BABY ... IS ALL I'M GONNA DO ...
UNDER MY AIR CONDITIONER ... UNTIL SUMMER IS THRU.
     I'LL BE DRINKING COLD DRINKS ... UNTIL I DROWN ...
BECAUSE THIS OLD BOY ... HAS GOT TO COOL DOWN.

VERSE FOUR:

     I HAD TO RESIGN ... FROM THAT TYPE OF WORK ...
I'LL HAVE TO FIND A WAY ... TO MAKE EASIER PAY DIRT.
     I DON'T CARE IF TOMORROW ... DON'T EVER COME AROUND ...
BECAUSE THIS OLD BOY ... HAS GOT TO COOL DOWN.

CHORUS:

     JUST COOLIN' IT BABY ... IS ALL I'M GONNA DO ...
UNDER MY AIR CONDITIONER ... UNTIL SUMMER IS THRU.
     I'LL BE DRINKING COLD DRINKS ... UNTIL I DROWN ...
BECAUSE THIS OLD BOY ... HAS GOT TO COOL DOWN.

HAPPY DAYS

CHORUS :
    I WISH HAPPY DAYS ... WERE HERE AGAIN ...
JUST LIKE THEY WERE ... AWAY BACK THEN.
    WHEN FRIENDS WERE FRIENDS ... UNTIL THE END ...
I WISH HAPPY DAYS ... WERE HERE AGAIN.

VERSE ONE :
    I REMEMBER BACK ... WHEN A FRIEND WAS A FRIEND ...
THEY WOULD STICK TOGETHER ... THRU THICK AND THIN.
    THEY WERE ALWAYS GLAD ... TO LEND A HELPING HAND ...
I WISH HAPPY DAYS ... WERE HERE AGAIN.

VERSE TWO :
    NOW IT DON'T MATTER ... WHO YOU ARE ...
GOOD FRIENDS ARE FEW ... AND VERY FAR.
    BUT IF YOU HAVE ONE ... YOU'RE A LUCKY MAN ...
I WISH HAPPY DAYS ... WERE HERE AGAIN.

CHORUS :
    I WISH HAPPY DAYS ... WERE HERE AGAIN ...
JUST LIKE THEY WERE ... AWAY BACK THEN.
    WHEN FRIENDS WERE FRIENDS ... UNTIL THE END ...
I WISH HAPPY DAYS ... WERE HERE AGAIN.

VERSE THREE :
    IT'S GOOD TO KNOW LIFE ... WAS NOT ALL THAT BAD ...
WHEN YOU THINK BACK ... TO ALL THE FUN THAT YOU HAD.
    THINKING OF THOSE TIMES ... PUTS YOUR HEAD IN A SPIN ...
I WISH HAPPY DAYS ... WERE HERE AGAIN.

CHORUS :
    I WISH HAPPY DAYS ... WERE HERE AGAIN ...
JUST LIKE THEY WERE ... AWAY BACK THEN.
    WHEN FRIENDS WERE FRIENDS ... UNTIL THE END ...
I WISH HAPPY DAYS ... WERE HERE AGAIN.

HATIN' TO BE WAITIN'

CHORUS:

    I'M A HATIN' TO BE WAITIN' ... FOR YOUR LOVE AND LIVIN'...
I AM READY TO ACCEPT ... ALL THE LOVE YOU ARE GIVIN'.
    DON'T YOU THINK IT'S TIME ... FOR US TO GET IT DONE ...
WHY DON'T YOU COME ON ... AND LET'S HAVE US SOME FUN.

VERSE ONE:

    I LOVED YOU THE FIRST TIME ... THAT YOU PASSED MY WAY ...
I SAID THAT GIRL WILL BE MINE ... SOME SWEET DAY.
    I'LL KEEP ON AWAITIN' ... UNTIL MY WAITING DAYS ARE THRU ...
I HATE TO BE WAITIN' ... BUT THAT'S WHAT I'M GONNA DO.

VERSE TWO:

    I'M A HATIN' TO BE WAITIN' ... BUT THAT'S WHAT I HAVE
TO DO ...
I WANT WHAT I SEE ... EVERYTIME I SEE YOU.
    ALL I WANT IS YOU BABY ... AND YOUR LOVE TO BE TRUE ...
I'M A HATIN' TO BE WAITIN' ... BUT THAT'S WHAT I WILL DO.

CHORUS:

    I'M A HATIN' TO BE WAITIN' ... FOR YOUR LOVE AND LIVIN' ...
I AM READY TO ACCEPT ... ALL THE LOVE YOU ARE GIVIN'.
    DON'T YOU THINK IT'S TIME ... FOR US TO GET IT DONE ...
WHY DON'T YOU COME ON ... AND LET'S HAVE US SOME FUN.

VERSE THREE:

    I WILL ALWAYS REMEMBER ... I WAS HELPLESS AS A CHILD ...
THE DAY YOU BRUSHED MY ARM ... AND THE WAY I SAW YOU SMILE.
    I SAID RIGHT THEN ... THERE IS NOTHING I WOUL'NT DO ...
I'M A HATIN' TO BE WAITIN' ... BUT I'LL KEEP WAITIN TIL I HAVE YOU.

CHORUS:

    I'M A HATIN' TO BE WAITIN' ... FOR YOUR LOVE AND LIVIN' ...
I AM READY TO ACCEPT ... ALL THE LOVE YOU ARE GIVIN'.
    DON'T YOU THINK IT'S TIME ... FOR US TO GET IT DONE ...
WHY DON'T YOU COME ON ... AND LET'S HAVE US SOME FUN.

HE JUST WANTED TO LOVE

CHORUS:
       IT WAS WAY DOWN SOUTH ... IN THE FIELDS OF GRAIN ...
MY DADDY ALMOST DROVE ... MY MOMMA INSANE.
       HE WORKED ALL DAY ... IN THE SUMMER HOT SUN ...
THEN HE WANTED TO LOVE ... WHEN THE WORK WAS DONE.

VERSE ONE:
       WORKIN' AND LOVIN' ... AND TILLING IN THE DIRT ...
WITHOUT ANY LOVIN' ... THERE WAS NO NEED TO WORK.
       DADDY LOVED MOMMA ... AND MOMMA LOVED DAD ...
AND THEY BOTH LOVED ALL ... OF THE KIDS THAT THEY HAD.

VERSE TWO:
       MOMMA RAISED THE CHILDREN ... DADDY WORKED THE FIELDS ...
AND THAT'S THE WAT IT WAS ... UNTIL MY DADDY GOT ILL.
       MOTHER KEPT ON GOING ... EVEN AFTER DADDY GOT SICK ...
THEN HE DIED VERY YOUNG ... HE WAS ONLY FIFTY SIX.

CHORUS:
       IT WAS WAY DOWN SOUTH ... IN THE FIELDS OF GRAIN ...
MY DADDY ALMOST DROVE ... MY MOMMA INSANE.
       HE WORKED ALL DAY ... IN THE SUMMER HOT SUN ...
THEN HE WANTED TO LOVE ... WHEN THE WORK WAS DONE.

VERSE THREE:
       THEY WANTED TWELVE KIDS ... THAT'S WHAT THEY SAID ...
SO THEY CARRIED ON WITH IT ... UNTIL MY DADY WAS DEAD.
       MY MOTHER HAD TEN KIDS ... WITH ONE ON THE WAY ...
WHEN MY DADDY DIED ... WITH A HEART ATTACK ONE DAY.

VERSE FOUR:
       IT WAS HARD ON MOTHER ... BUT SHE KNEW WHAT TO DO ...
SHE RAISED HER KIDS ... THAT'S WHAT DADDY WANTED HER TO.
       THERE WAS A LOT OF LOVE ... IN THAT OLD HOUSE ...
BECAUSE THAT'S WHAT A FAMILY ... IS TRUELY ALL ABOUT.

CHORUS:

    IT WAS WAY DOWN SOUTH ... IN THE FIELDS OF GRAIN ...
MY DADDY ALMOST DROVE ... MY MOMMA INSANE.
    HE WORKED ALL DAY ... IN THE SUMMER HOT SUN ...
THEN HE WANTED TO LOVE ... WHEN THE WORK WAS DONE.

HE WAS A GREAT MAN

VERSE ONE:

 HE WAS A GREAT MAN ... IN HIS FATHERS EYES ...
IT SEEMED THAT THE PEOPLE ... JUST COULD'NT REALIZE.
 HE WAS PREPARING A PLACE ... FAR BEYOND THE SKIES ...
FOR ALL WHO BELIEVED ... TO GO TO WHEN THEY DIED.

VERSE TWO:

 HE WAS BORN OF A VIRGIN MARY ... WHO GAVE HIM BIRTH ...
SO'S HE COULD BE AN EXAMPLE ... RIGHT HERE ON EARTH.
 GOD WAS THE FATHER ... OF AN EARTHLY CHILD ...
THOUGH THE DISTANCE FROM HEAVEN ... WAS MANY MILES.

VERSE THREE:

 HE CAME NOT TO CONDEMN ... BUT TO SAVE THEM THAT WAS
 LOST ...
AND THE PRICE HE HAD TO PAY ... WAS THE ULTIMATE COST.
 IF THERE WERE PRIZES TO WIN ... HE WON THE TOP PRIZE ...
BECAUSE HE GAVE IT HIS ALL ... AND IT COST HIM HIS LIFE.

VERSE FOUR:

 HE NEVER DID NOBODY NO WRONG ... HE WAS A GREAT MAN ...
AND HE EARNED HIS PLACE ... AT THE FATHERS RIGHT HAND.
 NOW HE'S MANKINDS ATTORNEY ... FOR THE WHOLE HUMAN
 RACE...
HE'S OUR INTERSESSION TO GOD ... AND HE'S PLEADING OUR CASE.

VERSE FIVE:

 IF WE FIND OURSELVES DOING ... ANY KIND OF A SIN ...
WE MUST FALL ON OUR KNEE'S AND PRAY ... AND REPENT TO HIM.
 WE HAVE A HOME A WAITING ... IN HEAVENS PROMISED LAND ...
THAT WAS PAID FOR BY THE SACRIFICE ... OF ONE GREAT MAN.

HE WAS JUST A COUNTRY BOY

VERSE ONE :

   HE WAS BORNED IN THE COUNTRY ... A NORMAL BABY CHILD ...
HIS BIRTH WAS RECORDED ... AND HIS NAME WAS PUT ON FILE.
   SOON AFTER HE STARTED TALKING ... HE FOUND OUT ONE
   THING ...
THAT HE LOVED COUNTRY MUSIC ... SO HE LEARNED HOW TO
SING.

VERSE TWO :

   HIS OLDEST BROTHER BOUGHT HIM ... AN OLD USED GUITAR ...
HE NEVER PICTURED HIMSELF ... AS A COUNTRY MUSIC STAR.
   BUT EVERY CHANCE HE GOT ... HE WOULD GET IT OUT AND
   STRUM ...
SOON HE PUT ON SOME SHOWS ... AND LOTS OF PEOPLE COME.

CHORUS :

   HE WAS JUST A COUNTRY BOY ... BUT HE BROUGHT A LOT OF
   JOY ...
TO PEOPLE THAT HEARD HIM SING ... AND PLAY MUSIC ON HIS
STRINGS.
   HE NEVER WAS THE BEST ... BUT A LONG WAYS FROM THE
   WORST ...
BUT BEFORE YOU CAN JUDGE HIM ... YOU'VE GOT TO HEAR HIM
FIRST.

------- INSTRUMENTAL WITH ACOUSTIC GUITAR ----------

VERSE THREE :

   HE WOULD TAKE THAT OLD GUITAR ... AND HOLD IT IN HIS
   HANDS ...
AND WHEN HE PLAYED HIS MUSIC ... HE BECAME A DIFFERANT MAN.
   HIS MUSIC WOULD STAND OUT ... AND THE CROWDS WOULD
   ROAR ...
HE WAS JUST A COUNTRY BOY ... BUT HIS SONGS WOULD SOAR.

VERSE FOUR :

LOTS OF PEOPLE SAID HE'D MAKE IT ... RIGHT FROM THE START ...

AND THEN ONE DAY HIS MUSIC ... SHOWED UP ON THE COUNTRY CHARTS.

HE WAS KNOWN WORLD OVER ... FOR HIS MUSIC AND HIS SONGS ...

HE WAS A JUST COUNTRY BOY ... BUT HIS MUSIC WILL LIVE ON.

CHORUS :

HE WAS JUST A COUNTRY BOY ... BUT HE BROUGHT A LOT OF JOY ...

TO PEOPLE THAT HEARD HIM SING ... AND PLAY MUSIC ON HIS STRINGS.

HE NEVER WAS THE BEST ... BUT A LONG WAYS FROM THE WORST ...

BUT BEFORE YOU CAN JUDGE HIM ... YOU'VE GOT TO HEAR HIM FIRST.

HE WILL ALWAYS BE REMEMBERED

CHORUS:

HE WILL ALWAYS BE REMEMBERED ... AFTER HE IS DEAD ...
OF THE MAN WHO GOT BY ... FOR THE GOOD THINGS THAT HE DID.
HE NEVER HAD MUCH NONEY ... NOR DID HE HAVE FAME ...
BUT HE WILL ALWAYS BE ... REMEMBERED JUST THE SAME.

VERSE ONE:

LET ME TELL YOU THE STORY ... OF AN ALL AMERICAN BOY ...
WHO NEVER REALLY HAD ANYTHING ... BUT STILL HAD EVERYTHING.
HE TOUCHED PEOPLE'S HEART... WITH SONGS THAT HE WOULD SING ...
AND EVERYONE LOVED HIM ... FOR THE BLESSINGS HE WOULD BRING.

VERSE TWO:

HE WOULD JUST SAT AROUND ... AND THINK OF SONGS IN HIS MIND ...
THEN HE WOULD GRAB UP A PENCIL ... AND WRITE DOWN EVERY LINE.
IT WOULD BE ABOUT THINGS ... THAT WAS HAPPENING EVERY DAY ...
IT SEEMED THAT IT WAS THINGS ... THAT WILL NEVER GO AWAY.

CHORUS:

HE WILL ALWAYS BE REMEMBERED ... EVEN AFTER HE IS DEAD ...
OF THE MAN WHO GOT BY ... FOR THE GOOD THINGS THAT HE DID.
HE NEVER HAD MUCH NONEY ... NOR DID HE KNOW FAME ...
BUT HE WILL ALWAYS BE ... REMEMBERED JUST THE SAME.

VERSE THREE:

HE WOULD SING TO THE POOR ... AND HE SEEMED TO NEVER STOP ...
SO HE NEVER GOT THE BREAKS ... TO MAKE IT TO THE TOP.
BUT HE WILL STILL BE REMEMBERED ... FOR ALL OF HIS GOOD TIMES ...
AND THE JOY THAT HE BROUGHT ... WHILE READING BETWEEN THE LINES.

VERSE FOUR:
    HIS LIFE WAS WORTH MORE ... THAN ALL THE SILVER AND GOLD ...
BECAUSE IT LET HIM LIVE LONG ENOUGH ... FOR HIM TO GET OLD.
    HE HAD A LIFE OF MEMORIES ... SOMETHING THAT COULD'NT BE SOLD ...
HE WILL ALWAYS BE REMEMBERED ... FOR A LIFETIME OF RICHES UNTOLD.

HEAVEN'S ROCK AND ROLL

VERSE ONE:

JESUS SAVED MY SOUL ... AND HE GAVE ME A BRAND NEW GOAL ...
THE LIFE THAT I WAS LIVIN' ... WAS JUST DIGGING ME A HOLE.
I'M GOING A DIFFERANT DIRECTION ... SINCE HE MADE ME WHOLE ...
AND NOW I'M STANDING ON THE ROCK ... WITH MY NAME ON THE ROLL.

VERSE TWO:

NOW HEAVEN'S ROCK AND ROLL ... IS THE ONLY WAY TO GO ...
KEEP YOUR FOOT ON THE ROCK ... AND GET YOUR NAME ON THE ROLL.
YOU WILL BE IN HIS PRESENCE ... WHEN HE MAKES UP HIS FOLD ...
SO ROCK YOUR WAY TO HEAVEN... WITH HEAVEN'S ROCK AND ROLL.

CHORUS:

ROCK ROCK ROCK YOUR WAY ... TO HEAVEN'S ROCK AND ROLL ...
NOW YOU MAY NOT LIKE MUSIC ... BUT IT'S GOOD FOR YOUR SOUL.
GET YOUR FOOT ON THE ROCK ... AND YOUR NAME ON THE ROLL ...
THEN S-T-R-O-L-L ...THAT'S THE WAY TO GET TO HEAVEN'S ROCK AND ROLL.

VERSE THREE:

THERE WILL BE NO STOPPING ... AS LONG AS YOU KEEP ON ROCKING ...
THERE WILL BE NO STROLLING ... WHILE YOU KEEP ON A ROLLING.
DON'T EVER GIVE IT UP ... AND DON'T NEVER GROW COLD ...
KEEP YOUR EYES ON THE ROAD ... TO HEAVEN'S ROCK AND ROLL.

VERSE FOUR:

THE HIGHWAY TO HEAVEN ... IS ALWAYS FULL OF ROCKY ROADS ...

SO KEEP YOUR EYES ON JESUS ... AND WAYCH WHEREVER YOU MAY GO.
    IF YOU SHOULD STUMBLE AND FALL ... ON SOME ROCKS IN
    THE ROAD ...
JUST GET UP AND START AGAIN ... ON HEAVEN'S ROCK AND ROLL.

CHORUS:
    ROCK ROCK ROCK YOUR WAY ... TO HEAVEN'S ROCK AND
    ROLL ...
NOW YOU MAY NOT LIKE MUSIC ... BUT IT'S GOOD FOR YOUR SOUL.
    GET YOUR FOOT ON THE ROCK ... AND YOUR NAME ON THE
    ROLL ...
THEN S-T-R-O-L-L ...THAT'S THE WAY TO GET TO HEAVEN'S ROCK
AND ROLL.

HEALTH IS BETTER THAN WEALTH

CHORUS :

MONEY IS NOT EVERYTHING ... IT WILL SET YOUR SOUL ON FIRE ...
WHILE SOME HAS IT AND NOT BE HAPPY ... IT'S STILL THE POOR MAN'S DESIRE.
JUST BE HAPPY WITH WHAT YOU HAVE ... AND DON'T ASK FOR TOO MUCH ...
BECAUSE HEALTH IS BETTER THAN WEALTH ...SO FORGET THAT OTHER STUFF.

VERSE ONE :

I ONCE KNEW A RICH MAN ... THAT WORE OLD WORN OUT CLOTHES ...
AND WHY HE SAVE HIS MONEY ... I GUESS I'LL NEVER KNOW.
HE ATE POTTED MEAT AND BOLOGNA ... AND CANNED PORK AND BEANS ...
HE SAID HE HAD TO SAVE HIS MONEY ... AND LIVE WITHIN HIS MEANS.

VERSE TWO :

PEOPLE LOOKS AT ME AND SAY ...YOU SURE LOOK GOOD FOR YOUR AGE ...
I SMILE AND THEN SAY THANK YOU ... AND THEN I WALK AWAY.
THEY DON'T KNOW I CAN'T AFFORD ... THE HIGH COST OF LIVING TODAY ...
I HAVE TO STRUGGLE TO PAY MY BILLS ... BUT THAT DON'T MATTER ANYWAY.

CHORUS :

MONEY IS NOT EVERYTHING ... IT WILL SET YOUR SOUL ON FIRE ...
WHILE SOME HAS IT AND NOT BE HAPPY ... IT'S STILL THE POOR MAN'S DESIRE.
JUST BE HAPPY WITH WHAT YOU HAVE ... AND DON'T ASK FOR TOO MUCH ...
BECAUSE HEALTH IS BETTER THAN WEALTH ...SO FORGET THAT OTHER STUFF.

VERSE THREE :

PEOPLE THINK I HAVE MONEY ... BECAUSE I ALWAYS DRESS WELL ...

BUT THEY DON'T KNOW I BUY MY CLOTHES ... IN SOME YARD SALE.

I DON'T KNOW WHERE YOU GET YOURS ... I ONLY KNOW ABOUT MYSELF ...

BUT HEALTH IS BETTER THAN WEALTH ... SO TAKE CARE OF YOURSELF.

CHORUS :

MONEY IS NOT EVERYTHING ... IT WILL SET YOUR SOUL ON FIRE ...

WHILE SOME HAS IT AND NOT BE HAPPY ... IT'S STILL THE POOR MAN'S DESIRE.

JUST BE HAPPY WITH WHAT YOU HAVE ... AND DON'T ASK FOR TOO MUCH ...

BECAUSE HEALTH IS BETTER THAN WEALTH ...SO FORGET THAT OTHER STUFF.

HERE COMES JOE

VERSE ONE:

    WELL HERE COMES JOE ... WHAT IS HE TRYING TO DO ...
HE REALLY SHAKES PEOPLE UP ... WHEN HE COMES THROUGH.
    HE THINKS HE IS BAD ... WHEN HE'S ACTING LIKE THAT ...
WITH SPIKES ON HIS SHOES ... AND A BASEBALL BAT.

VERSE TWO:

    IF HE SPIKES YOU WITH HIS SHOES ... YOU'LL HAVE SCARS ...
AND IF HE HITS YOU WITH HIS BAT ... THEN YOU'LL SEE STARS.
    HE THINKS HE'S MEAN ... WHEN HE SWINGS THAT THING ...
I RECKON THE SUN ... MUST HAVE SCORCHED HIS BRAIN.

VERSE THREE:

    HE TELLS EVERYONE ... HE WANTS TO BE LEFT ALONE ...
WHILE EVERYONE WISHES ... HE WOULD JUST GO HOME.
    THEY ALL OVERLOOK HIM ... AND NOT TRY TO GET HURT ...
BUT THEY'RE GONNA LOOK AFTER ... THEIR OWNSELVES FIRST.

VERSE FOUR:

    SO NOW COME ON JOE ... LET'S JUST TRY TO SETTLE DOWN ...
AND STOP SWINGIN' ... THAT BASEBALL BAT AROUND.
    WE DON'T HAVE ANYTHING ... THAT WE HOLD AGAINST YOU ...
SO WHY DO TREAT US ... THE WAY THAT YOU DO.

CHORUS:

    WELL HERE COMES JOE BACK ... HE'S AT IT AGAIN ...
A'SWINGIN' THAT BAT ... LIKE SOME KIND OF A WILD MAN.
    IT MAKES YOU WONDER ... IF HE'S EVER HAD A FRIEND ...
AND HOW LONG WILL IT BE ... BEFORE HE COMES BACK AGAIN.

HIGH POINT MY HOMETOWN

VERSE ONE:

    A LITTLE CITY IN NORTH CAROLINA ... IS WHERE I LOVE TO BE ...
IT'S A LITTLE PLACE CALLED HIGH POINT ... HIGH POINT NC.
    LOTS OF PEOPLE VISIT ...THEY COME FROM MILES AROUND...
TO SEE NEW FURNITURE MADE ... IN HIGH POINT MY HOMETOWN.

VERSE TWO:

    I DROVE A LONG DISTANT TRUCK ... FOR TWENTY NINE YEARS ...
BUT I ALWAYS CAME BACK ... TO MY HOMETOWN RIGHT HERE.
    THERE IS NO BETTER PLACE ... THAT I HAVE FOUND ...
THAN RIGHT HERE IN HIGH POINT ... MY OWN HOMETOWN.

VERSE THREE:

    I HAVE BEEN EVERYWHERE ... BUT NOWHERE COULD I FIND ...
NO PLACE SO DEAR TO ME ... AS THAT HOMETOWN OF MINE.
    YOU CAN OPEN YOUR EYES ... SEE GOOD PEOPLE ALL AROUND ...
THEY WILL TREAT YOU RIGHT ... IN HIGH POINT MY HOMETOWN.

VERSE FOUR:

    THERE IS MONEY TO BE MADE ... AND GRASS IS GREENER HERE ...
IF IT'S FRIENDS YOU NEED ... YOU CAN FIND THEM RIGHT THERE.
    SO COME ON DOWN ... AND LET'S ALL GATHER AROUND ...
YOU CAN FIND WHAT YOU WANT ... IN HIGH POINT MY HOMETOWN.

VERSE FIVE:

    WE HAVE LIQUOR STORES AND BARS ... ALL OVER THE TOWN ...
WHATEVER ROAD YOU CHOOSE ... THERE'S CHURCH'S ALL AROUND.
    IF IT'S VARIETY YOU WANT ... WHY DON'T YOU COME ON
DOWN ...
YOU WON'T WANT TO LEAVE ... HIGH POINT MY HOMETOWN.

HIS OLD POCKET KNIFE

VERSE ONE:
> I ONCE KNEW A MAN ... WHO LED A LONELY LIFE ...
AND HE WOULD RUN AROUND ... ALMOST EVERY NIGHT.
> SOMETIMES HE WOULD ALWAYS ... GET INTO A FIGHT.
HE WOULD ALWAYS TURN TO ... HIS OLD POCKET KNIFE.

VERSE TWO:
> HE KEPT HIS OLD POCKET KNIFE ... SHARP AND SLICK ...
AND HE COULD PULL IT OUT ... OF HIS POCKET REAL QUICK.
> SOON THE NEWS GOT OUT ... ALL OVER TOWN ...
THE MAN WITH THE OLD POCKET KNIFE ... DID'NT PLAY AROUND.

VERSE THREE:
> HE WOULD CUT YOU BEFORE ... YOU COULD BAT AN EYE ...
AND HE WOULD'NT STOP ... UNTIL HE MADE THE BLOOD FLY.
> HE WOULD START AT YOUR BELLY ... AND RIP YOUR INSIDES...
YOU MIGHT GET BLOOD POISON ... FROM HIS OLD POCKET KNIFE.

VERSE FOUR:
> HE WAS FAST AND QUICK ... AND MEAN AS HE COULD BE ...
AND HE HAD NO FRIENDS ... BECAUSE HE WAS CRAZY.
> HE NEVER WOULD SMILE ... SOMETIMES HE WOULD CRY ...
THE ONLY FRIEND HE HAD... WAS HIS OLD POCKET KNIFE.

CHORUS:
> DON'T LET YOUR REPUTATION ... TAKE YOU TO THE GRAVE ...
ALWAYS MAKE FRIENDS ... AND JUST TRY TO BEHAVE.
> ALWAYS TREAT OTHERS ... AS YOU WANT THEM TO TREAT YOU ...
AND LEAVE A GOOD MEMORY ... WHEN YOUR LIFE IS THROUGH.

HONEY DEW

CHORUS:
    YOU CAN ALWAYS HEAR ... NO MATTER WHERE YOU'RE AT ...
THE SAME OLD THING ...HONEY DEW THIS AND HONEY DEW THAT.
    SOME PEOPLE DON'T CARE ... WHAT THEY PUT OTHERS THRU...
BUT WHAT WOULD THEY DO ... WITHOUT THIER HONEY DEW.

VERSE ONE:
    I WAS GOING TO THE STORE ... IT TOOK ME OVER AN HOUR ...
IT JUST SO HAPPENED ... I FORGOT TO GET THE FLOUR.
    MY WIFE WANTED TO MAKE BREAD ... WITH SOME BEEF STEW ...
SHE ASK IF I WAS GOING BACK ... THEN SHE SAID HONEY DEW.

CHORUS:
    YOU CAN ALWAYS HEAR ... NO MATTER WHERE YOU'RE AT ...
THE SAME OLD THING ...HONEY DEW THIS AND HONEY DEW THAT.
    SOME PEOPLE DON'T CARE ... WHAT THEY PUT OTHERS THRU...
BUT WHAT WOULD THEY DO ... WITHOUT THIER HONEY DEW.

VERSE TWO:
    I WAS RUNNING LOW ON CASH ... SHE WANTED TO GO OUT ...
SOMETIMES A WOMAN DON'T UNDERSTAND ... WHAT LIFE IS ABOUT.
    I SAID I DON'T HAVE ENOUGH MONEY ... TO SEE ME THROUGH ...
AGAIN THE SAME OLD WORDS ... HONEY PLEASE DEW.

VERSE THREE:
    THEN I SAID OKAY ... I KNOW I'LL HAVE TO PAY FOR IT LATER ...
SHE SAID THAT'S THEN AND THIS IS NOW ...SO WHAT'S THE MATTER.
    SOMETIMES SHE DON'T UNDERSTAND ... SHE HAS NO CLUE ...
WHAT ON EARTH SHE WOULD DO ... WITHOUT HER HONEY DEW.

CHORUS:
    YOU CAN ALWAYS HEAR ... NO MATTER WHERE YOU'RE AT ...
THE SAME OLD THING ...HONEY DEW THIS AND HONEY DEW THAT.
    SOME PEOPLE DON'T CARE ... WHAT THEY PUT OTHERS THRU...
BUT WHAT WOULD THEY DO ... WITHOUT THIER HONEY DEW.

HONKY TONK IDIOT

VERSE ONE:

ANYTIME I WANTED SOMETHING TO DRINK ... I COULD GET IT ...
BUT WHEN IT CAME TO SAVING MONEY ... I COULD FORGET IT.
I NEVER COULD FIND A GOOD FRIEND ... WHEN I NEED IT ...
I GUESS ALL I EVER WAS ... IS A HONKY TONK IDIOT.

VERSE TWO:

ALL I EVER DID WAS ... JUST GET DRUNK FIGHT AND CUSS ...
I KNEW ABOUT HONKY TONKS ... AND I KNEW WHERE THEY ALL WAS.
MY FAMILY WOULD SAY TO ME ... BOY YOU BETTER QUIT IT ...
BUT I WOULD'NT GIVE IT UP ... I WAS A HONKY TONK IDIOT.

VERSE THREE:

ONE DAY WHEN I WAS SOBERING UP ... FEELING DOWN AND OUT ...
SOMETHING GOT A HOLD OF ME ... I DID'NT KNOW WHAT IT WAS ABOUT.
IT WAS A FEELING LIKE I HAD ... NEVER KNOWN BEFORE ...
I TRIED TO GET ME A BEER ... I COULD'NT GET OFF THE FLOOR.

VERSE FOUR:

SOMETHING WAS KEEPING ME DOWN ... I GOT UP ON MY KNEE'S ...
THEN I BOWED MY HEAD AND SAID ... LORD HELP ME PLEASE.
THAT WAS WHEN EVERYTHING CHANGED ... I'LL NEVER FORGET IT ..
I REALIZED WHAT I REALLY WAS ... JUST A HONKY TONK IDIOT.

VERSE FIVE:

GOD SAID COME OUT FROM WHERE YOU ARE ... AND FOLLOW ME ...
I'LL SHOW YOU GREATER THINGS ... AND IN WHAT YOU CAN BE.

HE SAID TO COME TO MY HOUSE ... AND JOIN THE CHURCH
FAMILY ...
HE TOOK ME FROM HONKY TONKS ... AND MADE SOMETHING OUT
OF ME.

CHORUS:
FROM HONKY TONKS TO HEAVEN ... THAT'S WHAT GOD
PROMISED ME ...
ALL I HAD TO DO WAS REPENT ... AND THEN SALVATION CAME FREE.
I DID'NT NEED ANY MONEY ... I COULD'NT HAVE PAID FOR IT ...
NOW I'M PROUD TO BE A CHRISTIAN ... AND NOT A HONKY TONK
IDIOT.

I CAN'T REMEMBER

CHORUS:
  I REMEMBER LAST WEEK ... WHEN WE HAD SO MUCH FUN ...
OR STOP TO THINK ABOUT IT ... MAYBE IT WAS LAST MONTH.
  SOMETIMES I CAN'T REMEMBER ... AND I WANT TO CRY ...
IT'S NO LAUGHING MATTER ... HOW FAST TIME GOES BY.

VERSE ONE:
  I CAN'T REMEMBER ANYTHING ... ABOUT YESTERDAY ...
BUT I DON'T GUESS TO ME ... IT WOULD MATTER ANYWAY.
  TIME JUST GOES SO FAST ... ANOTHER DAY IS GONE ...
BUT I DON'T WORRY ... BECAUSE TIME KEEPS MOVING ON.

VERSE TWO:
  I DON'T EVEN KNOW ... WHAT I HAVE TO DO TOMORROW ...
I CAN ONLY HOPE ... IT DON'T BRING ON MORE SORROW.
  TODAY IS ALMOST OVER ... SOON IT WILL BE A NEW DAY ...
IT SURE IS SURPRISING ... HOW FAST TIME SLIPS AWAY.

VERSE THREE:
  I'M GLAD YESTERDAY IS GONE ... I WON'T WORRY ANYMORE...
I JUST HOPE THAT TOMORROW...WILL BE BETTER THAN BEFORE.
  THE HOURS OF THE DAY ... SURE DOES PASS FAST AWAY ...
BUT I REALLY DON'T CARE ... I WON'T REMEMBER IT ANYWAY.

VERSE FOUR:
  IT'S NIGHTTIME ONCE MORE ... AND IT'S DARK OUTSIDE ...
I DON'T REMEMBER WHAT I DID ... BUT I ALMOST DIED.
  I'M NOT A KID ANYMORE ... I HAVE LIVED TO BE AN OLD MAN ...
I WONDER COULD I REMEMBER ... IF I LIVED IT ALL OVER AGAIN.

I CAN'T EVEN REMEMBER

COURSE :

    I CAN'T TURN BACK THE TIME ... AND START ALL OVER AGAIN ...
AND I CAN'T GO BACK TO WHERE ... I HAVE ALREADY BEEN.

    I CAN'T TELL YOU HOW SORRY I AM ... FOR LIVING A LIFE IN
SIN ...
BUT I CAN'T EVEN REMEMBER ... ALL THE THINGS I DID BACK THEN.

VERSE ONE :

    BUT IF I HAD MY WHOLE LIFE ... TO LIVE OVER AGAIN ...
THERE IS A LOT OF THINGS ... THAT I AM SURE I WOULD AMEND.

    I THANK GOD FOR THE DAY ... THAT I LET JESUS COME IN ...
AND I PROMISED TO NEVER LIVE ... THAT WAY AGAIN.

VERSE TWO :

    I DID A LOT OF THINGS ... THAT I SHOULD'NT HAVE DONE ...
WHILE ALL THE TIME I NEVER ... MEANT TO HURT ANYONE.

    I ONLY THOUGHT OF MYSELF ... NOT THINKING OF OTHERS ...
BUT IT WOULD BE DIFFERENT NOW ... IF I COULD LIVE MY LIFE
OVER.

COURSE :

    I CAN'T TURN BACK THE TIME ... AND START ALL OVER AGAIN ...
AND I CAN'T GO BACK TO WHERE ... I HAVE ALREADY BEEN.

    I CAN'T TELL YOU HOW SORRY I AM ... FOR LIVING A LIFE IN
SIN ...
BUT I CAN'T EVEN REMEMBER ... ALL THE THINGS I DID BACK THEN.

COURSE :

    I CAN'T TURN BACK THE TIME ... AND START ALL OVER AGAIN ...
AND I CAN'T GO BACK TO WHERE ... I HAVE ALREADY BEEN.

    I CAN'T TELL YOU HOW SORRY I AM ... FOR LIVING A LIFE IN
SIN ...
BUT I CAN'T EVEN REMEMBER ... ALL THE THINGS I DID BACK THEN.

I HAVE WON AGAIN

VERSE ONE:
    I USED TO BE A LOSER ... IT SEEMED I COULD'NT WIN ...
EVERYTHING I TRIED TO DO WOULD ... SEND ME TO THE PEN.
    I GOT SO TIRED OF LOSING ... I HAD TO MAKE AMENDS ...
SO I CHANGED MY WAYS OF LIVING ... AND NEVER LOST AGAIN.

VERSE TWO:
    I CHANGED MY WAYS ABOUT ... HOW I THOUGHT BACK THEN ...
IT MADE MY LIFE MUCH BETTER BECAUSE ... I HAD WON AGAIN.
    MY CONFIDENCE GREW AS ... EACH MORNING I WOULD SAY...
I CAN FEEL IT IN MY VEINS NOW ... TODAY WOULD BE MY DAY.

CHORUS:
    I WON ... I WON ... I WON ... YES, I HAVE WON AGAIN ...
WHEN I BOUGHT A LOTTERY TICKET .. HAD THE WINNING HAND.
    IT ECHOED THRU MY MIND ... THAT'S WHEN IT ALL BEGAN ...
I WON ... I WON ... I WON ... YES, I HAVE WON AGAIN

VERSE THREE:
    EACH DAY I WOULD GO OUT SAYING .. EVERYTHING IS OKAY ...
AND BELIEVING IN MYSELF ... THAT THIS IS A GREAT DAY.
    WHEN MY MIND WENT BACK ... TO HOW IT WAS BACK THEN ...
IT DID'NT TAKE LONG TO FIGURE ... THAT I HAD WON AGAIN.

VERSE FOUR:
    EVERYONE TOLD ME THAT ... MY LIFE WOULD SOON END ...
THEY HAD NO WAY OF KNOWING ... HOW I FELT BACK THEN.
    I WANTED THINGS TO CHANGE ... I FELT THE CHANGE WITHIN ...
NOW I HEAR IT OVER AND OVER ... YOU HAVE WON AGAIN.

I ALMOST MISSED HEAVEN

VERSE ONE:
 WHEN I WAS ONLY SEVENTEEN ... I HAD AN ACCIDENT.
I WRECKED MY CAR IN TENNESS EE ... AND I WAS REALLY SKIN'T.
 I WAS THROWN FROM MY CAR ... WHILE RUNNING EIGHTY
 FIVE ...
I ALMOST MISSED HEAVEN ... BUT THANK GOD I SURVIVED.

VERSE TWO:
 WHEN I WAS TWENTY THREE ... I WRECKED A MOTORCYCLE
 I HAD ...
TRYING TO JUMP A RAMP ... IT'S A WONDER THAT I AIN'T DEAD.
 I GUESS AT THE TIME ... I THOUGHT THAT I WAS LIVIN' ...
BUT THAT'S ANOTHER TIME ... I ALMOST MISSED HEAVEN.

VERSE THREE:
 WHEN I WAS TWENTY SEVEN ... I GOT IN A BAR ROOM BRAWL ...
WE WERE ALL OUT NUMBERED ... THAT'S THE LAST THAT I RECALL.
 I THOUGHT I WAS DOING GOOD ... TIL THEY TURNED OUT
 MY LIGHTS.
 I ALMOST MISSED HEAVEN ... ON THAT DARK AND DREARY NIGHT.

VERSE FOUR:
 THEN IN NINETEEN SIXTY SEVEN ... I HAD A WRECK IN MY
 TRUCK...
THAT WAS ONE YEAR IT SEEMED ... I WAS'NT HAVING MUCH LUCK'.
 I LAID IN THE BAPTIST HOSPITAL ... TEN DAYS IN A COMA.
I THOUGHT I WAS IN HEAVEN ... WHEN I SAW MY MOMMA.

VERSE FIVE:
 THEN IN NINETEEN SEVENTY SEVEN ... I REPENTED OF MY SIN ...
AND I PROMISED THE LORD ... I WOULD NEVER GO DOWN THAT
ROAD AGAIN.
 GOD SAID ALL THE BAD TIMES ... OF MY LIFE WAS FORGIVEN
AND NOW I'M ON MY JOURNEY ... TO MY HOME IN HEAVEN.

CHORUS:

    WHEN I THINK ABOUT THE TIMES ... I ALMOST MISSED HEAVEN ...

MY LEGS GETS TO KNOCKING ... AND MY KNEE'S STARTS TO BOWING.

    I CAN'T HARDLY WAIT ... UNTIL I SEE WHAT'S IN STORE ...

AND I SET MY FEET ... ON HEAVEN'S GOLDEN SHORE.

I APOLOGIZE

VERSE ONE:

DEAR GOD ... I KNOW I HAVE LET YOU DOWN AND I APOLOGIZE ... I KNOW I HAVE DONE A LOT OF WRONG ... THROUGH YOUR EYES.

PLEASE FORGIVE ME ... FOR THE THINGS THAT I HAVE DONE ... FOR I KNOW IT WAS FOR PEOPLE LIKE ME ... THAT YOU SENT YOUR SON.

VERSE TWO:

HAVE MERCY ON MY SOUL O' LORD ... AND GIVE ME A NEW LIFE ...
AND WHEN I EVER DO WRONG AGAIN ... I WANT YOU TO KNOW I APOLOGIZE.

I KNOW I'M NOT PERFECT ... BUT YOU DID'NT SAY I HAD TO BE ...
SO WHEN I FAIL IN DOING YOUR WORK ... PLEASE HAVE MERCY ON ME.

CHORUS:

I APOLOGIZE, I APOLOGIZE ... HOW MANY TIMES MUST I APOLOGIZE ...
AS MANY TIMES AS IT TAKES ... TO CHANGE FROM WRONG INTO RIGHT.

WIPE AWAY ALL MY TEARS ... AND LET ME SEE THROUGH YOUR EYES ...
THEN WHEN I STAND BEFORE YOU ... I WON'T HAVE TO APOLOGIZE.

VERSE THREE:

MAY I SEE THE THINGS OF THIS WORLD ... IN A DIFFERANT VIEW ...
WHEN THE DEVIL WORKS AROUND ME ... MAY I ALWAYS TURN TO YOU.

ALWAYS GIVE ME THE STRENGTH ... TO HELP ME TO GET THROUGH ...
AND I APOLOGIZE FROM MY HEART ... IF I EVER DO FAIL YOU.

VERSE FOUR:

FATHER I APOLOGIZE ... FOR NOT DOING WHAT'S RIGHT IN YOUR SIGHT ...
FOR YOU HAVE GIVEN ME THE SPIRIT ... TO KNOW WRONG FROM RIGHT.
BUT SOMETIMES I MAY SLIP AND FALL ... FROM YOUR LOVING GRACE ...
BUT YOU WILL PICK ME UP AGAIN ... AND PUT ME BACK IN MY PLACE.

CHORUS:

I APOLOGIZE, I APOLOGIZE ... HOW MANY TIMES MUST I APOLOGIZE ...
AS MANY TIMES AS IT TAKES ... TO CHANGE FROM WRONG INTO RIGHT.
WIPE AWAY ALL MY TEARS ... AND LET ME SEE THROUGH YOUR EYES ...
THEN WHEN I STAND BEFORE YOU ... I WON'T HAVE TO APOLOGIZE.

I DON'T KNOW WHY ... BUT I DO

VERSE ONE:

    LAST NIGHT AS I SAT HERE ... I WONDERED ...
WHAT ON EARTH ... AM I GONNA DO.
    AS MY MIND WENT BACK IN TIME ... I PONDERED ...
THIS TIME I KNOW ... THAT WE ARE REALLY THROUGH.

CHORUS:

    I DON'T KNOW WHY ... I FEEL THIS WAY...
I DON'T KNOW WHY ... I CAN'T FACE ANOTHER DAY.
    I ONLY KNOW ... THAT I REALLY LOVE YOU ...
I DON'T KNOW WHY ... BUT I DO.

VERSE TWO:

    I KNEW IT WOULD'NT LAST ... FOREVER ...
I KNEW SOMEDAY ... THAT IT WOULD ALL BE THROUGH.
    I STILL THINK ABOUT WHEN ... WE WERE TOGETHER ...
I DON'T KNOW WHY ... BUT I DO.

VERSE THREE:

    I'LL NEVER FORGET ... ABOUT THOSE DAYS ...
ESPECIALY THE DAY ... THAT YOU WENT AWAY.
    EVERY TIME I'M ALONE ... I THINK OF YOU ...
I DON'T KNOW WHY ... BUT I DO.

    CHORUS:

    I DON'T KNOW WHY... I HAVE TO FEEL THIS WAY...
I DON'T KNOW WHY ... I CAN'T FACE ANOTHER DAY.
    I ONLY KNOW ... I REALLY DO LOVE YOU ...
I DON'T KNOW WHY ... BUT I DO.

I HAVE SAID IT MANY TIMES

VERSE ONE:

FOLKS HAVE HEARD ME TALKING ... I HAVE SAID IT MANY TIMES ...
ABOUT A PLACE CALLED HEAVEN ... AND A HOME THAT IS MINE.
IT'S ALREADY BEEN BUILT ... AND IT'S READY TO MOVE IN ...
IT'S IN A VERY SPECIAL PLACE ... IN A CITY FREE FROM SIN.

CHORUS:

I HAVE SAID IT MANY TIMES ... AND I WILL SAY IT AGAIN ...
THAT I AM GOING TO A CITY ... WHERE LIFE HAS NO END.
IT WAS MADE BY GOD HIMSELF ... AND NOT BY HUMAN HANDS ...
THE BEAUTY OF THE CITY ... THE HUMAN MIND CAN'T COMPREHEND.

VERSE TWO:

I HAVE SAID IT MANY TIMES ... IT KEEPS RUNNING THRU MY MIND ...
THE FEELING HAS A SWEET SAVOR ... LIKE WALKING THRU THE PINES.
WITH ALL THAT IS AROUND ... IS PINE NEEDLES AND CONES ...
AND A SWEET THOUGHT OF KNOWING ... SOMEDAY I'M GOING HOME.

VERSE THREE:

THERE IS SOMEONE WALKING WITH ME ... I FEEL IT IN MY BONES ...
HE PROMISED WHEN HE SAVED ME ... I WOULD NEVER WALK ALONE.
HE MAKES ME FEEL SO HAPPY ... TO KNOW THAT HE IS MINE ...
HE LIVES WITHIN MY HEART ... AND I HAVE SAID IT MANY TIMES.

CHORUS:

I HAVE SAID IT MANY TIMES ... AND I WILL SAY IT AGAIN ...
THAT I AM GOING TO A CITY ... WHERE LIFE HAS NO END.

IT WAS MADE BY GOD HIMSELF ... AND NOT BY HUMAN HANDS ...
THE BEAUTY OF THE CITY ... THE HUMAN MIND CAN'T COMPREHEND.

VERSE FOUR:
MANY DON'T HAVE SOMEONE THAT ... THEY CAN CALL THEIR FRIEND ...
BUT JESUS PROMISED TO BE WITH YOU ... EVEN UNTO THE END.
SO GIVE YOUR HEART TO HIM ... HE WILL NEVER LET YOU DOWN ...
AND I HAVE SAID IT MANY TIMES ... HE WILL ALWAYS BE AROUND.

I HUNG MY HEAD AND CRIED

VERSE ONE:

SO MANY TIMES ... I HAVE BEEN WRONG ...
WHEN I THOUGHT ... THAT I WAS RIGHT.
SOMETIMES MY PAST ... WOULD HAUNT ME ...
AND I HAD TROUBLE ... TO SLEEP AT NIGHT.

VERSE TWO:

I PROMISED MYSELF ... I'M GONNA DO BETTER ...
THAT I WAS GOING ... TO MAKE THINGS RIGHT.
WHEN I THOUGHT OF... THE OTHER SIDE ...
I HUNG MY HEAD ... AND CRIED.

CHORUS:

I HUNG MY HEAD AND CRIED... DEAR JESUS ...
FOR THINGS I DID ... TO MAKE ME SATISFIED.
BUT FROM THE PAST ... I COULD'NT HIDE ...
SO I HUNG MY HEAD ... AND CRIED.

VERSE THREE:

IT HURTS ME TO THINK ... HOW HARD MOMMA TRIED ...
AND THE WAY I MUST HAVE ... MADE HER FEEL INSIDE.
THE DAY THEY TOLD ME ... THAT MOMMA HAD DIED ...
I HUNG MY HEAD ... AND CRIED.

CHORUS:

I HUNG MY HEAD AND CRIED... DEAR JESUS ...
FOR THINGS I DID ... TO MAKE ME SATISFIED.
BUT FROM THE PAST ... I COULD'NT HIDE ...
SO I HUNG MY HEAD ... AND CRIED.

I CAN'T REMEMBER

CHORUS:
    I REMEMBER LAST WEEK ... WHEN I HAD SO MUCH FUN ...
BUT WHEN I THINK ABOUT IT ... MAYBE IT WAS LAST MONTH.
    SOMETIMES I CAN'T REMEMBER ... AND I WANT TO CRY ...
IT'S NO LAUGHING MATTER ... HOW FAST TIME GOES BY.

VERSE ONE:
    I CAN'T REMEMBER ANYTHING ... ABOUT YESTERDAY ...
BUT I DON'T GUESS TO ME ... IT REALLY MATTERS ANYWAY.
    TIME JUST GOES SO FAST ... ANOTHER DAY IS GONE ...
BUT I DON'T WORRY ... BECAUSE TIME KEEPS MOVING ON.

VERSE TWO:
    I DON'T EVEN KNOW ... WHAT I HAVE TO DO TOMORROW ...
I CAN ONLY HOPE ... IT DON'T BRING ON MORE SORROW.
    TODAY IS ALMOST OVER ... SOON IT WILL BE A NEW DAY ...
IT SURE IS SURPRISING ... HOW FAST TIME SLIPS AWAY.

VERSE THREE:
    I'M GLAD YESTERDAY IS GONE ... I WON'T WORRY ANYMORE...
I JUST HOPE THAT TOMORROW...WILL BE BETTER THAN BEFORE.
    THE HOURS OF THE DAY ... SURE DOES PASS FAST AWAY ...
BUT I REALLY DON'T CARE ... I WON'T REMEMBER IT ANYWAY.

VERSE FOUR:
    IT'S NIGHTTIME ONCE MORE ... AND IT'S DARK OUTSIDE ...
I DON'T REMEMBER WHAT HAPPENED ... BUT I ALMOST DIED.
    I'M NOT A KID ANYMORE ... I HAVE LIVED TO BE AN OLD MAN ...
I WONDER COULD I REMEMBER ... IF I LIVED IT ALL OVER AGAIN.

I JUST FORGET

CHORUS:

 MY MOMMA SAID SON ... WHAT HAVE YOU DONE ...
WHAT MADE YOU DO ... A THING LIKE THAT.
 I SAID MOMMA ... I DON'T KNOW ...
I GUESS SOMETIMES ... I JUST FORGET.

VERSE ONE:

 I WENT AND GOT DRUNK ... WENT OUT OF MY HEAD ...
AND MY HEAD WAS SPINNIN' ... WHEN I WENT TO BED.
 I LAYED THERE AND WONDERED ... WHAT I HAD DONE ...
I FELT SO ASHAMED ... TO FACE ANYONE.

VERSE TWO:

 THIS TIME I REALLY MADE ... A BIG FOOL OF MYSELF ...
AND BELIEVE YOU ME ... I DID'NT NEED NO HELP.
 I THOUGHT I COULD DO ... WHATEVER I WANTED TO ...
SOMETIMES I FORGET ... WHAT I'M SUPPOSE TO DO.

CHORUS:

 MY MOMMA SAID SON ... WHAT HAVE YOU DONE ...
WHAT MADE YOU DO ... A THING LIKE THAT.
 I SAID MOMMA ... I DON'T KNOW ...
I GUESS SOMETIMES ... I JUST FORGET.

VERSE THREE:

 I HEARD A KNOCK ON MY DOOR ... IT WAS THE POLICE ...
AND THEY HAD A WARRANT ... FOR DISTURBING THE PEACE.
 THEY SAID DID'NT YOU KNOW ... THAT YOU CAN'T DO THAT ...
I SAID YES BUT SOMETIMES ... I JUST FORGET.

I JUST FORGOT

VERSE ONE:

ONE NIGHT AS I WAS RIDING ... RIGHT ON DOWN SOUTH MAIN ...
WHEN ALL OF A SUDDEN ... IT BEGAN TO RAIN.

I ROLLED UP MY WINDOWS ... AND TURNED MY HEADLIGHTS ON ...
THEN I STARTED WISHING ... I HAD STAYED AT HOME.

VERSE TWO:

MY WINDSHIELD WIPERS STOPPED WORKING ... AND I HAD
TO STOP ...
THEN I STARTED TO REMEMBER ... WHAT I JUST FORGOT.

LIKE WHERE WAS I GOING ... TO BEGIN WITH ...
AND WHAT DID I DO ... TO GET IN A FIX LIKE THIS.

CHORUS:

WHEN THEY ASK ME WHY ... I SAY I JUST FORGOT ...
EVEN I DON'T LIKE IT ... CAUSE IT SEEMS TO HAPPEN A LOT.

THEN I JUST SMILE ... WHETHER THEY LIKE IT OR NOT ...
BUT I CAN'T HELP IT ... I GUESS I JUST FORGOT.

VERSE THREE:

SO I GUESS I'LL HAVE TO WAIT ... UNTIL THE RAIN IS ALL GONE ...
BUT BOY I SURE DO HOPE ... IT DON'T LAST VERY LONG.

I HAD THINGS TO DO ... BUT I DON'T REMEMBER WHAT ...
IF ONLY I COULD REMEMBER ... BUT I JUST FORGOT.

VERSE FOUR:

NOW DON'T ASK ME WHY ... I DO THE THINGS I DO ...
BECAUSE YOU MAY NOT BELIEVE ... WHAT I HAVE TO TELL YOU.

I CAN'T REMEMBER TO DO ... THE THINGS THAT I NEED DONE ...
AND FORGETTING TO REMEMBER ... SURE AIN'T NO FUN.

CHORUS:

WHEN THEY ASK ME WHY ... I SAY I JUST FORGOT ...
EVEN I DON'T LIKE IT ... CAUSE IT SEEMS TO HAPPEN A LOT.

THEN I JUST SMILE ... WHETHER THEY LIKE IT OR NOT ...
BUT I CAN'T HELP IT ... I GUESS I JUST FORGOT.

I JUST WANTED TO TALK

LORD, I JUST WANT TO TALK ... TO YOU TODAY...
WHILE I SIT HERE ... AND TAKING MY BREAK.
IT'S BEEN ROUGH ON ME ... ALONG LIFE'S WAY ...
FOR SOME OF THE THINGS ... I HAVE HAD TO TAKE.
YOU KNOW LORD ... I HAVE HAD TO STRUGGLE...
AND WITH ME IT'S HARD ... TO MAKE ENDS MEET.
BUT I STILL BELIEVE ... IN YOU LORD...
AND I KNOW ... YOU AIN'T FORGOT ABOUT ME.
SOMETIMES LORD ... I FEEL LIKE I MUST BE ...
THE POOREST MAN THERE IS ... UNDER THE SUN.
OH! BUT I KNOW LORD ... I HAVE TO PAY FOR...
SOME OF THE THINGS ... THAT I HAVE DONE.
LORD, I KNOW I HAVE HAD .. SEVERAL CHANCES...
TO EVEN MAKE A FORTUNE ... OR MAYBE TWO.
BUT I AIN'T A'GONNA ... QUESTION YOU LORD...
OR ASK WHY MY PLANS ... JUST DID'NT GO THROUGH.
SOMETIMES LORD ... I CAN'T HELP BUT TO WONDER...
IF IN THIS LIFE THINGS WILL EVER ... GET ANY BETTER .
SOMETIMES I CAN'T GO TO SLEEP ... AND I LAY AWAKE...
I ASK MYSELF HOW MUCH LONGER ... DO I HAVE TO WAIT.
LORD YOU KNOW THE THINGS ... I'M GOING THRU..
AND YOU ALSO KNOW ... HOW I FEEL TOWARDS YOU.
BUT SOMETIMES LORD ... I CAN GET SO FLUSTRATED...
THAT I JUST DON'T EVEN KNOW ... JUST WHAT TO DO.
AH! NOW WON'T YOU LISTEN ... TO ME LORD...
YOU MIGHT THINK ... THAT I'M UNFAITHFUL.
BUT THE HEALTH AND LIFE ... THAT I STILL HAVE...
LORD, I JUST FEEL ... DOWN RIGHT GRATEFUL.
I WAS ABLE TO GET UP ... EARLY THIS MORNING...
AND I WAS ABLE ... TO GO OUT FOR A WALK.
SO I AIN'T A'GONNA ASK YOU... FOR ANYTHING ...
WHILE ON MY BREAK LORD, I JUST WANTED TO TALK.

I LOVED RUNNING THE ROADS

VERSE ONE:

    I'VE RUN A LOT MILES ... DELIVERING MY LOADS ...
I'VE SPENT A LOT OF MY LIFE ... A RUNNING THE ROADS.
    I WAS ALWAYS GONE ... HARDLY EVER AT HOME ...
I LOVED THE LIFE I LIVED ... I WAS A ROLLING STONE.

VERSE TWO:

    I'D CLIMB UP IN MY TRUCK ... AND GET BEHIND THE WHEEL ...
I'D FEEL BETTER ALL OVER ... IT WOULD GIVE ME A THRILL.
    I WOULD WARM UP THE ENGINE ... BEFORE I PUT IT IN GEAR ...
RUNNING THE ROADS IS ALL ... THAT I'VE DONE FOR YEARS.

CHORUS:

    I LOVED RUNNING THE ROADS ... ALWAYS RUNNING THE ROADS ...
I'VE BEEN THERE AND DONE THAT ... DELIVERING MY LOADS.
    MAKING A CUSTOMER HAPPY ... WAS A GREAT GLORY ...
AND RUNNING THE ROADS ... WAS THE END OF THE STORY.

VERSE THREE:

    I WOULD STOP AT TRUCK STOPS ... ALL ALONG THE WAY ...
SOMETIMES I'D MEET A FRIEND ... THAT WANTED ME TO STAY.
    I WOULD'NT STAY FOR LONG ... I HAD A JOB TO DO ...
I WAS ALWAYS RUNNING THE ROADS ... UNTIL THE JOB WAS THRU.

VERSE FOUR:

    WHEN I'D GET TO THE CUSTOMER .. I'D BACK UP TO THE DOCK ...
I'D GET THE ORDER OFF ... THEN I'D HEAD FOR THE NEXT STOP.
    AFTER I GOT THE BILLS SIGNED ... I'D GET ANOTHER LOAD ...
I WOULD'NT BE HOME LONG ... BEFORE I WAS BACK ON THE ROAD.

CHORUS:
>   I LOVED RUNNING THE ROADS ... ALWAYS RUNNING THE
>   ROADS ...
I'VE BEEN THERE AND DONE THAT ... DELIVERING MY LOADS.
>   MAKING A CUSTOMER HAPPY ... WAS A GREAT GLORY ...
AND RUNNING THE ROADS ... WAS THE END OF THE STORY.

I SHOULD HAVE KEPT ON GOIN'

CHORUS:
    IF YOU DRIVE THEM TRUCKS... UP AND DOWN THE LINE ...
TAKE MY ADVICE ... AND DON'T WASTE YOUR TIME ...
    ALWAYS KEEP THEM ... BIG WHEELS A'ROLLIN' ...
AND DON'T LOOK BACK ... JUST KEEP ON A'GOIN'.

VERSE ONE:
    I USED TO DRIVE A TRUCK ... FROM STATE TO STATE ...
SOME OF THOSE LOADS ... WOULD JUST HAVE TO WAIT.
    I WOULD STOP AT ... SOME CAT HOUSE IN BETWEEN ...
AND START PLAYING ... SOME OLD PINBALL MACHINE.

VERSE TWO:
    IT'S NOT THE MILES ... BUT SOME OF THE STOPS ...
THAT GAVE ME THE ACKES ... AND PAINS THAT I GOT.
    THE RESULTS IN MY BODY ...\ ARE REALLY SHOWIN' ...
FOR MAKING THE STOPS ... INSTEAD OF KEEP ON GOIN'...

VERSE THREE:
    I DROVE EVEN ... IF THE WEATHER WAS'NT CLEAR ...
I SPENT MY LIFE ... JUST JAMMING THOSE GEARS.
    I WASTED A LOT OF TIME ... NOT REALLY KNOWING ...
THAT I SHOULD HAVE JUST ... KEPT ON A'GOIN'.

VERSE FOUR:
    THERE WAS ONE TIME ... WHEN IT WAS A SNOWIN' ...
I STOPPED WHEN I SHOULD HAVE ... KEPT ON A'GOIN'.
    I OFFERED TO HELP ... SOMEONE THAT WAS STUCK ...
I'D WISHED LATER ... I HAD STAYED IN MY TRUCK.
    ..... SING CHORUS AGAIN ....

I SURE DO FEEL SORRY FOR YOU

VERSE ONE:

I'M GOING THRU BAD TIMES NOW ... WHEN EVERYTHING IS WRONG ...

SO I'M SITTING HERE PUTTING ... SOME OF THEM IN THIS SONG.

I KNOW I'M NOT THE ONLY ONE ... SOMETIMES THEY HAPPEN TO YOU TOO ...

BUT IF YOU'RE GOING THRU WHAT I AM ... I SURE DO FEEL SORRY FOR YOU.

VERSE TWO:

I'VE HEARD MY MOMMA SAY ... THERE'LL BE DAYS LIKE A STROKE ...

BUT I WOULD JUST LAUGH AND THOUGHT THAT IT WAS JUST A JOKE.

WHEN SOMETHING BAD HAPPENED ... I'D SAY IT'LL SOON GO AWAY.

BUT THEY STARTED HAPPENING IN BUNCHES ... ALL ON THE VERY SAME DAY.

CHORUS:

I SURE DO FEEL SORRY FOR YOU ... BUT I'LL CALL YOU MY FRIEND ...

SOMETIMES I FEEL LIKE THIS MISERY ... WILL NEVER HAVE AN END.

ONE DAY SEEMS LIKE FOREVER ... WHEN YOU'RE HAVING A BAD DAY ...

THANK GOD THERE'S HOPE FOR TOMORROW ... BUT IT SEEMS SO FAR AWAY.

VERSE THREE:

THE COUNTY GARNISHED MY BANK ACCOUNT ... FOR MY PROPERTY TAX ...

THAT'S MONEY GONE OUT THE WINDOW ... AND I'LL NEVER GET IT BACK.

THEN THE BANK CHARGED A SERVICE FEE ... ON TOP OF ALL
OF THAT ...
A POOR MAN DON'T HAVE A CHANCE ... NO MATTER WHO COMES
TO BAT.

VERSE FOUR:
MY SISTER GAVE ME A SIDE BY SIDE ... WITH WATER IN THE
FRONT DOOR ...
I WENT TO GET A GLASS OF ICE ... IT WAS'NT MAKING ANYMORE.
I SAID THAT I AIN'T A GONNA WORRY ... BECAUSE I CAN DO
WITHOUT ...
THEN ONE DAY I HEARD THE WATER ... IT WAS SHOOTING THRU
THE SPOUT.

CHORUS:
I SURE DO FEEL SORRY FOR YOU ... BUT I'LL CALL YOU MY
FRIEND ...
SOMETIMES I FEEL LIKE THIS MISERY ... WILL NEVER HAVE AN END.
ONE DAY SEEMS LIKE FOREVER ... WHEN YOU'RE HAVING A
BAD DAY ...
THANK GOD THERE'S HOPE FOR TOMORROW ... BUT IT SEEMS SO
FAR AWAY.

I WANT TO SEE WHO I'LL SEE

VERSE ONE:

NOW THE TIME IS A'COMIN' ... AND I CAN HARDLY WAIT ...
TO SEE WHO I'LL SEE ... JUST INSIDE THE PEARLY GATES.
THERE WILL BE SOME FAMILY ... AND SOME FRIENDS OF MINE ...
I CAN'T WAIT TO SEE ... WHO'S ON THE OTHER SIDE OF THE LINE.

VERSE TWO:

I'VE HEARD IT BEFORE ... GRASS IS GREENER ON THE OTHER
SIDE ...
BUT THERE WILL BE NO GRASS ... WHEN THE GATES ARE OPENED
WIDE.
THE STREETS ARE PURE GOLD ... ALONG SIDE THE TREE OF
LIFE ...
AND I CAN'T WAIT TO SEE WHO I'LL SEE ... OVER ON THE OTHER
SIDE.

CHORUS:

I WANT TO SEE WHO I'LL SEE ... A LOOKING BACK AT ME ...
WHEN MY NAME IS CALLED ... I DON'T KNOW WHERE I WILL I BE.
IT COULD BE ANY MOMENT ... IT COULD EVEN BE TODAY ...
I WANT TO SEE WHO I'LL SEE ... ON THE OTHER SIDE OF THE GRAVE.

VERSE THREE:

I WANT TO SEE WHO I'LL SEE ... WALKING ON THE STREETS OF
GOLD ...
I WANT TO SEE WHO I'LL SEE ... AMONG THE YOUNG AND THE OLD.
I WANT TO SEE WHO I'LL SEE ... WHEN I SEE THE ONE WHO
DIED FOR ME ...
I WANT TO SEE WHAT HE'LL SAY ... WHEN I FALL DOWN AT HIS FEET.

VERSE FOUR:

I CAN HEAR MY MOTHER CALLING ...THE TIME IS GETTING
NEAR ...
WE'RE SETTING THE LORD'S SUPPER ... WE'RE WAITING FOR YOU
DEAR.

I WANT TO SEE WHO I'LL SEE ... AND BE WITH THRU ETERNITY ...
I MIGHT REALLY BE SURPRISED ... SO I WANT TO SEE WHO I'LL SEE.

CHORUS:
I WANT TO SEE WHO I'LL SEE ... A LOOKING BACK AT ME ...
WHEN MY NAME IS CALLED ... I DON'T KNOW WHERE I WILL I BE.
IT COULD BE ANY MOMENT ... IT MIGHT EVEN BE TODAY ...
I WANT TO SEE WHO I'LL SEE ... ON THE OTHER SIDE OF THE GRAVE.

I WILL WRITE YOU THIS LETTER

VERSE ONE:

    I WILL WRITE YOU THIS LETTER ... AND TELL YOU ALL ABOUT IT THEN ...

I DON'T KNOW WHY IT HAPPENED ... BUT I'LL NEVER BE THE SAME AGAIN.

    I WILL TRY TO EXPLAIN EVERYTHING ... AND THE WAY THAT THINGS WENT ...

I DON'T KNOW WHAT HAPPENED TO ME ... BUT IT WILL NEVER HAPPEN AGAIN.

VERSE TWO:

    I THOUGHT THAT I LOVED YOU ... AND NOTHING COULD PULL US APART ..

BUT SOMETHING HAPPENED TO ME ... AND IT SEEMED TO NUMB MY HEART.

    IT HAD TO BE SOME KIND OF A DEMON ... THAT GOT A HOLD OF ME ...

I ONLY KNOW THAT I WANT THINGS ... TO BE LIKE THEY USED TO BE.

CHORUS:

    I'M NO GOOD AT WRITTING LETTERS ... BUT I DON'T KNOW WHAT TO DO ...

I'M SORRY FOR WHAT I DID ... AND I REALLY DID'NT MEAN TO HURT YOU.

    BUT LET'S PUT THE PAST BEHIND US ... AND START ALL OVER AGAIN ...

I HOPE WHEN YOU READ THIS LETTER ... WE WILL BE MORE THAN FRIENDS.

VERSE THREE:

    I KNEW WHEN I FIRST MET YOU ... THAT YOU WERE A VERY SPECIAL GIRL ...

AND I WOULD'NT HAVE TRADED YOU ... FOR THE WHOLE WORLD.

    BUT I WAS THE JEALOUS TYPE ... AND I SHOULD HAVE KNOWN BETTER ...

BUT I'LL TELL YOU ALL ABOUT IT ... BUT I WILL WRITE YOU A LETTER.

VERSE FOUR:

WHEN YOU RECIEVE THE LETTER ... I HOPE IT FINDS YOU WELL ...
BUT I WANT YOU TO KNOW I LOVE YOU ... MORE THAN I CAN TELL.
I HOPE YOU CAN FIND FORGIVENESS ... HIDDEN WITHIN YOUR HEART ...
AND I HOPE YOU CAN FIND A WAY ... TO NEVER LET IT TEAR OUR LOVE APART.

CHORUS:

I'M NO GOOD AT WRITTING LETTERS ... BUT I DON'T KNOW WHAT TO DO ...
I'M SORRY FOR WHAT I DID ... AND I REALLY DID'NT MEAN TO HURT YOU.
BUT LET'S PUT THE PAST BEHIND US ... AND START ALL OVER AGAIN ...
I HOPE WHEN YOU READ THIS LETTER ... WE WILL BE MORE THAN FRIENDS.

I WON'T BE LONG

VERSE ONE:
  I ONCE FELT DOWN ... AND THEN I GOT UP ...
AND WALKED OUTSIDE ... TO MY PICK-UP TRUCK.
  I TURNED MY RADIO ON ... AND I HEARD A SONG ...
IT SAID I'M WORRIED NOW ... BUT I WON'T BE LONG.

VERSE TWO:
  YOU MAY NOT KNOW ... THAT I'M WORRIED NOW ...
BUT I'M GONNA MAKE ... IT THRU SOMEHOW.
  THAT SONG SURE DID... MAKE ME FEEL STRONG ...
I MAY BE WORRIED NOW ... BUT I WON'T BE LONG.

VERSE THREE:
  SOMETIMES I LET PROBLEMS ... JUST WORRY ME ...
I MAY NOT BE AS STRONG ... AS I USED TO BE.
  I STILL HAVE THE URGE ... TO KEEP GOING ON ...
I MAY BE WORRIED NOW ... BUT I WON'T BE LONG.

VERSE FOUR:
  NOW ALL OF MY TROUBLES ... JUST GET ME DOWN ...
EVERYTIME THE MAILMAN ... COMES AROUND.
  I FEEL LIKE A DOG ... A'DRAGGING A BONE ...
I'M WORRIED NOW ... BUT I WON'T BE LONG.

VERSE FIVE:
  I'M GETTING TOO OLD ...TO LET IT GET ME DOWN ...
AND I SURE DON'T FEEL ... LIKE WORRYING NOW.
  SO I'LL TAKE MY TROUBLES... AND CARRY THEM ON ...
I MAY BE WORRIED NOW ... BUT I WON'T BE LONG.

I WON'T DO IT AGAIN

CHORUS:
     MOMMA DON'T WHIP ME ... I WON'T DO IT AGAIN ...
THESE WORDS KEEPS COMIN' BACK ... TIME AND TIME AGAIN.
     MOMMA WOULD WEAR ME OUT...WITH A SWITCH IN HER
     HAND...
AND WHEN MOMMA WHIPPED ME ... I KNEW NOT TO DO IT AGAIN.

VERSE ONE:
     MOMMA WANTED ME TO BE ... HER GOOD LITTLE BOY ...
BUT WHEN I DID WRONG ... THAT WAS ANOTHER STORY.
     SHE WOULD TELL ME TO GO ... AND GET HER A SWITCH ...
DON'T COME BACK WITH A LITTLE ONE ... OR YOU'LL REGRET IT.

VERSE TWO:
     SHE TAUGHT ME RIGHT FROM WRONG... RIGHT FROM THE
     START ...
SOMETIMES I COULD SEE ... THAT IT WOULD BREAK HER HEART.
     WHEN SHE WOULD WHIP ME ... FOR SOMETHING I HAD DONE ...
IT WAS HER RESPONSIBILITY ... BECAUSE I WAS HER SON.

     .... SING CHORUS AGAIN ....

VERSE THREE:
     I DON'T HOLD THESE WHIPPINGS ... AGAINST MY MOTHER ...
IT ONLY MADE ME BETTER ... AND MORE PROUD OF HER.
     IT'S A SHAME THINGS AIN'T LIKE ... IT WAS BACK THEN ...
WHEN MOMMA CORRECTED ME ... TIME AND TIME AGAIN.

     ... SING CHORUS AGAIN ...

I WONDER WHAT THEY'D SAY

VERSE ONE:

I DID'NT TAKE MUCH TIME ... TO GET A CLEAN SHAVE TODAY ... I DID'NT SLEEP TO GOOD ... BECAUSE THINGS WAS'NT GOING MY WAY.

PEOPLE SAID I LOOKED BAD ... WITH HAIR ALL OVER MY FACE ... BUT IF THEY LOOKED IN A MIRROR ... I WONDER WHAT THEY'D SAY ...

VERSE TWO:

THEY TALK ABOUT OTHERS ... NOT THINKING OF THEIR OWNSELVES ...

THEY ALWAYS JUST WANT ... TO TALK ABOUT SOMEONE ELSE.

IF ONLY THEY WOULD ASK THEMSELVES ... WHAT WOULD THEY DO ...

I WONDER WHAT THEY'D SAY ... IF THEY HAD TO WALK IN THIER SHOES.

CHORUS:

NOW DON'T LAUGH AT THE PEOPLE ... THAT ARE WORSE OFF THAN YOU ...

BECAUSE THE SAME GOD THAT MADE YOU ... ALSO MADE THEM TOO.

SO WHEN YOU SEE SOMEONE ... THAT NEEDS A HELPING HAND ...

JUST ASK YOURSELF WHAT YOU CAN DO ... AND DO WHATEVER YOU CAN.

VERSE THREE:

I SAW A BLIND MAN SITTING ... ON THE SIDE OF THE STREET TODAY ...

HE WAS ASKING FOR SOME COINS ... FROM PEOPLE THAT PASSED HIS WAY.

I SAW ONE GUY LAUGH ... AS HE P ITCHED A PENNY IN THE TRAY ...

BUT IF IT WAS HIM SITTING THERE ... I WONDER WHAT HE'D WOULD SAY.

VERSE FOUR:

HOW MANY PEOPLE THINKS ABOUT... HOW WELL OFF THEY ARE TODAY ...
I WONDER IF THEY THANK THE LORD ... AND TAKE TIME OUT TO PRAY.
THEY SAY THEY WORKED HARD FOR ... EVERYTHING THAT THEY HAVE ...
BUT I WONDER WHAT THEY'D SAY ... IF THEY LOST IT ALL SOMEHOW.

VERSE FIVE:

I WONDER WHAT THEY'LL SAY ... ON THAT LAST JUDGEMENT DAY ...
WHEN THEY STAND BEFORE THE ALMIGHTY GOD ... ASHAMED AND AFRAID.
WILL THEY BEG FOR MERCY ... LIKE THE BLIND MAN ON THE STREET ...
OR WILL THEY BE REWARDED ... FOR HELPING THE POOR AND THE WEAK.

CHORUS:

NOW DON'T LAUGH AT THE PEOPLE ... THAT ARE WORSE OFF THAN YOU ...
BECAUSE THE SAME GOD THAT MADE YOU ... ALSO MADE THEM TOO.
SO WHEN YOU SEE SOMEONE ... THAT NEEDS A HELPING HAND ...
JUST ASK YOURSELF WHAT YOU CAN DO ... AND DO WHATEVER YOU CAN.

I WONDER WHY

VERSE ONE:
  SINCE YOU LEFT ... MY HEART CRYS AND CRYS ...
AND IT'S DRAINING ALL THE TEARS ... FROM MY EYES.
  MY HEART CALLS FOR YOU ... AND WILL UNTIL I DIE ...
I CAN'T GO ON LIKE THIS ... AND I WONDER WHY.

VERSE TWO:
  I WONDER WHY ... BECAUSE I DID'NT DO NOTHING ...
MAYBE THAT'S WHY ... I SHOULD HAVE DONE SOMETHING.
  I SHOULD HAVE TOLD YOU ... AS THE DAYS WENT BY ...
THAT I STILL LOVE YOU ... BUT I DID'NT I WONDER WHY.

CHORUS:
  I WONDER WHY ... I FEEL THE WAY THAT I DO ...
AND I WONDER WHY ... I CARED SO MUCH FOR YOU.
  I WONDER WHY ... I HAVE TEARS IN MY EYES ...
SINCE YOU TOLD ME GOODBYE ... I WONDER WHY.

VERSE THREE:
  IN MY HEART I BELIEVE ... THAT I'LL LOVE YOU TIL I DIE ...
I'VE TOLD YOU THAT BEFORE ... AS THE YEARS WENT BY.
  NOW YOU TELL ME ... YOU BELIEVE THAT IT WAS A LIE ...
BUT WHY DON'T YOU BELIEVE ME ... I WONDER WHY.

VERSE FOUR:
  IF ONLY YOU OPENED YOUR EYES ... YOU WOULD REALIZE ...
THERE HAS BEEN NO ONE ELSE ... FOR ME IN MY LIFE.
  BUT YOU IGNORED ME ... AND SAID THAT IT WAS A LIE ...
AND IT TORE ME TO PIECES ... AND I WONDER WHY.

CHORUS:
  I WONDER WHY ... I FEEL THE WAY THAT I DO ...
I WONDER WHY ... I CARED SO MUCH FOR YOU.
  I WONDER WHY ... I HAVE TEARS IN MY EYES ...
SINCE YOU TOLD ME GOODBYE ... I WONDER WHY.

4

I WOULD'NT LISTEN

VERSE ONE:
    MOMMA BEGGED ME ... NOT TO GO OUT THAT NIGHT ...
BUT HOW WAS I TO KNOW ... I WOULD WIND UP IN A FIGHT.
    THERE WAS AN ARGUMENT ... THE GUY PULLED A KNIGHT ...
AND THAT ONE INCIDENT ... THAT CHANGED MY WHOLE LIFE.

VERSE TWO:
    I DID'NT REALLY MEAN TO ... BUT I KILLED THE MAN ...
AND HE DIED RIGHT THERE ... WITH HIS KNIFE IN HIS HAND.
    I AM SO SORRY ... I DID'NT MEAN IT THAT WAY ...
BUT I WOULD'NT LISTEN ... AND SOMEONE HAD TO PAY.

VERSE THREE:
    I GUESS MOMMA KNEW ... JUST HOW IT WOULD BE ...
IF I DID'NT CHANGE MY WAYS ... WHERE IT WOULD TAKE ME.
    IF IT WAS'NT IN SELF DEFENCE ... I WOULD BE IN PRISON ...
AND ALL BECAUSE ... I MADE THE WRONG DECISION.

VERSE FOUR:
    I DREAMED OF HEAVEN ... IT WAS BEAUTIFUL AND BRIGHT ...
ST. PETER AT THE GOLDEN GATE ... READING THE BOOK OF LIFE.
    I LISTENED FOR MY NAME ... BUT IT WAS'NT WRITTEN ...
I HAD HEARD PREACHERS PREACH ... BUT I WOULD'NT LISTEN.

CHORUS:
    SO LOOK BEFORE YOU LEAP ... DON'T TAKE IT TOO FAR ...
AND SLOW DOWN AND LIVE ... AND REMEMBER WHO YOU ARE.
    DON'T TAKE IT FOR GRANTED... IF THEY SAY YOU'RE WRONG ...
AND DON'T GET CAUGHT UP ... LIVING IN A SAD SONG.

I'LL BE HOME

VERSE ONE:

    I HAVE A HOME IN GLORYLAND ... THAT'S PAID FOR BY GOD'S
SON ...
.IT WAS HIS OWN CHOICE ... NOT FOR SOMETHING I HAD DONE.
    WELL SOON I'LL BE LEAVING ... AND IT WON'T BE TOO LONG ...
SO DON'T LOOK FOR ME ... I WON'T BE HERE CAUSE I'LL BE HOME.

CHORUS:

    I'LL BE HOME .. I'LL BE HOME ... PRAISE GOD I'LL BE HOME ...
THIS OLD LIFE HERE ON EARTH ... HAS BEEN MUCH TOO LONG.
    THE DEVIL HAS TEMPTED ME ... HE WON'T LEAVE ME ALONE ...
BUT HE HAS LOST THE BATTLE ... BECAUSE SOON I'LL BE HOME.

VERSE TWO:

    I'LL SEE MY FRIENDS AND FAMILY ... THAT HAS GONE ON
BEFORE ...
WE'LL WALK DOWN STREETS OF GOLD ... ON HEAVENS BRIGHT
SHORE.
    FIRST I WANT TO SEE JESUS ... WHO BUILT THE MANSION
FOR ME ...
AND HE PAID FOR IT WITH BLOOD ... WHEN HE DIED ON CALVARY.

VERSE THREE:

    IT WILL BE A GREAT REUNION ... AROUND GOD'S GOLDEN
THRONE ...
THOSE OLD HEARTACHES AND TROUBLES ... THERE ALL WILL BE
GONE.
    I KNOW MOTHER IS WAITING ... SHE PRAYED MANY TIMES
ALONE ...
AND HER PRAYERS WAS ANSWERED ... NOW SOON I'LL BE HOME.

CHORUS:

    I'LL BE HOME .. I'LL BE HOME ... PRAISE GOD I'LL BE HOME ...
THIS OLD LIFE HERE ON EARTH ... HAS BEEN MUCH TOO LONG.
    THE DEVIL HAS TEMPTED ME ... HE WON'T LEAVE ME ALONE ...
BUT HE HAS LOST THE BATTLE ... BECAUSE SOON I'LL BE HOME.

CHORUS:

    I'LL BE HOME .. I'LL BE HOME ... PRAISE GOD I'LL BE HOME ...
THIS OLD LIFE HERE ON EARTH ... HAS BEEN MUCH TOO LONG.
    THE DEVIL HAS TEMPTED ME ... HE WON'T LEAVE ME ALONE ...
BUT HE HAS LOST THE BATTLE ... BECAUSE SOON I'LL BE HOME.

I'LL JUST BE SITTING HERE

CHORUS:

      I'LL JUST BE SITTING HERE ... BESIDE THE CHRISTMAS TREE ...
WISHING THAT SANTA CLAUS ... WOULD BRING YOU BACK TO ME.

      THE TREE IS ALL LIT UP ... WITH LIGHT'S AND ALL IT'S CHARMS ...
JUST THE WAY THAT I WOULD BE ... IF YOU WERE IN MY ARMS.

VERSE ONE:

      EVERYONE IS SO HAPPY ... BUT SOMETHING IS WRONG
      WITH ME ...
I CAN'T FIND THE LOVE I NEED ... UNDERNEATH THE CHRISTMAS
TREE.

      I NEED YOU SO MUCH ... THAT YOU ARE ALL I WANT THIS
      YEAR ...
SO WHILE EVERYONE ELSE IS HAPPY ... I'LL JUST BE SITTING HERE.

VERSE TWO:

      THIS CHRISTMAS WILL BE BLUE'R ... THAN THE LIGHTS OF
      BLUE ...
IF I HAVE TO SPEND IT HERE ... THIS SEASON WITHOUT YOU.

      WHILE I'M SITTING HERE WISHING ... FOR MY DREAMS TO COME
      TRUE ...
I'LL JUST BE SITTING HERE ... THINKING OF NO ONE ELSE BUT YOU.

CHORUS:

      I'LL JUST BE SITTING HERE ... BESIDE THE CHRISTMAS TREE ...
WISHING THAT SANTA CLAUS ... WOULD BRING YOU BACK TO ME.

      THE TREE IS ALL LIT UP ... WITH LIGHT'S AND ALL IT'S CHARMS ...
JUST THE WAY THAT I WOULD BE ... IF YOU WERE HERE IN MY ARMS.

VERSE THREE:

      WHEN YOU LEFT YOU KNEW THAT ... I'LL JUST BE SITTING HERE ...
YOU THOUGHT THAT ALL I WANTED ... WAS ANOTHER BOTTLE OF
BEER.

      IT'S NOT THE SPIRIT OF CHRISTMAS ... AND THINGS WE ONCE
      KNEW ...
SO WHILE YOU ENJOY YOURSLF ... I'LL STILL BE THINKING OF YOU.

VERSE FOUR:

SO IF YOU DECIDE TO MAKE ME HAPPY ... YOU KNOW WHERE I WILL BE ..

YOU CAN WRAP UP YOUR LOVE ... AND BRING IT ON HOME TO ME.

IF YOU HAVE ANY FEELINGS AT ALL ... THEN LISTEN TO MY PLEA ...

I'LL JUST BE SITTING HERE ... WAITING AROUND THE CHRISTMAS TREE.

I'LL SOON BE GONE

VERSE ONE:

THERE'LL BE NO USE TO CALL ME ... ON THE TELEPHONE ...
DON'T WASTE YOUR TIME BECAUSE ... I WON'T BE AT HOME.
I'M GONNA BE LIKE HANK SNOW ... AND I'M A MOVING ON ...
YOU CAN LOOK AROUND FOR ME ... BUT I'LL SOON BE GONE.

CHORUS:

YOU MAY LAUGH AT ME AND WONDER ... WHAT IS GOING ON ...
HOW COULD A POOR BOY LIKE ME ... HAVE A MANSION OF HIS OWN ...
PRAYER HAS BUILT IT ... AND FAITH UNLOCKS THE DOOR ...
AND I KNOW I'LL SOON BE GONE ... I WON'T BE HERE ANYMORE.

VERSE TWO:

I'VE INHERITED ME A MANSION ... THAT I CAN CALL MY OWN ...
IT WAS HANDED DOWN BY JESUS ... GOD'S BEGOTTEN SON.
IT'S AN OPEN HOUSE ... ALL THE WORK HAS BEEN DONE ...
I JUST CAN'T WAIT TO GET THERE ... AND I'LL SOON BE GONE.

VERSE THREE:

HOME FOLKS ARE WAITING ... THEY WON'T HAVE TO WAIT LONG ...
I'LL GET A GLORIFIED BODY ... AND SHED THESE FRESH AND BONES.
I'LL MEET PEOPLE FROM ALL AGES ... AND I WON'T BE ALONE ...
I CAN ALMOST FEEL IT NOW ... THAT I'LL SOON BE GONE.

CHORUS:

YOU MAY LAUGH AT ME AND WONDER ... WHAT IS GOING ON ...
HOW COULD A POOR BOY LIKE ME ... HAVE A MANSION OF HIS OWN ...
PRAYER HAS BUILT IT ... AND FAITH UNLOCKS THE DOOR ...
AND I KNOW I'LL SOON BE GONE ... I WON'T BE HERE ANY MORE.

VERSE FOUR:

I HAVE A HOME IN HEAVEN ... AND I HAVE THE KEY TO THE
DOOR ...
I DON'T HAVE ANYTHING ON EARTH ... FOR ME TO STAY HERE FOR.
I'M ANXIOUS NOW TO GO ... I WANT TO SEE MY NEW HOME ...
AND WHEN THEY CALL MY NAME ... THEN I'LL SOON BE GONE.

I'LL TELL YOU AGAIN

CHORUS:
> WELL I'VE TOLD YOU BEFORE ... AND I'LL TELL YOU AGAIN ...
I'M NOT IN LOVE WITH YOU ... AND I NEVER HAVE BEEN.
> WE HAD A LONG FRIENDSHIP ... WE WERE JUST FRIENDS ...
I DON'T KNOW WHY YOU THOUGHT ... IT WOULD NEVER END.

VERSE ONE:
> WE WOULD LAUGH AND CARRY ON ... JUST AT TIMES ...
BUT I NEVER THOUGHT SOMEDAY ... YOU MIGHT BE MINE.
> THAT'S NOT THE WAY ... I INTENDED IT TO BE ...
SO I'LL TELL YOU AGAIN ... I NEVER WANTED YOU FOR ME.

VERSE TWO:
> I DON'T MEAN TO HURT YOU ... BUT THIS HAS TO END ...
IT HURTS ME TO TELL YOU ... THERE'S NO WAY YOU CAN WIN.
> I KEEP SAYING THIS ... AND I'VE SAID IT 'OR AND 'OR ...
BUT I'LL TELL YOU AGAIN ... IT'S THE VERY SAME AS BEFORE.

VERSE THREE:
> WHY CAN'T YOU REALIZE ... IT AIN'T LIKE IT WAS BACK THEN ...
I NEVER LOVED YOU ... I JUST TRIED TO BE YOUR FRIEND.
> I'VE SAID IT MANY TIMES BEFORE ... I'LL TELL YOU AGAIN ...
FIND SOMEONE WHO CARES,,, AND LET A NEW LIFE BEGIN.

CHORUS:
> WELL I'VE TOLD YOU BEFORE ... AND I'LL TELL YOU AGAIN ...
I'M NOT IN LOVE WITH YOU ... AND I NEVER HAVE BEEN.
> WE HAD A LONG FRIENDSHIP ... WE WERE JUST FRIENDS ...
I DON'T KNOW WHY YOU THOUGHT ... IT WOULD NEVER END.

I'M A DIFERANT ME

VERSE ONE:

      BACK WHEN I WAS YOUNG ... I WAS WILD AND FREE ...
BUT THE OLDER I GOT ... IT WAS MORE PLAIN FOR ME TO SEE.
      I WAS MISSING SOMETHING ... MY LIFE WAS'NT COMPLETE...
SO I AM NOT LIKE I USED TO BE ... I'M A DIFFERANT ME.

VERSE TWO:

      I WANTED SELF RESPECT ... BUT NOT FOR THINGS I DID ...
I WAS ALWAYS INTO TROUBLE ... LIKE A LITTLE KID.
      I HAD TO GROW UP ... LIKE A LITTLE OAK TREE ...
SO I'M NOT LIKE I USED TO BE ... I'M A DIFFERANT ME.

CHORUS:

      I'M A DIFFERANT ME ... YES I'M A DIFFERANT ME ...
AND I'LL NEVER GO BACK ... TO WHAT I USED TO BE.
      EVEN A BLIND MAN ... THOUGH HE'S BLIND CAN SEE ...
HE CAN SENSE THE DIFFERANCE ... I'M A DIFFERANT ME.

VERSE THREE:

      MY MOMMA SAID SON ... WHEN ARE YOU GOING TO CHANGE?..
ALL YOU ARE DOING IS ... HURTING THE FAMILY'S NAME.
      SO I TOOK IT TO MY HEART ... NOW IT'S PLAIN TO SEE ...
THAT I'M NOT LIKE I USED TO BE ... I'M A DIFFERANT ME.

VERSE FOUR:

      I FINALY GREW UP ... LIKE THAT BIG OAK TREE ...
AND MY LIFE IS BLOOMING ... WITH JOY ALL AROUND ME.
      I'LL NEVER GO BACK ... TO THE LIFE OF MISERY ...
I'M NOT LIKE I USED TO BE ... I'M A DIFFERANT ME.

CHORUS:

      I'M A DIFFERANT ME ... YES I'M A DIFFERANT ME ...
AND I'LL NEVER GO BACK ... TO WHAT I USED TO BE.
      EVEN A BLIND MAN ... THOUGH HE'S BLIND CAN SEE ...
HE CAN SENSE THE DIFFERANCE ... I'M A DIFFERANT ME.

I'M A LONELY COWBOY

VERSE ONE:

     I'M A LONELY COWBOY ... I RIDE A LONESOME TRAIL ...
MY CANTEEN IS ON MY SADDLE ... THAT JINGLES LIKE A BELL.
     THE TRAILS ARE ALL DUSTY ... AND I RIDE THEM ALONE ...
I'M A LONELY COWBOY ... AND MY SADDLE IS MY HOME.

VERSE TWO:

     I'M A LONELY COWBOY ... I RIDE THE TRAILS ALONE ...
MY GUNS MY HORSE AND MY SADDLE ... IS ALL THAT I OWN.
     I SLEEP UNDER THE STARS ... ON THE TRAIL EACH NIGHT ...
I LOOK UP AT THE SKY ... AND WATCH A PALE MOONLIGHT.

CHORUS:

     I'M A LONELY COWBOY ... AND I RIDE TO THE UNKNOWN ...
SOMEWHERE UP THE ROAD I'LL FIND ... A PLACE OF MY OWN.
     IT WILL TAKE MY WHOLE LIFETIME ... FOR ME TO GET THERE ...
BUT MY LONELY DAYS WILL BE OVER ... WITH NO BURDENS TO BEAR.

VERSE THREE:

     I'M A LONELY COWBOY ... WITH WEATHER BEAT'UN SKIN ...
I HAVE NO TABLE TO EAT ON ... AND NO BED TO SLEEP IN.
     I HAVE SOMETHING INSIDE OF ME ... THAT WILL NEVER PART ...
I KEEP A SMILE ON MY FACE ... AND A SONG IN MY HEART.

VERSE FOUR:

     WHEN I GET OLD AND LOOK BACK ... AT MY LONELY PAST ...
I HOPE I FIND WHERE I AM GOING ... WHEN I GET HOME AT LAST.
     I'LL MEET GOOD PEOPLE I'VE KNOWN ... ALL FILLED UP WITH
JOY ...
AND UP THERE I'LL NEVER KNOW ... ANOTHER LONELY COWBOY.

CHORUS:

     I'M A LONELY COWBOY ... AND I RIDE TO THE UNKNOWN ...
SOMEWHERE UP THE ROAD I'LL FIND ... A PLACE OF MY OWN.
     IT WILL TAKE MY WHOLE LIFETIME ... FOR ME TO GET THERE ...
BUT MY LONELY DAYS WILL BE OVER ... WITH NO BURDENS TO BEAR.

I'M GONNA LOOK FOR JESUS

VERSE ONE:

I ONCE HAD A VISITOR ... THAT CAUGHT ME BY SURPRISE ...
AND WHEN I MET HIM FACE TO FACE ... HE HAD TEARS IN HIS EYES.
HE SAID YOU HAVE HURT ME ... BY THINGS THAT YOU HAVE
DONE ...
THEN HE TOLD ME THAT HE WAS JESUS ... GOD's BEGOTTEN SON.

VERSE TWO:

I HAD NO WAY OF KNOWING ... BUT IF ONLY I HAD KNOWN ...
I WOULD'NT BE CAUGHT DOING ... THE THINGS THAT I HAVE DONE.
HE CAUGHT ME UNSUSPECTED ... I WAS'NT LOOKING FOR HIM
TO COME ...
I WOULD HAVE BEEN MORE PREPARED ... IT MADE ME FEEL SO DUMB.

VERSE THREE:

I LOOKED UP TOWARD HEAVEN ... AND THEN I BEGAN TO
CRY ...
I SAID LORD HAVE MERCY ON ME ... ON JUDGEMENT DAY WHEN
I DIE.
HE SAID MY SON I HEAR YOU ... AND YOUR SINS ARE FORGIVEN ...
AND I HAVE A PLACE PREPARED FOR YOU ... IN A PLACE CALLED
HEAVEN.

CHORUS:

I'M GONNA LOOK FOR JESUS ... THROUGHOUT LIFE'S DREARY
WAY ...
AND I KNOW THAT HE IS WITH ME ... EVERY MINUTE OF THE DAY.
WHENEVER TROUBLE SURROUNDS ME ... HE ALWAYS LEADS
THE WAY ...
I'M GONNA LOOK FOR JESUS ... ON THAT LAST JUDGEMENT DAY.

VERSE FOUR:

I KNOW IT WON'T BE LONG ... AND THEN I'M GOING HOME ...
ALL THE HARDSHIPS OF THIS LIFE ... WILL ALL BE DEAD AND GONE.

IT'LL BE A LONG HARD TRIP ... WITH MANY DETOURS ON THE WAY ...
BUT SOON I'LL BE WITH GOD ... AND FOREVER THERE I'LL STAY.

CHORUS:
I'M GONNA LOOK FOR JESUS ... THROUGHOUT LIFE'S DREARY WAY ...
BUT I KNOW THAT HE IS WITH ME ... EVERY MINUTE OF THE DAY.
WHENEVER TROUBLE SURROUNDS ME ... HE ALWAYS LEADS THE WAY ...
I'M GONNA LOOK FOR JESUS ... ON THAT LAST JUDGEMENT DAY.

I'M GONNA SING HAPPY BIRTHDAY TO ME

CHORUS:
      I'M GONNA SING ... HAPPY BIRTHDAY TO ME ...
IT MAKES ME ... FEEL SO HAPPY.
      I'M A YEAR OLDER ... AND STILL HEALTHY ...
AND SO I'LL SING ... HAPPY BIRTHDAY TO ME.

      IT'S A VERY ... VERY SPECIAL DAY ...
AND I WANT THINGS TO ... GO MY WAY.
      IT'S ABOUT TIME ... NOT TO BE DECIEVED ...
SO I'M GONNA SING ... HAPPY BIRTHDAY TO ME.

      AND NOW AS I LOOK ... BACK IN TIME ...
I SEE WHERE A LOT OF STRIFE ... WAS ALL MINE.
      BUT THAT'S ALL BEHIND ME ... AND DONE ...
SO I'M GONNA SING NOW ... JUST FOR FUN.

      MY BIRTHDAY IS IN ... THE MONTH OF MAY ...
AND IT'S ON ... THE TWENTY EIGHT DAY.
      WHATEVER COMES ... AND WHAT MAY ...
I'M GONNA HAVE ... A HAPPY BIRTHDAY.

      IF THERE'S NO PARTY ... YOU'LL SEE ...
I'LL BE AS HAPPY ... AS I CAN BE.
      IF EVERYONE'S FILLED ... WITH JEALOUSY ...
I'M STILL GONNA SING ... HAPPY BIRTHDAY TO ME.
CHORUS:
      I'M GONNA SING ... HAPPY BIRTHDAY TO ME ...
IT MAKES ME ... FEEL SO HAPPY.
      I'M A YEAR OLDER ... AND STILL HEALTHY ...
AND SO I'LL SING ... HAPPY BIRTHDAY TO ME.

IF I DID'NT HAVE

VERSE ONE:

    I HAVE A ROOF TO GET UNDER ... AND A HOME I CALL MY DEN ...
I HAVE FOOD ON MY TABLE ... AND A BED TO SLEEP IN.

    I HAVE CLOTHES ON MY BACK ... AND SHOES ON MY FEET ...
BUT I HAVE TO WEAR GLASSES ... SO THAT I CAN STILL SEE.

VERSE TWO:

    I HAVE TO MOVE REAL SLOW ... LIKE AN OLD ANTIQUE TANK ...
AND I DON'T HAVE NO MONEY ... STORED AWAY IN SOME BANK.

    BUT I DON'T HAVE NO COMPLAINTS...I HAVE GOOD HEALTH ...
AND I HAVE THE ABILITY ... TO STILL HELP MYSELF.

VERSE THREE:

    SOMETIMES I LOOK AROUND ... AND IT HURTS ME TO SEE ...
THOSE PEOPLE WHO DON'T HAVE ... HALF AS MUCH AS ME.

    THERE'S A LOT OF FOLKS ... WHO WOULD GIVE ANYTHING ...
TO HAVE A PEACE OF MIND ... THAT THE SIMPLE LIFE CAN BRING.

CHORUS:

    IF I DID'NT HAVE A MOUTH ... I WOULD'NT NEED FALSE TEETH ...
AND IF I DID'NT HAVE NO EYES... I WOULD'NT NEED GLASSES TO SEE.

    AND IF I DID'NT HAVE A TONGUE ... I COULD'NT EVEN TALK ...
AND IF I DID'NT HAVE NO LEGS ... I COULD'NT EVEN WALK.

VERSE FOUR:

    IF YOU HEAR PEOPLE CRYING... ABOUT THINGS THEY DON'T
HAVE...
IT MAY BE THAT THEIR WANTS ... ARE TOO HIGH IN THE CLOUDS.

    YOU DON'T NEED ALL THE LUXURIES... TO LIVE A SIMPLE LIFE ...
BE THANKFUL FOR WHAT YOU DO HAVE ...THINGS WILL BE ALRIGHT.

IF HEARTACHES WERE DOLLARS

VERSE ONE:

I'VE HAD NOTHING BUT HEARTACHES ... EVER SINCE I MET
YOU ...

MANY TIMES I HAVE WONDERED ... HOW DID I MAKE IT THROUGH.

MY LIFE HAS BEEN SO MISERABLE ... AND I FEEL SO LOW ...

IF HEARTACHES WERE DOLLARS ... I'D A BEEN RICH LONG AGO.

VERSE TWO:

I'VE HAD HEARTACHES UNNUMBERED ... MAYBE A MILLION
OR TWO ...

IT SEEMS YOU LIKE TO BREAK MY HEART ... IN EVERYTHING YOU DO.

I'LL PROBABLY END UP IN A POOR HOUSE ... JUST A NO NAME
JOE ...

IF HEARTACHES WERE DOLLARS ... I'D A BEEN RICH LONG AGO.

CHORUS:

IF I DID'NT LOVE YOU ... I WOULD'NT TAKE IT ANYMORE ...

I THOUGHT YOU WOULD CHANGE ... BUT IT'S WORSE NOW THAN
BEFORE.

YOU'RE SO FULL OF LIES ... THAT'S ALL THAT YOU KNOW ...

IF HEARTACHES WERE DOLLARS ... I'D A BEEN RICH LONG AGO.

VERSE THREE:

YOU STAY OUT EVERY NIGHT ... UNTIL ONE OR TWO OR
THREE ...

THEN YOU COME KNOCKING ON MY DOOR ... CRAWLING BACK
TO ME.

YOU SAY THAT YOU ARE SORRY ... BUT THAT'S THE LIFE YOU
CHOSE ...

IF HEARTACHES WERE DOLLARS ... I'D A BEEN RICH LONG AGO.

VERSE FOUR:

I KEEP PUTTING UP WITH YOU ... CAUSE YOU HAVE NO WHERE
TO GO ...

YOU ALWAYS DO AS YOU PLEASE ... EVEN THOUGH IT HURTS ME SO.

I SHOULD HAVE THROWN YOU OUT ... AS FAR AS I COULD
    THROW ...
IF HEARTACHES WERE DOLLARS ... I'D A BEEN RICH LONG AGO.

CHORUS:
    IF I DID'NT LOVE YOU ... I WOULD'NT TAKE IT ANYMORE ...
I THOUGHT YOU WOULD CHANGE ... BUT IT'S WORSE NOW THAN
BEFORE.
    YOU'RE SO FULL OF LIES ... THAT'S ALL THAT YOU KNOW ...
IF HEARTACHES WERE DOLLARS ... I'D A BEEN RICH LONG AGO.

IF HEARTACHES WERE MONEY

VERSE ONE:

I'VE HAD NOTHING BUT HEARTACHES ... EVER SINCE I MET YOU ...
MANY TIMES I HAVE WONDERED ... HOW I MADE IT THROUGH.
MY LIFE HAS BEEN SO MISERABLE ... A FEELING SO MIGHTY LOW ...
IF HEARTACHES WERE MONEY ... I'D A BEEN RICH LONG AGO.

VERSE TWO:

I'VE HAD HEARTACHES UNNUMBERED ... MORE THAN JUST A FEW ...
IT SEEMS YOU LIKE TO BREAK MY HEART ... IN EVERYTHING YOU DO.
I'LL PROBABLY END UP IN A POOR HOUSE ... JUST A NO NAME JOE ...
IF HEARTACHES WERE MONEY ... I'D A BEEN RICH LONG AGO.

CHORUS:

IF I DID'NT LOVE YOU ... I WOULD'NT TAKE IT ANYMORE ...
I HOPED THAT YOU WOULD CHANGE ... BUT IT'S WORSE NOW THAN BEFORE.
YOU'RE SO FULL OF APOLOGISE ... THAT'S ALL THAT YOU KNOW ...
IF HEARTACHES WERE MONEY ... I'D A BEEN RICH LONG AGO.

VERSE THREE:

YOU STAY OUT EVERY NIGHT ... UNTIL ONE OR TWO OR THREE ...
THEN YOU COME KNOCKING ON MY DOOR ... CRAWLING BACK TO ME.
YOU SAY THAT YOU ARE SORRY ... BUT THAT'S THE LIFE YOU CHOSE ...
IF HEARTACHES WERE MONEY ... I'D A BEEN RICH LONG AGO.

VERSE FOUR:

YOU THINK I HAVE TO HAVE YOU ... CAUSE I HAVE NO WHERE TO GO ...
YOU ALWAYS DO AS YOU PLEASE ... EVEN THOUGH IT HURTS ME SO.

I SHOULD HAVE THROWN YOU OUT ... AS FAR AS I COULD THROW ...
IF HEARTACHES WERE MONEY ... I'D A BEEN RICH LONG AGO.

CHORUS:
IF I DID'NT LOVE YOU ... I WOULD'NT TAKE IT ANYMORE ...
I HOPED THAT YOU WOULD CHANGE ... BUT IT'S WORSE NOW THAN BEFORE.
YOU'RE SO FULL OF DISAPPOINTMENTS ... THAT'S ALL THAT YOU KNOW ...
IF HEARTACHES WERE MONEY ... I'D A BEEN RICH LONG AGO.

IF I COULD ONLY LIVE

VERSE ONE:

    IF I COULD ONLY LIVE ... MY WHOLE LIFE AGAIN ...
I'M SURE I WOULD CHANGE ... HOW I LIVED BACK THEN.
    I'D SHOW MORE LOVE ... AND HAVE A LOT MORE FRIENDS...
IF I COULD ONLY LIVE ... MY WHOLE LIFE AGAIN.

VERSE TWO:

    IT'S BAD TO GET OLD ... AND REGRET THE WAY YOU LIVED ...
AND NEVER HAVE ANYTHING ... WITH NOTHING THERE TO GIVE.
    YOU THINK OF THE TIMES ... WHEN SOMEONE WAS IN NEED ...
BUT I DID'NT WORRY ABOUT THEM ... I ONLY THOUGHT OF ME.
CHORUS:

    IF I COULD ONLY LIVE ... MY WHOLE LIFE AGAIN ...
IF I COULD ONLY LIVE ... IT WOULD DIFFERANT THAN THEN.
    IF I COULD ONLY LIVE ... MY LIFE I WOULD AMEND ...
IF I COULD ONLY LIVE ... MY WHOLE LIFE AGAIN.

VERSE THREE:

    I NEVER HAD PLANS TO LIVE ... IN A MANSION OF GOLD ...
AND I NEVER DID EXPECT ... TO LIVE TO BE OLD.
    BUT NOW THAT I AM THERE ... I'M SURE THAT CAN SAY ...
I WISH THAT I HAD LIVED ... MY LIFE ANOTHER WAY.

VERSE FOUR:

    NOW I HAVE MORE REASONS ... TO LIVE AND DIE FOR ...
I HEARD THE MASTER KNOCKING ... ON MY HEARTS DOOR.
    HE FORGAVE ME OF BAD THINGS ... AND WIPED AWAY MY SIN ...
AND NOW I CAN LIVE ... A BRAND NEW LIFE AGAIN.

       .... SING CHORUS AGAIN ......

IF I WAS YOU

CHORUS:

    IF I WAS YOU ... I TELL YOU WHAT I'D DO ...
I SURE WOULD'NT DO ... THE THINGS THAT YOU DO.
    BUT IF YOU WAS ME ... I HAVE NEWS FOR YOU ...
YOU'D STILL DO ... THE SAME THINGS THAT I DO.

VERSE ONE:

    EVERYONE ALWAYS SAY ... I TELL YOU WHAT I'D DO ...
IF IT WAS ME ... INSTEAD OF YOU.
    BUT IF IT WAS YOU ... A WEARING MY SHOES ...
YOU'D STILL DO ... THE SAME THINGS THAT I DO.

VERSE TWO:

    HOW CAN YOU KNOW ... WHAT I'M GOING THRU ...
WHEN YOU DON'T EVEN HAVE ... ONE SMALL CLUE.
    IT MAKES GOOD SENSE ... IF YOU ONLY KNEW ...
YOU'D HAVE TO DO ... THE SAME THINGS THAT I DO.

VERSE THREE:

    IF YOU WAS ME ... AND THEN IF I WAS YOU ...
DON'T YOU THINK ... I'D DO THE SAME THINGS YOU DO.
    WHY DO YOU THINK ... YOU COULD CHANGE MY DESTINY.
IF I WAS YOU ... AND YOU WERE ME.

CHORUS:

    IF I WAS YOU ... I TELL YOU WHAT I'D DO ...
I SURE WOULD'NT DO ... THE THINGS THAT YOU DO.
    BUT IF YOU WAS ME ... I HAVE NEWS FOR YOU ...
YOU'D STILL DO ... THE SAME THINGS THAT I DO.

IN THAT LITTLE OLD COUNTRY CHURCH

VERSE ONE :
    ONE DAY AS I WAS WALKING ... BY A LITTLE OLD COUNTRY
    CHURCH ...
MY WHOLE WORLD WAS TURNED UPSIDE DOWN ... WHEN I HEARD
WHAT I HEARD.
    THE PREACHER PREACHED ON HELL ... RIGHT STRAIGHT FROM
    GOD'S OWN WORD ...
AND MY LIFE WAS CHANGED THAT DAY ... IN THAT LITTLE OLD
COUNTRY CHURCH.

CHORUS :
    IN THAT LITTLE OLD COUNTRY CHURCH ... GOD'S SPIRIT WAS
    AT WORK ...
NO MATTER WHO CAME THRU THE DOOR ... GOD WAS SAVING THE
RICH AND POOR.
    SATIN'S KNEE'S WAS A KNOCKIN' ... HIS WHOLE PLAN HAD
    GONE BESERK ...
ALL BECAUSE OF WHAT WAS HAPPENING ... IN THAT LITTLE OLE
COUNTRY CHURCH.

VERSE TWO :
    GOD INTERVINED THAT DAY ... BECAUSE OF THE LIFE THAT I
    WAS LIVING ...
HE SAID HE'D REVEAL TO ME A NEW WAY ... IF I WAS ONLY WILLING.
    HE SAID THAT I WAS HEADED FOR HELL ... IF I DID'NT SLOW
    DOWN ...
BUT HE'D SEND ME TO NEW GROUND ... IF I'D TURN MY LIFE
AROUND.

VERSE THREE :

I LOOKED UP TOWARD HEAVEN ... AND ASKED WHERE DO I
START ? ...
HE SAID TO JUST BOW YOUR HEAD ... AND REPENT FROM YOUR
HEART.
THEN GET YOUR LIFE OUT OF DARKNESS ... AND WALK AWAY
FROM SIN ...
AND YOU WILL NEVER WANT TO GO BACK ... DOWN THAT LONG
LOST ROAD AGAIN .

CHORUS :

IN THAT LITTLE OLD COUNTRY CHURCH ... GOD'S SPIRIT WAS
AT WORK ...
NO MATTER WHO CAME THRU THE DOOR ... GOD WAS SAVING THE
RICH AND POOR.
SATIN'S KNEE'S WAS A KNOCKIN' ... HIS WHOLE PLAN HAD
GONE BESERK ...
ALL BECAUSE OF WHAT WAS HAPPENING ... IN THAT LITTLE OLE
COUNTRY CHURCH.

VERSE FOUR :

I USED TO HEAR MY MOTHER MENTION ... THAT LITTLE OLD
COUNTRY CHURCH ...
AND THE MIRACLES THAT WAS HAPPENING ... RIGHT THERE BY
GOD'S OWN WORK.
HE WORKED A MIRACLE IN MY LIFE ... WHEN I WENT TO THE
ALTER AND PRAYED ...
I WILL NEVER FORGET WHAT HAPPENED ... IN THAT LITTLE
COUNTRY CHURCH THAT DAY.

CHORUS :
     IN THAT LITTLE OLD COUNTRY CHURCH ... GOD'S SPIRIT WAS
     AT WORK ...
NO MATTER WHO CAME THRU THE DOOR ... GOD WAS SAVING THE
RICH AND POOR.
     SATIN'S KNEE'S WAS A KNOCKIN' ... HIS WHOLE PLAN HAD
     GONE BESERK ...
ALL BECAUSE OF WHAT WAS HAPPENING ... IN THAT LITTLE OLE
COUNTRY CHURCH.

IT HURTS

CHORUS:
    IT HURTS TO BE BLAMED ... FOR THINGS YOU'RE NOT GUILTY OF ...
IT HURTS WHEN YOU LOSE ... SOMEONE THAT YOU. REALLY LOVE.
    IT HURTS WHEN YOU SEE SOMEONE ... THAT YOU CARE ABOUT
    DIE ...
IT HURTS WHEN YOU BOW YOUR HEAD ... AND CAN'T DO NOTHING
BUT CRY.

VERSE ONE:
    IT HURTS WHEN YOU DON'T HAVE ... MONEY TO PAY YOUR
    BILLS ...
AND YOU DON'T KNOW HOW YOU'LL MAKE IT ... OVER THE NEXT
HILL.
    WHEN YOU NEED A VACATION ... AND CAN'T GET OFF OF WORK ...
THE BOSS MAN DON'T UNDERSTAND ... JUST HOW BAD IT HURTS.

VERSE TWO:
    FEELINGS IS ONE THING ... YOU CAN'T HIDE UNDER YOUR
    SHIRT ...
BUT NO ONE REALLY CARES ABOUT ... JUST HOW BAD YOU HURT.
    SOMETIMES YOU MAY WALK AROUND ... BEING IN A DAZE ...
AND PEOPLE WONDERS WHY ... YOU MAKE MISTAKES YOU MAKE.

CHORUS:
    IT HURTS TO BE BLAMED ... FOR THINGS YOU'RE NOT GUILTY OF ...
IT HURTS WHEN YOU LOSE ... SOMEONE THAT YOU REALLY LOVE.
    IT HURTS WHEN YOU SEE SOMEONE ... THAT YOU CARE ABOUT
    DIE ...
IT HURTS WHEN YOU BOW YOUR HEAD ... AND CAN'T DO NOTHING
BUT CRY.

VERSE THREE:
    YOU MAY GET SICK AND HAVE TO STAY ... IN A HOSPITAL BED ...
YOU WANT TO GET UP AND GO SOMEWHERE ... BUT YOU FEEL HALF
DEAD.

YOUR BODY IS ACKING WITH PAIN ... AND THERE'S NOTHING YOU CAN DO ...
AND IT HURTS EVEN MORE ... WHEN YOU DON'T EVEN HAVE A CLUE.

VERSE FOUR:
IT HURTS WHEN YOU HAVE PROBLEMS ... AND LOSE YOUR WILL TO TRY ...
SOMETIMES IT HURTS SO BAD ... THAT YOU WANT TO LAY DOWN AND DIE.
SOME MAY LOSE THEIR FAITH ... AND FEEL AS CHEAP AS DIRT ...
WHEN YOU LOSE YOUR REASON TO LIVE ... THAT'S WHEN IT REALLY HURTS.

IT'S ABOUT TIME

VERSE ONE:
>   WHEN IT COMES TIME ... TO CAST YOUR VOTE ...
TAKE TIME TO BE SERIOUS ... FOR THIS IS NO JOKE.
>   IT'S THE LEAST WE CAN DO ...TO SHOW THAT WE CARE ...
SO CAST YOUR VOTE ... WHEN ELECTION TIME IS HERE.

VERSE TWO:
>   IF YOU HAVE NEVER VOTED ... THEN IT'S ABOUT TIME ...
GO UP AND REGISTER ... EVEN IF YOU HAVE TO STAND IN LINE.
>   BECAUSE VOTING IS LIKE ... GETTING IN OUT OF THE RAIN ...
IF YOU FAIL TO VOTE ... YOU HAVE NO RIGHT TO COMPLAIN.

VERSE THREE:
>   IT'S ABOUT TIME ... TO DO SOMETHING RIGHT ...
LET YOUR VOICE BE HEARD ... STAND UP AND FIGHT.
>   THE ONE YOU VOTE FOR ... MAY NOT GET IN ...
BUT DON'T GIVE UP ... YOU'VE DONE ALL THAT YOU CAN.

CHORUS:
>   WE ARE AMERICANS ... AND THE LAND OF THE FREE...
THE CONSTITUTION WAS WRITTEN ... FOR YOU AND FOR ME.
>   SO FIGHT FOR THE RIGHTS ... THAT'S YOUR'S AND MINE ...
AND STAND UP AND SAY ... IT'S ABOUT TIME.

IT'S JUST ONE OF THEM DAYS

VERSE ONE:

    IT LOOKS LIKE IT'S JUST ONE ... OF THEM DAYS AGAIN ...
WHEN NO MATTER HOW HARD I TRY ... I JUST CAN'T WIN.
    IT SEEMS LIKE EVERYTHING I DO ... IS JUST ALL IN VAIN ...
SO I GUESS IT'S SAFE TO SAY ... IT'S ONE OF THEM DAYS AGAIN.

VERSE TWO:

    WHEN I FIRST WOKE UP ... IT LOOKED LIKE A GOOD DAY ...
UNTIL I REALIZED ... THINGS WAS'NT GOING TO GO MY WAY.
    IT STARTED AS SOON ... AS I PUT MY FEET ON THE FLOOR ...
I KNEW THAT I HAD HAD THIS FEELING ... MANY TIMES BEFORE.

VERSE THREE:

    I STUMBLED DOWN THE HALLWAY ... LIKE A LAMED DUCK ...
IT WAS ONE OF THEM DAYS ... THAT I DREADED TO GET UP.
    I WENT TO WASH MY FACE ... AND TRIED TO GET AWAKE ...
BUT I HAD NO HOT WATER ... I THOUGHT FOR HEAVENS SAKE.

VERSE FOUR:

    THEN I COULD'NT SHAVE ... WITHOUT ANY HOT WATER ...
AND WHEN I GOT TO WORK ... THEY ASKED WHAT'S THE MATTER.
    I JUST SMILED AND SAID ... EVERYTHING WILL BE OKAY ...
I'VE BEEN THRU THIS BEFORE ... IT'S JUST ONE OF THEM DAYS.

CHORUS:

    SO IF YOU THINK ... THAT IT CAN'T GET MUCH WORSE ...
AT LEAST NOT UNTIL ... IT GETS A LOT BETTER FIRST.
    YOU CAN'T JUST GIVE UP ... TRY TO JUST SMILE AND SAY ...
IT SURE LOOKS LIKE IT'S GONNA BE ... JUST ONE OF THEM DAYS.

IT'S NOT HOW OLD YOU ARE

CHORUS:
SOME PEOPLE SAYS THEY'RE OLD ... WHEN THEY GET UP IN AGE...
BUT FOR EACH DAY THAT PASSES ... I JUST TURN ANOTHER PAGE.
THE LAST CHAPTER OF MY LIFE ... HAS NOT YET BEEN READ ...
BECAUSE IT WON'T BE WRITTEN ... UNTIL AFTER I AM DEAD.

VERSE ONE:
I LOVE TO WATCH THE BIRDS ... ESPECIALLY THE SPARROWS ...
THEY FIND FOOD FOR TODAY... NOT WORRYING ABOUT TOMORROW.
THAT'S HOW I LIVE TODAY ... NOT WORRYING WHAT LIES
AHEAD...
AND I DON'T DWELL ON THINGS ... SOMEONE ELSE HAS SAID.

VERSE TWO:
I HAVE PUT YEARS BEHIND ME ... SOME GOOD AND SOME BAD ...
I DON'T THINK ABOUT THE PAST ... OR TIMES THAT I HAVE HAD.
NOW AGE IS NOT EVERYTHING ... IT JUST FLIES ON BY ...
IT'S NOT HOW OLD YOU ARE ... IT'S HOW YOU FEEL INSIDE.

VERSE THREE:
JUST TRY TO ENJOY YOUR LIFE ... WITH EACH PASSING DAY...
DON'T LET THIS THING CALLED TIME ... STAND IN YOUR WAY.
AGE IS JUST A NUMBER ... IT'S NOT THE YEARS BY FAR ...
IT'S HOW YOU LIVE WHILE LIVING ... NOT HOW OLD YOU ARE ...

VERSE FOUR:
BE THANKFUL YOU ARE LIVING ... ALWAYS WEAR A SMILE ...
YOU CAN STILL BE YOUNG AT HEART ... THINK BACK AS A CHILD.
I'VE SEEN REPAIR SHOPS ... REBUILD BROKEN DOWN CARS...
TAKE CARE OF WHAT YOU HAVE ... IT'S NOT HOW OLD YOU ARE.

IT'S NOT WHAT YOU SEE

CHORUS:
>
> NOW IT'S NOT WHAT YOU SEE ... BUT WHAT YOU CAN NOT SEE ...

THAT WILL LIVE FOREVER ... AND WILL FOREVER BE.

> FOR EVERYTHING THAT YOU SEE ... WILL VANISH AWAY ...

AND ONLY THINGS YOU CANNOT SEE ... WILL FOREVER STAY.

VERSE ONE:

> WHEN YOU LOSE SOMETHING IN LIFE ... THAT REALLY HURTS YOU ...

IT TEARS YOUR WORLD APART ... AND YOU WONDER WHAT WILL YOU DO.

> YOU MIGHT SAT DOWN AND CRY ... BECAUSE YOU JUST CAN NOT SEE ...

THAT IT'S ONLY WHAT YOU CAN NOT SEE ... IS FOR ALL ETERNITY.

VERSE TWO:

> I'VE LOST MANY THINGS ON EARTH ... I DID'NT GRIEVE HOWEVER ...

I KNEW IT'S ONLY THINGS YOU CAN'T SEE ... THAT WILL LAST FOREVER.

> IT DON'T BOTHER SOME PEOPLE ... THEY JUST SMILE AND AGREE ...

THEN SHAKE THEIR HEAD AND SAY ... IT JUST WAS'NT MEANT TO BE.

CHORUS:

> NOW IT'S NOT WHAT YOU SEE ... BUT WHAT YOU CAN NOT SEE ...

THAT WILL LIVE FOREVER ... AND WILL FOREVER BE.

> FOR EVERYTHING THAT YOU SEE ... WILL VANISH AWAY ...

AND ONLY THINGS YOU CANNOT SEE ... WILL FOREVER STAY.

VERSE THREE:

> DON'T EVER SET YOUR HEART ... ON THE THINGS OF THIS EARTH ...

THEY WILL ROB YOU OF TREASURES ... AND THEY'LL ALL GO BACK TO DIRT.

THERE ARE BETTER THINGS ... LAYED UP FOR US IN SECRECY ... AND IT'S NOT WHAT YOU SEE ... THAT WILL LAST THROUGHOUT ETERNITY.

CHORUS:
NOW IT'S NOT WHAT YOU SEE ... BUT WHAT YOU CAN NOT SEE ...
THAT WILL LIVE FOREVER ... AND WILL FOREVER BE.
FOR EVERYTHING THAT YOU SEE ... WILL VANISH AWAY ... AND ONLY THINGS YOU CANNOT SEE ... WILL FOREVER STAY.

IT'S ONE OF THEM TIMES

VERSE ONE:

    TODAY LOOKS LIKE ... IT'S ONE OF THEM TIMES ...
WHEN I CAN SAY ... I'M NOT FEELING SO FINE.
    THINGS AIN'T GOING ... THE WAY THEY SHOULD ...
BUT I CAN'T EXPECT ... EVERYDAY TO BE GOOD.

VERSE TWO:

    I CAN SAY IT'S VERY SELDOM ... THAT I COMPLAIN ...
BUT HERE IT IS ... ONE OF THEM TIMES AGAIN.
    I WISH I FELT BETTER ... THAN I DO RIGHT NOW ...
DON'T WORRY ABOUT ME ... I'LL MAKE IT SOMEHOW.

VERSE THREE:

    IT'S ONE OF THEM TIMES ... I DON'T FEEL RIGHT ...
BUT I HOPE BETTER TIMES ... SOON COMES TO LIGHT.
    I HOPE IT WON'T BE ... TOO MUCH LONGER ...
OR I'LL SOON BE ... A REAL GONE GONER.

VERSE FOUR:

    BUT IT SURE IS GOOD ... TO BE ALIVE TODAY ...
EVEN IF I DON'T ... FEEL GOOD ANYWAY.
    I KNOW SOME PEOPLE ... ARE WORSE OFF THAN ME ...
BUT WHEREVER THEY ARE ... YOU DON'T WANT TO BE.

VERSE FIVE:

    SO PLEASE DON'T ASK ME ... HOW I FEEL TODAY ...
YOU PROBABLY WOULD'NT BELIEVE ME ... ANYWAY.
    JUST BE THANKFUL ... THAT IT AIN'T YOU ...
NO MATTER HOW BAD ... YOU MIGHT FEEL TOO.

CHORUS:

    LET'S STOP COMPLAINING ... AND SING OUR SONGS ...
BE THANKFUL THAT SOME ... OF THEM DAYS ARE GONE.
    IT MAY SEEM LIKE ... THE SUN WILL NEVER SHINE ...
BUT THINGS WILL GET BETTER ... IT'S ONE OF THEM TIMES.

IT'S THAT TIME OF THE YEAR

VERSE ONE:
    SPRING TIME IS A'COMIN' ... IT'S RIGHT AROUND THE CORNER ...
IT'S THAT TIME OF THE YEAR ... AND IT WON'T BE MUCH LONGER.
    THERE WILL BE HOT DAYS ... AND A LOT OF HOT NIGHTS ...
BUT HANG ON TO YOUR FAITH BOYS ... AND GIVE IT A GOOD FIGHT.

VERSE TWO:
    SOON SUMMERTIME WILL BE OVER ... AND WINTER IS VERY
    NEAR ...
GET YOUR FURNACE READY BOYS ... IT'S THAT TIME OF THE YEAR.
    WHEN SNOW FLAKES STARTS TO FALLING ... A TIME WE ALL
    LOVE DEAR ...
HAVE YOUR SNOW SHOVELS READY BOYS ... IT'S THAT TIME OF THE
YEAR.

VERSE THREE:
    SOON WINTER TIME WILL BE OVER ... AND SPRING IS IN THE
    AIR ...
SO NOW GET YOUR MOWERS READY BOYS ... IT'S THAT TIME OF THE
YEAR.
    THE GRASS WILL GROW FASTER ... THAN ANYONE MAY KNOW ...
SO SHARPEN UP THE BLADES BOYS ... AND GET READY TO START
TO MOW.

VERSE FOUR:
    THEN COMES THE FALL SEASON ... WITH A REAL COOL BREEZE ...
THE GROUND WILL BE COVERED ... WITH LEAVES FROM THE TREE'S.
    SO GET THAT RAKE READY NOW ... AND DO IT WITHOUT
    FEAR ...
AND DON'T START COMPLAINING BOYS ... IT'S THAT TIME OF THE
YEAR.

VERSE FIVE:
    YOU CAN ALWAYS FIND SOMETHING ... YOU CAN COMPLAIN
    ABOUT ...

AND YOU'RE ALWAYS BUYING THINGS ... THAT YOU CAN LIVE WITHOUT.
>BUT IT'S TIME TO WISE UP ... AND BE THANKFUL THAT YOU'RE HERE ...
JUST GO AHEAD AND GIVE THANKS ... IT'S THAT TIME OF THE YEAR.

CHORUS:
>LIFE IS SO BEAUTIFUL ... AND SO ARE THE SEASONS THAT WE SHARE ...
IT'S WHATEVER WE MAKE OF IT ... SO LIVE IT AND ENJOY IT WITH CARE.
>SUMMERTIME SPRING WINTER AND FALL ... ARE FULL OF GOOD CHEER ...
SO GO AHEAD AND HAVE YOUR PARTY BOYS ... IT'S THAT TIME OF THE YEAR.

IT'S TIME I'M A LEAVING

CHORUS:
     I'VE BEEN SAYING THIS ... FOR MUCH TOO LONG ...
IT'S TIME I'M A LEAVING ... SO I'LL SOON BE GONE.

VERSE ONE:
     THE DAY OF OUR MARRIAGE ... WE BOTH FELT GREAT ...
BUT NOW THAT I'M A LEAVING ... I CAN'T HARDLY WAIT.
     I HAVE TRIED MY BEST ... TO GET ALONG WITH YOU ...
IT'S TIME I'M A LEAVING ... CAUSE THIS TIME WE'RE THRU.

VERSE TWO:
     ALL WE EVER DO ... IS FIGHT FIGHT FIGHT ...
I NEVER HAVE NO PEACE ... NEITHER DAY OR NIGHT.
     YOU MADE ME FEEL ... LIKE A DOG WITHOUT A BONE ...
SO IT'S TIME I'M A LEAVING ... AND I'LL SOON BE GONE.

VERSE THREE:
     NOW DON'T TELL ME YOUR LIES ... LIKE YOU DID BEFORE ...
AND DON'T STAND IN MY WAY ... WHEN I WALK TO THE DOOR.
     I CAN'T TAKE IT ANYMORE ... IT'S EATING UP MY INSIDES ...
SO IT'S TIME I'M A LEAVING ... CAUSE YOU NEVER TRIED.

VERSE FOUR:
     I WILL NEVER LOOK BACK ... I'LL LEAVE THE PAST BEHIND ...
I'M A'GONNA DO SOMETHING ... WITH THIS LIFE OF MINE.
     I WON'T BE HERE NO MORE ... WHEN THE MORNINGS DAWN ...
CAUSE IT'S TIME I'M A LEAVING ... AND I'LL SOON BE GONE.

JESUS CAME TO VISIT ME

VERSE ONE:
> WHILE LYING IN MY BED ONE NIGHT ... I COULD'NT GO TO SLEEP ...

WHEN SOMETHING SUDDENLY HAPPENED ... JESUS CAME TO VISIT ME.
> I KNEW IT COULD'NT BE A DREAM ... THIS TIME IT WAS FOR REAL ...

AS HE TOLD ME WHO HE WAS AND WHY ... HE DIED UP ON THAT HILL.

VERSE TWO:
> I WILL NEVER FORGET THAT NIGHT ... WHEN JESUS CAME TO VISIT ME ...

HE KNEW MY TROUBLES AND TOLD ME WHY ... I COULD'NT GO TO SLEEP.
> HE SAID IF I WOULD LISTEN ... HE WOULD LIKE TO SEE ME THRUOGH ...

BUT YOU MUST BELIEVE AND THAT IS ALL ... THAT YOU WILL HAVE TO DO.

CHORUS:
> WHEN JESUS CAME TO VISIT ME ... HE MADE EVERYTHING ALL RIGHT ...

HE TOOK AWAY ALL MY SINS ... AND HE GAVE ME A BRAND NEW LIFE.
> MY FRIENDS ALL ASK WHAT HAPPENED ... I'M NOT LIKE I USED TO BE ...

I TELL THEM MY LIFE WAS CHANGED ... WHEN JESUS CAME TO VISIT ME.

VERSE THREE:
> HE SAID GATHER ALL YOUR PROBLEMS ... AND LAY THEM AT MY FEET ...

AND I WILL PUT THEM IN ORDER ... THE WAY THAT THEY SHOULD BE.

SO I DONE AS HE TOLD ME ... BECAUSE I HAVE FAITH AND BELIEVE ...
MY LIFE WAS CHANGED THAT NIGHT ... WHEN JESUS CAME TO VISIT ME.

VERSE FOUR:
MANY TIMES I HAD WONDERED ... IF THE STORY OF HIM WAS TRUE ...
AND IF HE COULD DO THE THINGS ... THAT PREACHERS SAID HE COULD DO.
BUT WHEN I OPENED UP MY HEART ... IT WAS VERY PLAIN TO SEE ...
HE'S ALIVE AND NOW LIVES IN MY HEART ... SINCE JESUS CAME TO VISIT ME.

CHORUS:
WHEN JESUS CAME TO VISIT ME ... HE MADE EVERYTHING ALL RIGHT ...
HE TOOK AWAY ALL MY SINS ... AND HE GAVE ME A BRAND NEW LIFE.
MY FRIENDS ALL ASK WHAT HAPPENED ... I'M NOT LIKE I USED TO BE ...
I TELL THEM MY LIFE WAS CHANGED ... WHEN JESUS CAME TO VISIT ME.

JESUS IS THE LIGHT

VERSE ONE:

      I AM GOING TO A CITY ... WHERE YOU NEVER GROW OLD ...
AND I'LL BE WALKING ON STREETS ... THAT ARE MADE OF GOLD.
      THE ANGELS WILL BE SINGING ... I SAW THE LIGHT ...
IN THAT HEAVENLY CITY ... WHERE THERE IS NO NIGHT.

VERSE TWO:

      JESUS IS THE LIGHT ... AND HE BLAZED ME A TRAIL ...
TO TAKE ME TO A LAND ... WHERE ALL IS WELL.
      HE SAID REPENT OF YOUR SINS ... AND FOLLOW ME ...
YOU WILL LIVE IN A MANSION ... FOR ALL ETERNITY.

CHORUS:

      WALKING, TALKING, SINGING ... AND PRAISING THE LORD ...
I'LL BE SINGING WITH THE ANGELS ... THAT WILL BE MY REWARD.
      THERE WILL BE NO DARKNESS ... JESUS IS THE LIGHT ...
UP THERE IN HEAVEN ... WHERE THERE IS NO NIGHT.

VERSE THREE:

      ALL ETERNITY ... IS A LONG LONG TIME ...
AND THERE WILL NEVER BE ... NO END OF THE LINE.
      WHEN ETERNITY STARTS ... THERE WILL BE NO END ...
WE WILL LIVE FOREVER ... AND NEVER DIE AGAIN.

VERSE FOUR:

      JESUS IS THE LIGHT ... AND IN HIM IS NO DARKNESS ...
WHEN YOU FOLLOW HIM ... YOU WILL ONLY DO GOODNESS.
      SO LIFT UP YOUR HEAD ... AND LEAVE YOUR PAST BEHIND ...
YOU WILL NEVER REGRET THE JOY ... THAT YOU WILL FIND.

CHORUS:

      WALKING, TALKING, SINGING ... AND PRAISING THE LORD ...
I'LL BE SINGING WITH THE ANGELS ... THAT WILL BE MY REWARD.
      THERE WILL BE NO DARKNESS ... JESUS IS THE LIGHT ...
UP THERE IN HEAVEN ... WHERE THERE IS NO NIGHT.

JESUS PASSED MY WAY

VERSE ONE:

IT WAS ON A COLD AND DARK DAY ... WHEN JESUS PASSED MY WAY ...
THINGS WAS'NT LOOKING SO GOOD ... THAT'S WHEN I HEARD HIM SAY.
NOW THINGS ARE NOT AS HOPELESS ... AS THEY MAY SEEM TODAY ...
HE TOOK THE DARKNESS AWAY ... AND MADE IT A BEAUTIFUL DAY.

VERSE TWO:

IT WAS THE WORST DAY OF MY LIFE ... I FELT SO DOWN AND OUT ...
I'M SO THANKFUL THAT I SAW HIM ... HE TOLD ME WHAT IT WAS ABOUT.
HE SAID DON'T PUT IT OFF ... DON'T YOU WAIT ANOTHER DAY ... ...
I FELL DOWN ON MY KNEE'S ... WHEN JESUS PASSED MY WAY ...

CHORUS:

WHEN JESUS PASSED MY WAY ... WHEN JESUS PASSED MY WAY ...
HE SAID I'LL BE WITH YOU ... AND IN MY PRESANCE HE WILL STAY.
HE MOLDED ME FROM CLAY ... AND TURNED MY NIGHT INTO DAY ...
NOW I HAVE MORE TO DIE FOR ... SINCE JESUS PASSED MY WAY.

VERSE THREE:

HE SAID ALL HOPE IS NOT GONE ... AND YOU ARE NOT ALONE ...
I'LL BE WALKING WITH YOU ... UNTIL THE BAD TIMES ARE GONE.
I WILL NEVER LEAVE YOU ... EVEN ON JUDGEMENT DAY ...
AND EVERYTHING'S BEEN BETTER ... SINCE JESUS PASSED MY WAY.

VERSE FOUR:

I KNOW THERE'LL COME A TIME ... I WILL FACE JUDGEMENT DAY ...
BUT I'M MORE PREPARED TO DIE ... SINCE JESUS PASSED MY WAY.

I'M ON MY WAY TO GLORY NOW ... TO GIVE HIM ALL THE PRAISE ...
I HAVE NEVER FELT SO GOOD ... SINCE JESUS PASSED MY WAY.

CHORUS:
SINCE JESUS PASSED MY WAY ... SINCE JESUS PASSED MY WAY ...
HE SAID I'LL BE WITH YOU ... AND IN MY PRESANCE HE WILL STAY.
HE MOLDED ME FROM CLAY ... AND TURNED MY NIGHT INTO DAY ...
NOW I HAVE MORE TO DIE FOR ... SINCE JESUS PASSED MY WAY.

JUDGE ME NOT

CHORUS:

    NOW JUDGE ME NOT ... EVEN IF I AM WRONG ...
CAUSE I'M NOT PERFECT ... JUST TRYING TO GET ALONG.
    JUST TRY TO BE YOURSELF ... IN EVERYTHING YOU DO ...
MAYBE OTHERS THEN ... WOULD THINK MORE OF YOU.

VERSE ONE:

    NOW DON'T JUDGE ME ... BY WHAT YOU'D LIKE TO BE ...
BECAUSE MY LIFE AIN'T BEEN ... NOTHING BUT MISERY.
    A LOT OF PEOPLE THINKS ... I HAVE PLENTY OF MONEY ...
WHEN IT COMES DOWN TO IT ... THAT AIN'T SO FUNNY.

VERAE TWO:

    I NEVER SPEND MONEY ... TO BUY A NEWSPAPER ...
I GO TO A RESTURANT ... AND GET A CUP OF COFFEE.
    I WON'T BUY ANYTHING ... JUST TO THROW IT AWAY.
WHEN I CAN READ THE NEWSPAPER ... FREE EVERYDAY.

VERSE THREE:

    NOW JUDGE ME NOT ... BECAUSE MY LIFE IS A MESS ...
I HAVE TRIED TO DO BETTER ... BUT I AIN'T DONE IT YET.
    I ALWAYS TRY TO DO ... THE VERY BEST THAT I CAN ...
THAT'S NOT GOOD ENOUGH ... FOR A SPECIAL KIND OF MAN.

CHORUS:

    NOW JUDGE ME NOT ... EVEN IF I AM WRONG ...
CAUSE I'M NOT PERFECT ... JUST TRYING TO GET ALONG.
    JUST TRY TO BE YOURSELF ... IN EVERYTHING YOU DO ...
MAYBE OTHERS THEN ... WOULD THINK MORE OF YOU.

JUST A MAN WITH NO PLAN

VERSE ONE:

MOST OF HIS FAMILY ... DROVE A BRAND NEW AUTOMOBILE ... SOMETIMES HE WONDERED ... IF HIS WOULD GET OVER THE NEXT HILL.

HE NEVER REALLY WANTED ... TO BUY A BRAND NEW CAR ... HE WAS RUNNING ON TREADS ... HE COULD'NT EVEN BUY A NEW TIRE.

VERSE TWO:

HE ALWAYS HAD AT LEAST... ONE DOLLAR IN HIS HAND ... AND HE FELT THAT'S ALL HE NEEDED ...JUST A MAN WITH NO PLAN.

HE HAVE WORKED VERY HARD ... JUST TRYING TO SURVIVE ... BUT ALL HE EVER WANTED IN LIFE ... WAS JUST TO STAY ALIVE.

CHORUS:

JUST A MAN WITH NO PLAN ... HE ATE HIS BEANS FROM A CAN ... THAT'S HOW HE LIVED HIS LIFE ... AND PEOPLE COULD'NT UNDERSTAND.

THERE HAVE BEEN TIMES ... HE DID'NT EVEN HAVE A FRYING PAN ...

BUT HE DID'NT WORRY THOUGH ... HE'S JUST A MAN WITH NO PLAN.

VERSE THREE:

SOME PEOPLE LIKES BIG HOUSES ... AND FANCY CARS TO DRIVE ...

BUT HE JUST WANTED QUITING TIME ... TO HURRY UP AND ARRIVE.

THEN HE WOULD GO SOMEWHERE ... AND GET A BEER IN HIS HAND ...

AND HE ALWAYS FELT CONTENT ... HE'S JUST A MAN WITH NO PLAN.

VERSE FOUR:

PEOPLE ASK HIM WHY HE DID THAT ... HE COULD'NT TELL THEM WHY ...

HE SAID IT'S JUST HIS WAY OF LIVING ... AND IT WILL BE UNTILHE DIE.

HE DON'T LOOK FOR TOMORROW ...HE WAS JUST A FREE MAN ...
I JUST LIVE FOR TODAY ... BECAUSE I'M A MAN WITH NO PLAN.

CHORUS:
    HE'S JUST A MAN WITH NO PLAN ... HE ATE HIS BEANS FROM
    A CAN ...
THAT'S HOW HE LIVED HIS LIFE ... AND PEOPLE COULD'NT
UNDERSTAND.
    THERE HAVE BEEN TIMES ... HE DID'NT EVEN HAVE A FRYING
    PAN ...
HE DID'NT SEEM TO WORRY THOUGH ...HE'S JUST A MAN WITH NO
PLAN.

JUST A MEMORY

VERSE ONE:

    IT SEEMS THAT EVERYONE ... IS TOO BUSY TO SLOW DOWN ...
THEY CAN'T FIND TIME TO VISIT... FAMILY IN THEIR HOMETOWN.
    I HAVE LIVED IN THE SAME HOUSE ... FOR FORTY ONE YEARS...
MY LIFE HAS BEEN AS MEANINGLESS... AS AN EMPTY CAN OF BEER.

VERSE TWO:

    ONLY MY OLDER BROTHER ... WHO LIVED ONE BLOCK AWAY ...
AND MY DEAR MOTHER ... WOULD COME BY EVERY FEW DAYS.
    THEY WOULD VISIT OFTEN ... NOW THAT'S JUST A MEMORY...
GOD HAS TAKEN THEM BOTH AWAY ... THEY HAD TO LEAVE ME.

VERSE THREE:

    WHY CAN'T PEOPLE SLOW DOWN ... TAKE A LOOK AROUND ...
SEE WHAT THEY'RE DOING ... WHEN THEY LET OTHERS DOWN.
    THERE IS VOID IN MY LIFE ... FOR FELLOWSHIP OF MY FAMILY ...
SOMEDAY THEY'LL REGRET IT... WHEN I'M JUST A MEMORY.

VERSE FOUR:

    TO STOP AND SEE THE PRESENT...THEY DON'T HAVE TIME ...
THEY LOOK FOR THE FUTURE ... AND THINGS LEFT BEHIND.
    THINK OF THIS VERY MOMENT... IT CAN NEVER AGAIN BE ...
AS OF RIGHT NOW THAT ONE MOMENT ... IS JUST A MEMORY.

VERSE FIVE:

    TIME GOES BY SO FAST... IT WON'T WAIT FOR ANYONE ...
WE'RE HERE TODAY ... BUT TOMORROW WE MAY BE GONE.
    I WONDER THEN ... WILL THEY EVER REMEMBER ME ...
WHEN I'M DEAD AND BURIED ... WILL I EVEN BE A MEMORY.

JUST BE ME

CHORUS:
NOW I'M NOT YOU, I'M JUST ME ... THAT IS ALL I'LL EVER BE ...
LEAVE ME ALONE AND LET IT BE ... ALL I WANTA DO IS JUST BE ME.

VERSE ONE:
NOW I MAY NOT BE ... WHAT THEY WANT ME TO BE ...
BECAUSE ALL I'M EVER GONNA BE ... IS JUST ME.
DON'T SAY I'M NOT WHAT ... YOU THOUGHT I WOULD BE...
BECAUSE ALL YOU'RE EVER GONNA SEE ... IS JUST ME.

VERSE TWO:
NOW I DON'T WANT TO BE ... JUST A MEMORY ...
I WANT TO BE REAL ... I JUST WANT TO BE FREE.
SO DON'T EXSPECT ME ... TO GO DOWN IN HISTORY ...
BECAUSE MY ONLY DESIRE ... IS JUST BE ME.

VERSE THREE:
NOW I DON'T CLAIM TO BE ... SOMEONE I'M NOT ...
AND I DON'T CLAIM TO HAVE THINGS ... THAT I AIN'T GOT.
BUT WHEN YOU LOOK AT ME ... YOU CAN PLAINLY SEE ...
THAT ALL I'M EVER GONNA BE ... IS JUST ME.

VERSE FOUR:
WHY CAN'T PEOPLE LET ME BE ... AND LET ME JUST BE ME ...
THEY TRY TO TELL ME ... MY WHOLE LIFE'S HISTORY.
THEY SHOULD LOOK BACK ... AND MAYBE THEY COULD SEE ...
SOME OF THEIR PROBLEMS ... AND LET ME JUST BE ME.

JUST HANG IT UP

CHORUS:
      ALWAYS LET LIFE ... JUST KEEP ROLLING ON...
AND KEEP IN YOUR HEART ... A HAPPY SONG.
      YOU'RE NOT DRINKING ... FROM AN EMPTY CUP ...
SO DON'T END YOUR LIFE ... BY JUST HANGING IT UP.

VERSE ONE:
      WHEN THINGS GETS OUT OF HAND ... AND TIMES GET ROUGH ...
AND IT SEEMS YOU CAN'T HANDLE IT ... THEN JUST HANG IT UP.
   IF THE PRESSURE GETS TO YOU ...AND YOU FEEL YOU'VE HAD ENOUGH ..
DON'T LET IT REALLY GET YOU DOWN ... JUST HANG IT UP.

VERSE TWO:
      WHEN SOMEONE CALLS YOU ... AND TELLS YOU BAD NEWS ...
AND YOU START ASKING YOURSELF ... WHAT AM I GCING TO DO ...
   JUST TAKE A DEEP BREATH ... TRY NOT TO THINK ABOUT IT MUCH ...
THEN PULL YOURSELF TOGETHER ... AND JUST HANG UP.

CHORUS:
      ALWAYS LET LIFE ... JUST KEEP ROLLING ON...
AND KEEP IN YOUR HEART ... A HAPPY SONG.
      YOU'RE NOT DRINKING ... FROM AN EMPTY CUP ...
SO DON'T END YOUR LIFE ... BY JUST HANGING IT UP.

VERSE THREE:
   A COLLECTOR CALLS ... AND THREATENS TO DESTROY YOUR CREDIT ...
IT MIGHT EVEN DRIVE YOU HALF CRAZY ... IF YOU LET IT.
   BUT DON'T LISTEN TO HIM ... ABOUT ANY OF THAT STUFF ...
YOU HAVE THE POWER TO TURN HIM OFF ... JUST HANG UP.

CHORUS:

     ALWAYS LET LIFE ... JUST KEEP ROLLING ON...
AND KEEP IN YOUR HEART ... A HAPPY SONG.
     YOU'RE NOT DRINKING ... FROM AN EMPTY CUP ...
SO DON'T END YOUR LIFE ... BY JUST HANGING IT UP.

JUST IN SIGHT

CHORUS:

JUST IN SIGHT, JUST IN SIGHT ... YES, HEAVEN IS JUST IN SIGHT...
I CAN HEAR THE ANGELS SINGING ... IT'S A ROYAL DELIGHT.
SUCH HARMONY I'VE NEVER KNOWN ... SINCE I GOT MY LIFE
RIGHT ...
AND I HAVE FOUGHT THE FIGHT ... NOW HEAVEN IS JUST IN SIGHT.

VERSE ONE:

I STILL REMEMBER WHEN ... MY MOTHER PASSED AWAY ...
AND I WILL NEVER FORGET ... THE WORDS SHE HAD TO SAY.
SHE SAID SOON THE TIME WILL COME ... FOR ME TO DIE ...
BUT I DON'T WANT ANY OF YOU ... YOUNG'UNS TO CRY.

VERSE TWO:

SHE SAID SOON I'LL BE LEAVING ... IT COULD BE TONIGHT ...
BUT I'M READY TO GO ... TO TAKE MY HEAVENLY FLIGHT.
NOW DON'T YOU WORRY ... MOMMA IS GONNA BE ALRIGHT ...
I CAN SEE THE ANGELS NOW ... CAUSE HEAVEN IS JUST IN SIGHT.

CHORUS:

JUST IN SIGHT, JUST IN SIGHT ... YES, HEAVEN IS JUST IN SIGHT...
I CAN HEAR THE ANGELS SINGING ... IT'S A ROYAL DELIGHT.
SUCH HARMONY I'VE NEVER KNOWN ... SINCE I GOT MY LIFE
RIGHT ...
AND I HAVE FOUGHT THE FIGHT ... NOW HEAVEN IS JUST IN SIGHT.

VERSE THREE:

SHE LOOKED AT US AND SMILED ... THEN SHE CLOSED HER
EYES ...
IT WAS A PEACEFUL ENDING ... WHEN SHE GAVE UP THIS LIFE.
WE BOWED OUR HEADS AND PRAYED ... BUT NONE OF US
CRIED ...
SHE IS IN A BETTER PLACE ... BECAUSE HEAVEN IS JUST IN SIGHT.

CHORUS:
    JUST IN SIGHT, JUST IN SIGHT ... YES, HEAVEN IS JUST IN SIGHT...
I CAN HEAR THE ANGELS SINGING ... IT'S A ROYAL DELIGHT.
    SUCH HARMONY I'VE NEVER KNOWN ... SINCE I GOT MY LIFE
    RIGHT ...
AND I HAVE FOUGHT THE FIGHT ... NOW HEAVEN IS JUST IN SIGHT.

JUST ONE MISTAKE

VERSE ONE:

    I WENT DOWNTOWN ... ONE BRIGHT MORNING ...
AND IT LOOKED LIKE ... IT WAS A BEAUTIFUL DAY.
    WHEN SUDDENLY THINGS CHANGED ... WITHOUT A WARNING ...
AND ALL MY BLUE SKIES ... TURNED INTO GRAY.

CHORUS:

    JUST ONE MISTAKE ... CHANGED MY LIFE THAT DAY ...
BECAUSE OF WHAT I DID ... AND NOW I HAVE TO PAY.
    SO DON'T EVER THINK ... THAT IT CAN'T HAPPEN TO YOU ...
YOU NEVER KNOW WHAT ... YOU MIGHT HAVE TO GO THRU.

VERSE TWO:

    WHILE I WAS A WALKING ... RIGHT DOWN MAIN STREET ...
MY DREAMS WAS TRAMPLED ... RIGHT UNDERNEATH MY FEET.
    WHEN I NOTICED A CAR ... THAT HAD STOPPED NEAR BY ...
AND I SAW YOU GET OUT ... WITH ANOTHER GUY.

VERSE THREE:

    I WATCHED AS BOTH OF YOU ... WALKED INTO THE BAR ...
THEN MY HEART WAS BROKEN ... LIKE AN OLD GLASS JAR.
    MY KNEES BEGAN TREMBLING ... AS I WALKED IN THE DOOR ...
A FEELING I HAD NEVER HAD ... IN MY LIFE BEFORE.

CHORUS:

    JUST ONE MISTAKE ... CHANGED MY LIFE THAT DAY ...
BECAUSE OF WHAT I DID ... AND NOW I HAVE TO PAY.
    SO DON'T EVER THINK ... THAT IT CAN'T HAPPEN TO YOU ...
YOU NEVER KNOW WHAT ... YOU MIGHT HAVE TO GO THRU.

VERSE FOUR:

    I TOLD THE MAN ... HE WAS SITTING WITH MY WIFE ...
AND HE SAID SO WHAT ... SHE'S WITH ME TONIGHT.
    I REACHED IN MY POCKET ... AND PULLED OUT MY KNIFE ...
BUT I REALLY DID'NT MEAN ... TO TAKE THE MAN'S LIFE.

CHORUS:
     JUST ONE MISTAKE ... CHANGED MY LIFE THAT DAY ...
BECAUSE OF WHAT I DID ... AND NOW I HAVE TO PAY.
     SO DON'T EVER THINK ... THAT IT CAN'T HAPPEN TO YOU ...
YOU NEVER KNOW WHAT ... YOU MIGHT HAVE TO GO THRU.

JUST OUTSIDE OF LITTLE ROCK

VERSE ONE:

     I PULLED IN THE PARKING LOT ...OF A DIESEL TRUCK STOP...
I HAD BEEN HERE BEFORE ... IT WAS A FAVORITE SPOT .

     I ALWAYS STOPPED HERE ... EVERYTIME I CAME THIS WAY ...
AND I THOUGHT THAT TODAY ... WAS JUST ANOTHER DAY.

VERSE TWO:

     I WENT IN THE RESTURANT ...THE WAITRESS CAME AROUND ...
AND SHE SAID WELL LOOKY HERE ... AT WHAT I HAVE FOUND.

     SHE LOOKED ME OVER AND SAID ... NOW DON'T I KNOW YOU...
I SAID MAYBE YOU DO ... I'VE BEEN HERE A TIME OR TWO.

     ...... SING CHORUS ....

VERSE THREE:

     SHE TOOK MY ORDER ... THEN SHE BROUGHT ME MY FOOD ...
AND I TOLD HER THAT MY MEAL ... SURE DID LOOK GOOD.

     SHE ASK IS THERE ANYTHING ELSE ... THAT SHE COULD DO.
I SAID IF I THINK OF SOMETHING ... I WILL SURE CALL ON YOU .

VERSE FOUR:

     SHE LEANED OVER THE TABLE ... AND SHE GAVE ME A KISS ...
AND I SAID RIGHT THEN ... NOW I SURE DO LIKE THIS.

     BUT I HAD A JOB TO DO ... SO I TOLD HER I HAD TO GO ...
I SAID I HAVE TO GET MY LOAD OFF ... FURTHER ON DOWN THE ROAD.

     .... SING CHORUS ....

VERSE FIVE:

     SHE GOT OFF OF WORK ... AND WALKED OUT TO MY TRUCK...
AND WHEN I OPENED THE DOOR ... SHE WANTED TO CLIMB UP.

     IT WAS EARLY IN THE MORNING ... AROUND FOUR O'CLOCK ...
I'LL NEVER FORGET THAT NIGHT ...JUST OUTSIDE OF LITTLE ROCK.

CHORUS:

     I STILL REMEMBER ... THAT NIGHT AT THE TRUCK STOP...
AND THE GIRL THAT I MET ... I SURE LIKED A LOT.

     I LEFT HER STANDING THERE ... BUT HAVE NEVER FORGOT...
THE GIRL THAT I LEFT ... JUST OUTSIDE OF LITTLE ROCK.

JUST SAY NO

VERSE ONE:
YOU SAY YOUR SUGAR LEVEL ... IS A LITTLE TOO HIGH ...
BUT YOU COULD'NT LET THOSE COOKIES ... JUST PASS YOU BY.
EVERYONE ELSE IS EATING THEM ... WHY SHOULD'NT YOU ...
THEY DON'T HAVE HEALTH PROBLEMS ... LIKE YOU DO.

VERSE TWO:
YOUR DOCTOR TOLD YOU ... TO WATCH WHAT YOU EAT ...
AND TO ESPECIALY LAY OFF ... ALL OF THEM SWEETS.
IF YOU CARE ABOUT YOUR HEALTH ... AND DON'T WANT TO GO ...
YOU'VE GOT TO TRY TO FIND A WAY ... TO JUST SAY NO.

VERSE THREE:
IT'S JUST A TWO LETTER WORD ... THAT'S SPELLED N - O ...
SO WHY IS IT SO HARD ... TO JUST SAY NO.
MAYBE IT'S YOUR BRAINS ...YOU SHOULD BE WORRIED ABOUT ...
INSTEAD OF THE FOOD ... THAT YOU SHOULD DO WITHOUT.

VERSE FOUR:
I WISH YOU COULD FIND A WAY ... TO REALLY LIVE ...
AND ENJOY MORE OF THE THINGS ... THAT LIFE HAS TO GIVE.
I HATE TO SAY THIS ... BUT IT'S THE WAY IT GOES ...
YOU JUST AIN'T GOT SENSE ENOUGH ... TO JUST SAY NO.

JUST SOUTH OF LONELY STREET

VERSE ONE:

 IF YOU EVER WONDER ... JUST WHERE I MIGHT BE ...
YOU CAN ALWAYS FIND ME ... JUST SOUTH OF LONELY STREET.
 SINCE MY SWEET BABY LEFT ME ... I'VE BEEN IN MISERY ...
NOW YOU CAN FIND ME ... JUST SOUTH OF LONELY STREET.

CHORUS:

 SOUTH OF LONELY STREET ... SOUTH OF LONELY STREET ...
DOWN ON THE CORNER ... OF HEARTBREAK AND LONELY.
 I WORKED HARD FOR THIS .. AND HAD IT COMING TO ME ...
AND I BUILT ME A PLACE ... JUST SOUTH OF LONELY STREET.

VERSE TWO:

 I'M NOT HERE ALL BY MYSELF ... I HAVE A LOT OF COMPANY ...
THERE'S TEARDROPS EVERYWHERE ... FLOWING DOWN MY CHEEK.
 I HAVE THE MIDNIGHT BLUES ... WRITTEN ALL OVER ME ...
SO COME ON BY ANYTIME ... TO JUST SOUTH OF LONELY STREET.

VERSE THREE:

 I DON'T KNOW WHAT I EVER DID ... TO DESERVE THIS LUXURY ...
THESE DIRTY OLD CLOTHES ... AND WORN OUT SHOES ON MY FEET.
 I HAVE A DIRTY FACE ... WITH A BEARD ON MY CHEEK ...
BUT THAT'S THE WAY WE LIVE ... JUST SOUTH OF LONEY STREET.

CHORUS:

 SOUTH OF LONELY STREET ... SOUTH OF LONELY STREET ...
DOWN ON THE CORNER ... OF HEARTBREAK AND LONELY.
 I WORKED HARD FOR THIS .. AND HAD IT COMING TO ME ...
AND I BUILT ME A PLACE ... JUST SOUTH OF LONELY STREET.

VERSE FOUR:

 DON'T TRY TO TELL ME ... WHAT IT'S LIKE TO BE LONELY ...
I'M LIVING IT NOW EVERYDAY ... WITH NEW FRIENDS I MEET.
 IF YOU GET TO FEELING BLUE ... COME ON AND JOIN ME ...
AND WE'LL CRY TOGETHER ... JUST SOUTH OF LONEY STREET.

LEAVING A LEGACY

VERSE ONE:
EVERYONE THAT LIVES ... WILL LEAVE A LEGACY ...
SOME WILL EVEN GO DOWN ... INTO HISTORY.
SOME WILL BE REMEMBERED ... FOR THEIR BAD PAST ...
WHILE OTHERS WILL LEAVE ... A LEGACY THAT WILL LAST.

VERSE TWO:
THE LEGACY YOU CHOOSE ... IS ENTIRELY UP TO YOU ...
YOU WILL BE REMEMBERED ... BY THE THINGS THAT YOU DO.
SO DO SOMETHING GOOD ... WHILE LIVING YOUR LIFE ...
AND LEAVE A GOOD LEGACY ... WHEN YOUR TIME COMES TO DIE.

CHORUS:
NOW I KNOW I'M NOT PERFECT ... AND I'M NOT GONNA LIE ...
I'LL LEAVE A GOOD LEGACY ... WHEN MY TIME COMES TO DIE.
THEY'LL TALK ABOUT THINGS ... THAT I HAVE SAID AND DONE ...
THEY'LL REMEMBER ME BY ... THE SONGS I WROTE AND SUNG.

VERSE THREE:
SOMETIMES YOU DON'T CARE ... WHAT OTHERS MAY THINK ...
THAT'S HOW YOU'LL BE REMEMBERED...WHEN YOU BECOME EXTINCT.
YOU KNOW YOU ARE GOING TO DIE ... THERE IS NO DOUBT ...
SO LEAVE A GOOD LEGACY ... FOR THEM TO TALK ABOUT.

CHORUS:
NOW I KNOW I'M NOT PERFECT ... AND I'M NOT GONNA LIE ...
I KNOW I'LL LEAVE A GOOD LEGACY ... WHEN I DIE.
THEY'LL TALK ABOUT THINGS ... THAT I HAVE SAID AND DONE ...
THEY'LL REMEMBER ME BY... THE SONGS I WROTE AND SUNG.

LET'S PLAY BALL

VERSE ONE:
    LET'S ALL GO DOWN ... TO THE BASEBALL FIELD ...
AND GET ALL THE FEELINGS ... WE KNOW ARE REAL.
    HEARING THE UMPIRE ... A MAKING HIS CALLS ...
AND HEARING THE ANNOUNCER SAY ... LET'S PLAY BALL.

CHORUS:
    FIRST ONE UP GETS ON FIRST ... HE STEALS SECOND BASE ...
THEY BUNT HIM TO THIRD ... LOOKING FOR HOME PLATE.
    THEN NEXT THING YOU KNOW ... IT'S A DIFFERENT SONG ...
GET 'EM ON AND HIT'EM LONG ... AND BRING 'EM ON HOME ...

VERSE TWO:
    WATCH THE BASEBALL ... AND DON'T PLAY AROUND ...
AND HIT 'EM HARD ... KEEP THEM UP OFF THE GROUND.
    AND LISTEN TO THE ECHOES ... OF AMERICA'S SONG ...
BASEBALL AND HOT DOGS ... AND BRING 'EM ON HOME.

VERSE THREE:
    IT'S ONE STRIKE TWO ... THREE STRIKES YOU'RE OUT ...
FOR THE OPPOSITE TEAM ... LISTEN TO THAT CROWD.
    NOW IN THIS LIFE ... THERE ARE THREE BEST THINGS ...
LIKE EATING CAKE AND ICE CREAM ... AND YOUR FAVORITE TEAM.

CHORUS:
    FIRST ONE UP GETS ON FIRST ... HE STEALS SECOND BASE ...
THEY BUNT HIM TO THIRD ... LOOKING FOR HOME PLATE.
    THEN NEXT THING YOU KNOW ... IT'S A DIFFERENT SONG ...
GET 'EM ON AND HIT'EM LONG ... AND BRING 'EM ON HOME ...

        .... SING CHORUS AGAIN ....

LIFE ON THE FARM

VERSE ONE:

    NOW DOWN ON THE FARM ... IS WHERE I WANT TO BE ...
THAT IS THE ONLY PLACE ... WHERE I CAN REALLY FEEL FREE.
    SITTING OUT IN THE YARD ... IN THE EVENING BREEZE ...
I REALLY FIND PEACE ... WHEN I'M WAY OUT IN THE COUNTRY.

VERSE TWO:

    I LOVE THE LIFE ON THE FARM ... THAT'S WHERE I BELONG ...
IT'S WHERE PEACE ON EARTH ... IS LIKE A BEAUTIFUL SONG.
    THERE ARE WONDERFUL HEAVENLY VISIONS ... ALL AROUND ME.
AND THAT IS WHY LIFE ON THE FARM... IS WHERE I WANT TO BE.

VERSE THREE:

    THERE ARE NO FAST CARS ... RUNNING HERE AND THERE ...
AND THERE IS NO POLLUTION ... THAT FILLS THE AIR.
    IT'S EASY TO SEE WHY ... LIFE ON THE FARM GOT TO ME ...
WITH NO PEOPLE SHOUTING ... AND WALKING THE STREETS.

VERSE FOUR:

    EVERYTHING ON THE FARM LIFE ... IS PEACE AND QUIET ...
WITH NO SIRENS OR HORNS ... WHEN I LAY DOWN AT NIGHT.
    IF ONLY I HAD KNOWN ... HOW NICE IT REALLY IS ...
I WOULD HAVE BEEN HERE YEARS AGO ... TO ENJOY ALL THIS.

VERSE FIVE:

    NOW LIFE ON THE FARM ... IS A HOME WHERE LIFE IS FREE ...
GROWING YOUR OWN GARDEN ... HAVING YOUR OWN FRUIT TREES ...
    GETTING UP WHEN YOU WANT TO ... AND LIVING LIFE WITH
    EASE ...
WITH NO ONE BOSSING YOU AROUND ... JUST DOING AS YOU PLEASE.

VERSE SIX:

    WHETHER YOU GO BY DIRT ROAD ... OR THE STATE HIGHWAY ...
YOU CAN ALWAYS GET HERE ... TO THE OLD HOME PLACE.
    IN CASE YOU EVER DO DECIDE ... TO COME HERE AND STAY ...
YOU'LL HAVE TO AGREE LIFE ON THE FARM ... IS THE ONLY WAY.

LIFE'S OTHER GAME

VERSE ONE:

    WHEN I STARTED TO SCHOOL ... I WAS SCARED TO DEATH ...
IT WAS SOMETHING NEW ... I COULD'NT HELP BUT TO FRET.
    I REALLY MISSED MY FAMILY ... AND I FELT SO ASHAMED ...
WHEN THE TEACHER SCOLDED ME ... IT WAS LIFE'S OTHER GAME.

VERSE TWO:

    I GREW UP FAST ... AND NOW MY SCHOOL DAYS ARE GONE ...
NOW I'VE GOT TO USE WHAT I LEARNED ... BEFORE I LEFT HOME.
    I'M A GROWN UP MAN NOW ... AND NOTHING IS THE SAME ...
I LEARNED A LOT OF THINGS ... ABOUT LIFE'S OTHER GAME.

CHORUS:

    SOMETIMES LIFE CAN ALMOST ... DRIVE YOU INSANE ...
BUT I'M A GONNA LIVE AS GOOD ... AND AS LONG AS I CAN.
    WHEN IT COMES TO DYING ... I'LL GO THE WAY I CAME ...
IF I DON'T WIN THE GAME OF LIFE ... I'M THE ONLY ONE TO BLAME.

VERSE THREE:

    GOOD OLD NORTH CAROLINA .. IS WHERE I COME FROM ...
BACK WHERE I WAS NOT KNOWN ... MUCH BY ANYONE.
    THEN I WENT OUT WEST ... TO SEEK FORTUNE AND FAME ...
NOW I HAVE TO GO BACK HOME ... TO PLAY LIFE'S OTHER GAME.

VERSE FOUR:

    I ALWAYS WORKED HARD ... BUT PEOPLE COULD'NT SEE
THAT ...
SO I HAD TO GET AWAY ... LIKE A LONG GONE CAT.
    I STRUCK IT RICH ... IN THE CALIFORNIA LOTTERY CLAIMS ...
AND NOW I HAVE TO GO BACK ... TO PLAY LIFE'S OTHER GAME.

CHORUS:

    SOMETIMES LIFE CAN ALMOST ... DRIVE YOU INSANE ...
BUT I'M A GONNA LIVE AS GOOD...AND AS LONG AS I CAN.
    WHEN IT COMES TO DYING ... I'LL GO THE WAY I CAME ...
IF I DON'T WIN THE GAME OF LIFE... I'M THE ONLY ONE TO BLAME.

LIKE A KID AGAIN

VERSE ONE:
    AS I WALKED OUTSIDE ... OF MY HOME ONE NIGHT ...
THE SNOW WAS COMING DOWN ... IT WAS A BEAUTIFUL SIGHT.
    I THOUGHT BACK AS A KID ...THE MEMORIES WOULD'NT STOP...
SO I GOT ME A BIG BOWL ... AND I FILLED IT TO THE TOP.

VERSE TWO:
    I ADDED VANILLA FLAVORING ... AND SOME SUGAR TOO ...
THEN I POURED IN SOME MILK ... AND WHEN I GOT THRU.
    I HAD A FULL BOWL ... OF HOMEMADE SNOW CREAM ...
AND IT SURE MADE ME FEEL ... LIKE A KID AGAIN.

VERSE THREE:
    THEN I THOUGHT BACK ... TO WHEN I WAS VERY YOUNG ...
AND THOUGHT OF SOME OF THE THINGS ... US KIDS HAD DONE.
    LIKE EATING SNOW CREAM ... AND BUILDING SNOW MEN ...
AND IT MADE ME WANT TO GO BACK ... TO BEING A KID AGAIN.

VERSE FOUR:
    MY MOTHER WOULD WORRY ... THAT I MIGHT CATCH A COLD ...
NOW I LIKE TO THINK BACK ... TO THOSE MEMORIES OF OLD.
    WHEN I DID'NT HAVE NO WORRYS ... NO CARES AT ALL ...
AND I JUST COULD'NT WAIT ... FOR THE NEXT SNOW TO FALL.

VERSE FIVE:
    WE WOULD HAVE SNOW FIGHTS ... A BUNCH OF MY FRIENDS...
AND BOY BACK IN THOSE DAYS ... REAL JOY HAD NO END.
    BUT I KNOW THINGS CAN'T BE ... LIKE THEY WERE BACK THEN.
BUT I SURE WOULD LIKE TO BE ... LIKE A KID AGAIN.

LIKE IT AND LIVE WITH IT

VERSE ONE:
 THERE'S A LOT OF THINGS ... THAT WE DON'T LIKE ...
AND THERE IS A LOT OF THINGS ... THAT WE THINK AIN'T RIGHT.
 EVEN THOUGH WE KNOW ... IT AIN'T OUR WAY ...
W HA'VE GOT TO LIKE IT ... AND LIVE WITH IT ANYWAY.

VERSE TWO:
 WHEN WE SEE THINGS ... THAT WE DON'T APPROVE OF ...
LIKE PUSH AND SHOVE ... AND PEOPLE SHOWING NO LOVE.
 WE WANT TO GIVE UP ... SOMETIMES AND QUIT ...
WE FIND IT HARD TO LIKE IT ... AND LIVE WITH IT.

CHORUS:
 LIKE IT AND LIVE WITH IT ... WHETHER YOU LIKE IT OR NOT ...
THERE'S A LOT OF PEOPLE ... THAT DON'T HAVE WHAT WE GOT.
 WE HAD BETTER APPRECIATE ... JUST BEING FREE ...
BUT FOR THE GRACE OF GOD ... IT COULD BE YOU AND ME.

VERSE THREE:
 WE MUST UNDERSTAND ... WHAT MAKES THEM THIS WAY ...
AND TRY TO HELP THEM ... TO GET THROUGH ANOTHER DAY.
 SO SHOW SOMEONE PITY ... IF ONLY A LITTLE BIT ...
MAYBE THEY CAN LEARN ... TO LIKE IT AND LIVE WITH IT.

VERSE FOUR:
 I DON'T HAVE MUCH ... BUT I'M THANKFUL FOR IT ALL ...
AND I'M WILLING TO SHARE ... BEFORE I SEE SOMEONE FALL.
 PUT YOURSELF IN THEIR SHOES ... AND DON'T FALL IN THE PIT ...
AND HELP SOMEONE EVERY DAY ... AND LIKE IT AND LIVE WITH IT.

CHORUS:
 LIKE IT AND LIVE WITH IT ... WHETHER YOU LIKE IT OR NOT ...
THERE'S A LOT OF PEOPLE ... THAT DON'T HAVE WHAT WE GOT.
 WE HAD BETTER APPRECIATE ... JUST BEING FREE ...
BUT FOR THE GRACE OF GOD ... IT COULD BE YOU AND ME.

LOCOMO

VERSE ONE:

    I REMEMBER WHEN I WAS A LAD ... SOME OF THE DREAMS I
HAD ...

WHEN I WAS GROWING UP ... I WANTED TO DRIVE A BIG TRUCK.

    THEN WHEN I GOT GROWN ... I GOT ME A JOB OF MY OWN ...

DRIVING OVER THE ROAD ... THEY CALLED ME THE LOCOMO.

VERSE TWO:

    I STARTED PEDDLING FURNITURE ... THAT WORKED FOR A
WHILE ...

THEN I GOT ME A JOB DRIVING ... THAT PAID BY THE MILE.

    IT WAS IN A BIG OLD TRUCK ... AN EIGHTEEN WHEELER ...

THIRTEEN FOOT HIGH ... WITH A FORTY FIVE FOOT TRAILOR.

CHORUS:

    BREAKER BREAKER 1 - 9 ... THIS IS THE LOCOMO ...

IF YOU WANT TO SHOOT THE BREEZE ... WELL I'M AN OLD PRO.

    SO PUT YOUR EARS ON ... AND LET'S CHAT FOR A WHILE ...

ABOUT SOME OLD MEMORIES ... WHILE WE RUN THE MILES.

VERSE THREE:

    I LOVED THAT OLD TRUCK ... IT WAS JUST LIKE MY HOME ...

AND WHEN I WAS RUNNING THE ROADS ... I WAS NEVER ALONE.

    WHENEVER I WANTED SOMEONE ... TO JUST TALK TO ME ...

I WOULD GET ON CHANNEL 1 - 9 ... ON MY OLD CB.

VERSE FOUR:

    SOME SAID I WAS CRAZY ... THEY JUST COULD'NT UNDERSTAND ...

WHAT IT WAS THAT MADE ME ... WANT TO BE A TRUCK DRIVING MAN.

    BUT THAT'S THE LIFE THAT I CHOSE ... I WAS ALWAYS ON THE
ROAD ...

AND YOU COULD FIND ME ON THE CB ... AS THE LOCOMO.

CHORUS:
     BREAKER BREAKER 1 - 9 ... THIS IS THE LOCOMO ...
IF YOU WANT TO SHOOT THE BREEZE ... WELL I'M AN OLD PRO.
     SO PUT YOUR EARS ON ... AND LET'S CHAT FOR A WHILE ...
ABOUT SOME OLD MEMORIES ... WHILE WE RUN THE MILES.

     WELL I'M SIGNING OFF NOW ... SO KEEP THE GOOD WORK UP ...
AND KEEP ON A DRIVING ... THAT BIG OLD TRUCK..

LOOK OUT CALIFORNIA

CHORUS:
     I REMEMBER ONCE I HEARD ... A GOOD SONG SUNG ...
ABOUT LOOK OUT CALIFORNIA ... HERE I COME.
     IT WAS PLAYED BY ... AN OLD FASHION HILLBILLY BAND ...
AND SUNG BY A LITTLE ... OLD TIME COUNTRY MAN.

VERSE ONE:
     IT WAS ABOUT BIG CITIES ... AND VERY BRIGHT LIGHTS ...
AND GETTING LOST IN CROWDS ... ALMOST EVERY NIGHT.
     NOW DOWN IN THE COUNTRY ... IS WHERE I COME FROM ...
BUT LOOK OUT CALIFORNIA ... HERE I COME.

VERSE TWO:
     I WANT TO SEE JUST WHAT ... IT WOULD BE LIKE ...
TO WALK DOWN THE STREETS ... ALL LIT UP AT NIGHT.
     WITH PLENTY OF BARS ... AND HONKY TONKS IN TOWN...
WITH MUSIC EVERYWHERE ... I AM CALIFORNIA BOUND.

VERSE THREE:
     THERE'S PLENTY OF GIRLS ... FOR BOYS ALL AROUND ...
AND ALL KINDS OF THINGS TO DO ... ALL OVER TOWN.
     THE FUN STARTS AT DARK ... AND LASTS ALL NIGHT LONG ...
SO LOOK OUT CALIFORNIA ... HERE I COME.

VERSE FOUR:
     I HEARD THE SOUNDS ... OF THE STREETS CALLING ME ...
AND I HAVE A FEELING ... SOON LIGHTS IS WHAT I'LL SEE .
     NOW I'M ON THE ROAD ... I CAN HEAR THE MOTOR HUM ...
I SAID LOOK OUT CALIFORNIA ... HERE I COME.

LOVE AT CHRISTMAS TIME

VERSE ONE:

  IF CHRISTMAS WAS LIKE ... IT USED TO BE ...
I WOULD REALLY BE BLESSED ... THIS CHRISTMAS DAY .
  WHAT I REALLY WANT ... YOU CAN'T GET UNDER THE TREE ...
BUT JUST LISTEN ... AND I'LL TELL YOU ANYWAY.

VERSE TWO:

  I WANT YOU ... ALL WRAPPED UP IN MY LOVE ...
AND IN YOUR HEART ... IS WHERE I WANT TO BE.
  BUT FIRST PUT YOU HEART ... IN WHAT CHRISTMAS MEANS ...
AND THEN ALLTHE REST ... YOU CAN GIVE TO ME.

VERSE THREE:

  YOU BRIGHTEN UP THINGS ... WITH LOVE AT CHRISTMAS
TIME ...
AND YOU PUT JOY IN MY HEART ... ALL OF THE TIME.
  YOU MAKE ME SMILE ... BOTH DAY AND NIGHT ...
AS LONG AS YOU ARE AROUND ... MY FUTURE LOOKS BRIGHT.

VERSE FOUR:

  CHRISTMAS TIME IS THE HAPPIEST ... TIME OF THE YEAR ...
AND MY LIFE IS THE BRIGHTEST ... WHEN YOU ARE HERE.
  SO STAY CLOSE BY ME ... BECAUSE I NEED YOU ...
AND DON'T MAKE MY CHRISTMAS CHEER ... TURN INTO BLUE.

VERSE FIVE:

  LET'S SING SOME CHRISTMAS SONGS ... WITH OUR LIPS ...
BUT LET THE FEELING COME ... FROM WITHIN OUR HEARTS.
  CHRIST WAS BORN ... ON CHRISTMAS DAY ...
AND THAT IS WHERE ... SALVATION STARTS.

CHORUS:

  SING SING SING ... THOSE HAPPY CHRISTMAS SONGS ...
AND LET'S ALL REJOICE ... AS WE RIDE ALONG.
  KEEP THE JOY OF CHRISTMAS ... IN OUR HEARTS AND MINDS ...
AND PRAISE JESUS CHRIST ... AS LONG AS THERE IS TIME

MAKE IT ON WHEELS

VERSE ONE:

    I REMEMBER BACK WHEN ... WE USED TO HAVE CURB SERVICE ... YOU WOULD PULL INTO A PARKING SPACE ... WITH AN INTERCOM IN IT.

    I WOULD PUSH THE BUTTON ... AND ASK WHAT'S YOUR BEST DEAL ...

THEY'D SAY FOR HERE OR TO GO ... I WOULD SAY MAKE IT ON WHEELS.

VERSE TWO:

    WHEN I'D SAY MAKE IT ON WHEELS ... I SIMPLY MEANT TO GO ... I WOULD BE IN A HURRY ... BECAUSE I HAD OTHER THINGS TO DO.

    THEY'D BRING IT TO THE CAR ... WITH MY DRINKS AND MEAL ... I WOULD REACH IN MY POCKET FOR MONEY... TO PAY FOR THE BILL.

VERSE THREE:

    ONE OF MY FAVORITE SPOTS ... WAS THE A & W ROOT BEER ... I ALWAYS FELT WELCOME ... EACH TIME THAT I WAS THERE.

    I WOULD TALK WITH THE GIRLS ... FEELING FIT TO KILL... AND I WAS ALWAYS READY ... TO MAKE IT ON WHEELS.

VERSE FOUR:

    ANOTHER HOT SPOT IN TOWN ... WAS THE TOOT AND TELL ... JUST TOOT YOUR HORN ... AND TELL THEM WHAT YOU WANT .

    IT WAS A FRIENDLY FAST MOVING ... FAST FOOD RESTURANT ... THEY WOULD COOK IT ON THE GRILL ... THEN PUT IT ON WHEELS.

VERSE FIVE:

    AND THEN THERE WAS ... THE TOPPER DRIVE - IN ... WHERE A LOT OF US GUYS ... WOULD MEET AS FRIENDS.

    THOSE WERE THE GOOD OLD DAYS ... WHERE YOUTH WAS KING ...

WE DID'NT GO LOOKING FOR TROUBLE ... THANKS TO THE DRIVE IN'S.

CHORUS:

NOW I GO IN A RESTURANT ... THEY ASK FOR HERE OR TO GO ...
I JUST SMILE AT THEM AND SAY ... I THOUGHT YOU ALREADY KNOW.
THEY GET A KICK OUT OF THAT ... I CAN TELL THEY GET A THRILL .
WHEN I SAY THAT OLD SAYING ... JUST MAKE IT ON WHEELS.

ME AND THOSE OLD MEMORIES

VERSE ONE:

AS I SIT HERE TONIGHT ... I THINK BACK ON MY LIFE ...
I DID A LOT OF THINGS ... THAT I KNEW WASN'T RIGHT.

THERE WAS A LOT OF PEOPLE ... WHO DID NOT AGREE.
OF THE LIFE THAT I LIVED ... BUT IS NOW A MEMORY.

CHORUS:

NOW I'M NOT AS BAD ... AS THOSE OLD MEMORIES ...
AND I'M NOT AS GOOD ... AS I'M GOING TO BE.

AS MY MIND GOES BACK ... TO THAT MEMORY LANE ...
I KNOW I'M NOT GOING ... DOWN THAT SAME ROAD AGAIN.

VERSE TWO:

THERE WAS A LOT OF PEOPLE ... I THOUGHT I KNEW ...
THAT DID A LOT OF THINGS ... TO HELP ME GET THRU.

NOW WHEN I THINK BACK ... OF THINGS I DID THEN ...
I WOULD'NT HAVE DONE THEM ... IF WAS'NT FOR THEM.

VERSE THREE:

WE ALL HAVE DONE THINGS ... THAT WE'RE ASHAMED OF...
AND I GUESS WE ALL HAVE SOMETIMES ... FALLEN IN LOVE.

IF I DID HAVE FRIENDS ... THEY'VE ALL GONE AND LEFT ME...
AND ALL I HAVE LEFT IS ... ME AND THOSE OLD MEMORIES.

.... SING CHORUS AGAIN ....

MIND IN MOTION

VERSE ONE:

     I CAN GO ANYWHERE ... THAT I WANT TO GO ...
OR I CAN DO ANYTHING ... ANYWAY I WANT TO DO.
     WHEN I THINK ABOUT IT ... I WRITE IT DOWN AND THEN ...
I CAN GO BACK AND RELIVE IT ... TIME AND TIME AGAIN.

VERSE TWO:

     I CAN GO TO CHICAGO ... OR IT MAY BE SAN ANGELO ...
OR EVEN NEW YORK CITY ... OR PERHAPS OLD MEXICO.
     WITH MY MIND IN MOTION ... I CAN GO ANYWHERE ...
WHEN I SEE IT IN MY MIND ... THEN I AM ALREADY THERE.

CHORUS:

     PUT YOUR MIND OVER MATTER ... AND KEEP IT IN MOTION ...
AND YOU CAN DO ANYTHING ... THAT YOU TAKE A NOTION.
     LIFE CAN BE AS GOOD ... AS YOU WANT IT TO BE ...
IF YOU PUT YOUR MIND IN MOTION ... AND ONLY BELIEVE.

VERSE THREE:

     IT DON'T COST ME NOTHING ... TO TRAVEL IN THOUGHT ...
OR I CAN DO ANYTHING ... WITHOUT GETTING CAUGHT.
     WHEN MY MIND IS IDOL ... IT CAN REALLY GET ME DOWN ...
BUT WITH MY MIND IN MOTION ... IT WIPES AWAY THAT FROWN.

VERSE FOUR:

     WITH MY MIND IN MOTION ... I CAN BE WELL SATISFIED ...
EVEN THOUGH I AM A POOR MAN ... I STILL HAVE A LOT OF PRIDE.
     YOU CAN BELIEVE I'M STILL BE HAPPY ...IN RAGS OR RICHES ...
WHETHER I'M WORKING IN A BANK ... OR EVEN DIGGING DITCHES.

CHORUS:

     PUT YOUR MIND OVER MATTER ... AND KEEP IT IN MOTION ...
AND YOU CAN DO ANYTHING ... THAT YOU TAKE A NOTION.
     LIFE CAN BE AS GOOD ... AS YOU WANT IT TO BE ...
IF YOU PUT YOUR MIND IN MOTION ... AND ONLY BELIEVE.

MOMMA AND JESUS

VERSE ONE:
  WE KNEW SHE WOULD HAVE TO ... LEAVE US SOMEDAY ...
BUT IT WAS SO SAD ... WHEN OUR MOTHER PASSED AWAY.
  IT'S HARD TO EXPLAIN ... BUT SHE WAS A BIG PART OF ME ...
AND ALL I HAVE LEFT ... IS A LOT OF SWEET MEMORIES.

VERSE TWO:
  I WAS SO HURT ... THAT I BROKE DOWN AND CRIED ...
THE VERY SAME DAY ... THAT MY MOTHER HAD DIED.
  I SURE DO MISS HER ... SHE MEANT SO MUCH TO ME ...
AND NOW THAT SHE IS GONE ... I FEEL SO LONELY.

VERSE THREE:
  MOMMA ALWAYS TOLD ME ... ABOUT A MAN CALLED JESUS...
AND IF I SINNED... HE WOULD ALWAYS FORGIVE US.
  SHE WAS AS TRUE AS THE BLOOD...THAT RAN THRU HER VEINS ...
AND THE DAY THAT I LOST HER ... MY TEARS FELL LIKE RAIN.

VERSE FOUR;
  WHEN I GOT INTO TROUBLE ... SHE WAS ALWAYS THERE ...
NOT TO TELL ME I WAS WRONG ... BUT BECAUSE SHE CARED.
  I REALLY FEEL LIKE ... SHE DID'NT EVEN LEAVE US ...
AND SOMEDAY I'LL WALK ... WITH MOMMA AND JESUS.

VERSE FIVE:
  SOMEDAY WE'LL MEET AGAIN ... SO I HAVE BEEN TOLD ...
AND I'LL HOLD HER HAND ... LIKE I DID IN DAYS OF OLD.
  THE GREATEST PART OF MY LIFE ...WILL SOMEDAY UNFOLD...
WHEN I WALK WITH MOMMA AND JESUS ... ON STREETS OF GOLD.

MOMMA SAID

CHORUS:

    MY MOMMA SAID SON ... TRY TO LIVE RIGHT ...
BUT DON'T EVER RUN ... IF YOU HAVE TO FIGHT.
    DON'T LOOK FOR TROUBLE ... BUT IF IT COMES TO YOU ...
YOU'RE ALWAYS OBLIGATED ... TO SEE IT THROUGH.

VERSE ONE:

    I GOT PUT IN JAIL ... FOR SOMETHING I DID'NT DO ...
IT GOES TO SHOW YOU WHAT ... MOMMA SAID WAS TRUE.
    CAUSE WHEN I WENT TO COURT ... THE JUDGE DID'NT GRIN ...
WHEN THEY FOUND OUT ... THEY HAD THE WRONG MAN.

VERSE TWO:

    MY MOMMA SAID SON ... I'M SO PROUD OF YOU ...
FOR NOT DOING THE THINGS ... THEY SAY YOU DO.
    YOU'RE GONNA FIND OUT ... THAT IN DUE TIME ...
WHEN YOU'RE LIVING RIGHT ... YOU'LL WIN EVERYTIME.

VERSE THREE:

    ALWAYS BE HONEST ... STAND UP FOR WHAT'S RIGHT ...
AND DON'T STAY OUT ... TOO LATE AT NIGHT.
    JUST LET FOLKS KNOW ... YOU'RE A VERY FIRM MAN ...
AND YOU CAN HANDLE ... WHATEVER HITS THE FAN.

VERSE FOUR:

    PEOPLE STOP AND THINK ... BEFORE YOU DO WHAT YOU DO ...
THEN YOU'LL FIND OUT ... WHAT MOMMA SAID IS TRUE.
    THAT IF YOU DO WRONG ... YOU'LL HAVE TO EAT CROW ...
I CAN STILL HEAR MY MOMMA SAY ... I TOLD YOU SO.

    SING CHORUS:....

MOONLIGHT DRINKING

CHORUS:
    THIS DAYTIME THINKING ... AND MOONLGHT DRINKING ...
HAS GOT A BIG ... HOLD ON ME.
    OF ALL THE PEOPLE I KNOW ... I JUST CAN'T LET GO ...
WHY CAN'T I ... JUST LET IT BE.

VERSE ONE:
    ALL MY DAY DREAMING ... TURNED TO MOONLIGHT
    DRINKING ...
AND IT'S ALL ... BECAUSE OF YOU.
    I KEPT ON A TRYING ... BUT YOU KEPT ON A LYING ...
WHY DO YOU KEEP DOING ME .... LIKE YOU DO.

VERSE TWO:
    I HAVE ALWAYS WORKED HARD ... UNTIL I GOT FIRED ...
AND NOW YOU TELL ME ... THAT WE ARE THROUGH.
    BUT I STILL HAVE DREAMS ... OF ALL OF THOSE THINGS ...
AND THE THINGS THAT WE ... WANTED TO DO.

CHORUS:
    THIS DAY TIME THINKING ... AND MY MOONLGHT DRINKING ...
HAS GOT ... A HOLD ON ME.
    OF ALL THE PEOPLE I KNOW ... I JUST CAN'T LET GO ...
WHY CAN'T I ... LET IT BE.

VERSE THREE:
    YOU SAID YOU LOVED ME ... AND ALWAYS THOUGHT OF ME ...
AND YOU ALWAYS DID THE THINGS ... THAT YOU WANTED TO.
    WHY CAN'T YOU EVER SEE ... WHAT YOU'RE DOING TO ME ...
I'M NOT A BROKEN DOOR ... THAT YOU WALK THROUGH.

VERSE FOUR:
    WHY DO YOU TREAT ME ... THE WAY THAT YOU DO ...
WHEN ALL THE TIME YOU KNOW ... WHAT I'M GOING THROUGH.
    THIS MOONLIGHT DRINKING ... IS GOING TO STOP ...
I'M GOING TO CHANGE MY WAYS ... BELIEVE IT OR NOT.

MR MUSIC MAN

VERSE ONE:

    HE STANDS TALL ... WITH A GUITAR IN HIS HANDS ...
AND EVERYONE CALLS HIM ... MR MUSIC MAN.
    IF ANYONE CAN GET,,, THEIR ATTENTION HE CAN ...
AND THAT'S WHY THEY CALL HIM ... MR MUSIC MAN.

VERSE TWO:

    HE PUTS MUSIC TO MOTION ... LIKE NO ONE ELSE CAN ...
AND YOU'LL KNOW WHEN ... YOU HEAR MR MUSIC MAN.
    I'LL HAVE TO SAY HE'S THE BEST ...THAT I'VE EVER SEEN ...
WHEN THE WOMEN STANDS UP...THEY ALL BEGIN TO SCREAM.

VERSE THREE:

    WHEN HE WOULD SING ... THE PEOPLE WOULD SHOUT ...
THEY WOULD'NT HOLD BACK ... THEY WOULD LET IT ALL OUT.
    HE DID IT BY HIMSELF ... HE DID'NT NEED NO BAND ...
AND EVERYBODY CALLED HIM ... MR MUSIC MAN.

VERSE FOUR:
    NOW DON'T GET IN HIS WAY ... WHEN HE BEGINS TO PLAY ...
NO ONE WANTS TO LEAVE ... THEY ALL WANT TO STAY.
    SO GET THERE EARLY ... OR YOU'LL HAVE TO STAND ...
CAUSE EVERYBODY WANTS ... TO HEAR MR MUSIC MAN.

MUSIC DOCTOR

VERSE ONE:
    MUSIC MAKES ME FEEL ... MUCH YOUNGER THAN I AM ...
I ALWAYS PLAY AND SING ... WHEN I'M FEELING DOWN.
    IT MAKES ME FORGET ... ALL THE ACHES AND PAINS ...
WHEN THE MUSIC DOCTOR COMES ... ONTO THE SCHENE.

VERSE TWO:
    MUSIC COMES FROM MY HEART ... WHEN I SING EVERY LINE ...
AND THAT'S WHEN I START ... TO REALLY FEELING FINE.
    SOMETIMES I JUST WANT ... TO KICK UP MY HEELS ...
MUSIC IS A POWERFUL DOCTOR ... THAT'S HOW I FEEL.

VERSE THREE:
    IT'S GOOD TO KNOW THAT I HAVE ... A LOT OF FANS ...
DOCTOR MUSIC MAKES ME FEEL ... LIKE A VERY YOUNG MAN.
    WHEN I SING ... MUSIC COMES STRAIGHT FROM MY HEART ...
AND THAT IS WHY MUSIC PLAYS ... SUCH A BIG PART.

CHORUS:
    MUSIC MUSIC ... MUSIC IS MY DOCTOR ...
SOMETIMES IT MAKES ME ... JUST WANT TO HOLLER.
    MUSIC IS WAY DOWN ... DEEP IN MY SOUL ...
IT MAKES ALL THE GOOD TIMES ... JUST START TO ROLL.

MUSIC IS MY MEDICINE

VERSE ONE:
    WHEN EVER I FEEL BAD ... I GRAB UP MY GUITAR ...
I MIGHT BE AT HOME ... OR ON A TRIP IN MY CAR.
    MUSIC IS MY MEDICINE ... NO MATTER WHERE I GO ...
IT WILL ALWAYS PICK ME UP ... WHENEVER I FEEL LOW.

VERSE TWO:
    I GET TO PICK THE SONGS ... THAT I WANT TO SING ...
I SING THEM FROM MY HEART ...THAT MEANS EVERYTHING.
    WHEN SOMEONE HEARS MY SONGS ... AND I SEE THEM SMILE ...
MUSIC IS BETTER MEDICINE ...THAN ANY DRUG THERE IS ON FILE.

CHORUS:
    MUSIC IS MY MEDICINE ... IT CURES ME THRU AND THRU ...
IT TAKES AWAY THE PAIN ... LIKE NO OTHER DRUG CAN DO.
    IT DOES MORE FOR ME ... THAN TAKING ANY PILLS ...
I THINK OF WHAT I'M DOING ... NOT ABOUT HOW I FEEL.

VERSE THREE:
    MUSIC IS MY MEDICINE ... IT KEEPS ME FEELING YOUNG ...
THE PRESCRIPTION FOR MY SONGS... ARE THINGS I HAVE DONE.
    I TALK ABOUT GOOD TIMES ... AND PLACES I HAVE BEEN ...
AS LONG AS I PLAY MUSIC ... I CAN ALWAYS FIND A FRIEND.

VERSE FOUR:
    MUSIC MAKES ME HAPPY... AND IT MAKES PEOPLE SMILE ...
THEY EVEN TAP THEIR TOES ... AND CLAP THEIR HANDS A WHILE.
    THEY EVEN START TO JUMPING ... AND DANCING ALL AROUND...
MUSIC IS GOOD MEDICINE ... THE BEST THAT CAN BE FOUND.

MY BIG BROTHER HENRY

VERSE ONE:

    WHEN I WAS GROWING UP ... I THOUGHT THERE WAS NO OTHER ...
PERSON ON THIS WHOLE EARTH ... LIKE MY BIG BROTHER.
    HE WAS SIX YEARS OLDER THAN ME ... HIS NAME WAS HENRY.
NOW HE COULD GET MEAN ... BUT MOST OF THE TIME FRIENDLY.

VERSE TWO:

    WHEN I WAS SIXTEEN ... HE GOT ME A JOB WHERE HE WORKED ...
IT PUT A LOT OF PRESSURE ON HIM ... HE WORRIED I MIGHT GET HURT.
    WE ALWAYS GOT PAID ON FRIDAY ... THAT WAS OUR NIGHT ...
HE TAUGHT ME HOW TO DRINK ... I ALREADY KNEW HOW TO FIGHT.

VERSE THREE:

    WE'D GO OUT TO THE BARS ... AND PLAY THE PINBALL MACHINES ...
WE WOULD GET ABOUT HALF DRUNK ... BUT NEVER DID GET MEAN.
    HE HAD A GOOD WIFE ... THAT WOULD PUT UP WITH HIM ...
WE WOULD GO IN LATE AT NIGHT ... SHE WOULD BE WAITING UP FOR HIM.

VERSE FOUR:

    NOW HER NAME WAS BECKY ... SHE TREATED ME LIKE MY MOTHER ...
I KNOW WE MADE IT ROUGH ON HER ... ME AND MY BIG BROTHER.
    WE WENT TO CALIFORNIA ... SEEKING FOR FORTUNE AND FAME ...
BUT IT WAS JUST WORK WORK WORK ... THAT'S THE NAME OF THE GAME.

VERSE FIVE:

    BECAUSE I WAS SO MUCH YOUNGER ... HE THOUGHT I WAS A KID ...
AND HE WORRIED ABOUT ME ... FOR SOME OF THE THINGS THAT I DID.
    WE NEVER DID MAKE THE NEWS ... ON THE FRONT COVER ...
BUT I'LL NEVER FORGET THE DAYS ... OF ME AND MY BIG BROTHER.

MY BIG BROTHER

VERSE ONE:

WHEN I WAS GROWING UP ... I THOUGHT THERE WAS NO OTHER ...

PERSON ON THIS WHOLE EARTH ... LIKE MY BIG BROTHER.

HE WAS SIX YEARS OLDER THAN ME ... HIS NAME WAS HENRY.

NOW HE COULD GET MEAN ... BUT MOST OF THE TIME FRIENDLY.

VERSE TWO:

WHEN I WAS SIXTEEN ... HE GOT ME A JOB WHERE HE WORKED ... IT PUT A LOT OF PRESSURE ON HIM ... HE WORRIED I MIGHT GET HURT.

WE ALWAYS GOT PAID ON FRIDAY ... THAT WAS OUR NIGHT ...

HE TAUGHT ME HOW TO DRINK ... I ALREADY KNEW HOW TO FIGHT.

VERSE THREE:

WE'D GO OUT TO THE BARS ... AND PLAY THE PINBALL MACHINES ...

WE WOULD GET ABOUT HALF DRUNK ... BUT NEVER DID GET MEAN.

HE HAD A GOOD WIFE ... THAT WOULD PUT UP WITH HIM ...

WE WOULD GO IN LATE AT NIGHT ... SHE WOULD BE WAITING UP FOR HIM.

VERSE FOUR:

NOW HER NAME WAS BECKY ... SHE TREATED ME LIKE MY MOTHER ...

I KNOW WE MADE IT ROUGH ON HER ... ME AND MY BIG BROTHER.

WE WENT TO CALIFORNIA ... SEEKING FOR FORTUNE AND FAME ... BUT IT WAS JUST WORK WORK WORK ... THAT'S THE NAME OF THE GAME.

VERSE FIVE:

BECAUSE I WAS SO MUCH YOUNGER ... HE THOUGHT I WAS A KID ... AND HE WORRIED ABOUT ME ... FOR SOME OF THE THINGS THAT I DID.

WE NEVER DID MAKE THE NEWS ... ON THE FRONT COVER ...

BUT I'LL NEVER FORGET THE DAYS ... OF ME AND MY BIG BROTHER.

MY DADDY SAID SON

VERSE ONE:

   I WAS SITTIN' AT HOME ... A WATCHING T.V. ...
THEY KNOCKED ON THE DOOR ... WITH A WARRANT FOR ME.
   THEY SAID I ROBBED A MAN ... OVER IN TENNESSEE.
BUT I WAS AS INNOCENT ... AS I COULD BE.

VERSE TWO:

   THEY TOOK ME TO JAIL ... FOR SUMPTIN' I DID'NT DO ...
IT GOES TO SHOW YOU ... WHAT A MAN HAS TO GO THRU.
   WHEN I WENT TO COURT ... THE JUDGE DID'NT GRIN ...
WHEN HE FOUND OUT ... THEY HAD THE WRONG MAN.

CHORUS:

   MY DADDY SAID SON ... TRY TO LIVE RIGHT ...
BUT DON'T EVER RUN ... IF YOU HAVE TO FIGHT.
   DON'T LOOK FOR TROUBLE ... BUT IF IT COMES TO YOU ...
BE OBLIGATED ... TO SEE IT THROUGH.

VERSE THREE:

   MY DADDY SAID SON ... I'M SO PROUD OF YOU ...
FOR NOT DOING THE THINGS ... THEY SAY YOU DO.
   YOU'RE GONNA FIND OUT ... BAD TIMES WILL DECLINE ...
WHEN YOU'RE LIVING RIGHT ... YOU'LL WIN EVERYTIME.

VERSE FOUR:

   PEOPLE STOP AND THINK ... BEFORE YOU DO WHAT YOU DO ...
THEN YOU'LL FIND OUT ... WHAT MY DADDY SAID WAS TRUE.
   THAT IF YOU DO WRONG ... YOU'LL HAVE TO EAT CROW ...
I CAN STILL HEAR DADDY SAY ... I TOLD YOU SO.

   .... SING CHORUS AGAIN ....

MY DYING DAY

VERSE ONE:

    I WAS WALKING THROUGH ... AN OLD CEMETARY ONE DAY ...
AND I NOTICED SOME OF THE WRITTINGS ... THERE ON DISPLAY.
    THEN I STARTED TO WONDER ... WHAT MINE MIGHT SAY ...
WHEN I'VE LAYED DOWN FOR THE LAST TIME ... IN MY GRAVE.

VERSE TWO:

    IT PUT MY MIND TO THINKING ... WHEN THIS TIME DOES
COME ...
WILL I BE READY FOR THE JUDGEMENT ... FOR THINGS I HAVE DONE.
    I FELL DOWN ON MY KNEES ... AND SAID A LITTLE PRAYER ...
PLEASE LORD HAVE MERCY ON ME ... WHEN I DO GET THERE.

CHORUS:

    I KNOW MY DYING DAY ... WILL SOMEDAY COME MY WAY ...
AND I AM SO CONCERNED ... ABOUT WHAT PEOPLE MIGHT SAY.
    WHEN IT COMES TO MY REPUTATION ... I WANT TO
PROTECT IT ...
I KNOW MY DYING DAY WILL COME ... WHEN I LEAST EXPECT IT.

VERSE THREE:

    AS I WALKED A LITTLE FURTHER ... I WAS SUPRISED AT WHAT
I READ ...
I COULD'NT HOLD THE TEARS ... BECAUSE OF WHAT ONE TOMBSTONE
SAID.
    HERE LIES THE ONE I LOVED ... BUT GOD CALLED HER AWAY ...
AND NOW ALL I HAVE TO LIVE FOR ... IS MY DYING DAY.

VERSE FOUR:

    THESE WORDS TAUNTED ME ... BECAUSE I KNOW THE
FEELING ...
WHEN SOMEONE HAS TO DIE ... BECAUSE THERE WAS NO HEALING.
    I ASK MYSELF DID THEY SUFFER ... OR DID THEY DIE IN THEIR
SLEEP ...
WAS IT A WEALTHY PERSON ... OR DID THEY HAVE TO LIVE CHEAP.

VERSE FIVE:

THERE ARE MANY THINGS PEOPLE WONDER ... WHEN SOMEONE DIES ...

SO HELP OTHERS ALONG LIFE'S WAY ... AND DON'T EVEN ASK WHY. THEN WHEN THEY READ YOUR TOMBSTONE ... MAYBE THEY'LL DISCOVER ...

YOU DID'NT ALWAYS THINK OF YOURSELF ... YOU HELPED MANY OTHERS.

CHORUS:

I KNOW MY DYING DAY ... WILL SOMEDAY COME MY WAY ...

AND I AM SO CONCERNED ... ABOUT WHAT PEOPLE MIGHT SAY. WHEN IT COMES TO MY REPUTATION ... I WANT TO PROTECT IT ...

I KNOW MY DYING DAY WILL COME ... WHEN I LEAST EXPECT IT.

MY FIRST JOB

VERSE ONE:
    MY FIRST JOB ... WAS IN A PAPER PACKAGING PLANT ...
I WAS FIFTEEN ... AND I THOUGHT I WAS A MAN.
    IT WAS AT CELLU PRODUCTS ... OUT ON CLINTON STREET...
AND IT SURE WAS'NT AS EASY ... AS I THOUGHT IT WOULD BE.

VERSE TWO:
    I WAS RUNNING PAPER WADDING ...THRU A CRAPING MACHINE ...
IT WAS'NT MUCH OF A START ... FOR A TEENAGERS DREAM.
    I ALSO UNLOADED PAPER ROLLS ... FROM A BIG BOX CAR ...
AND THEN BY QUITTING TIME ... I WAS ALWAYS PRETTY TIRED.

VERSE THREE:
    MY FIRST DAY SURE WAS'NT LIKE ... MY EVERYDAY LIFE ...
BUT I KNEW IT WAS SOMETHING ... THAT WOULD GET ME BY.
    I SURE HAD NO TROUBLE ... TO GO TO SLEEP AT NIGHT ...
FOR EVERY BONE IN MY BODY ... WAS REALLY SORE AND TIGHT.

CHORUS:
    THE NEXT DAY I WAS READY ... TO GET W ITH IT AGAIN ...
HOPING IT WOULD BE BETTER ... THAN THE FIRST DAY HAD BEEN.
    I HAD LEARNED A WHOLE LOT ... ABOUT WHAT I WAS DOING ...
BUT I HAD NO WAY OF KNOWING ... JUST WHERE I WAS GOING.

VERSE FOUR:
    CAUSE AFTER A WEEK ... THEY FOUND OUT ABOUT MY AGE ...
AND WHEN THEY LAID ME OFF ... THAT TURNED ANOTHER PAGE.
    BUT THEM OLD MEMORIES ... ARE STILL WITH ME YET ...
AND MY FIRST JOB IS ONE JOB ... I'LL NEVER FORGET.

MY GOAT GOT GONE

THERE WAS A TIME ... I THOUGHT LIFE WAS A JOKE ...
I WENT OUT AND BOUGHT ME ... A LITTLE NANNY GOAT.
SHE GAVE GOOD MILK ... AND WAS A WONDERFUL PET ...
BUT MY GOAT GOT GONE... AND I AIN'T FOUND HER YET.

I SEARCHED AND I SEARCHED ... BUT TO NO AVAIL ...
IF ANYONE KNEW WHERE SHE WAS ... THEY WOULD'NT TELL.
I REALLY MISSED MY GOAT ... I FELT SO ALL ALONE ...
IT WAS A BAD TIME OF MY LIFE ... WHEN MY GOAT GOT GONE.

I WON'T GET ANOTHER GOAT ... AND LET THAT HAPPEN AGAIN ...
CAUSE THE DAY I LOST MY GOAT ... I LOST MY BEST FRIEND.
MY WORLD FELT LIKE ... IT WAS HIT BY A CYCLONE ...
THE DAY THAT I LEARNED ... THAT MY GOAT WAS GONE.

THERE'S AN OLD SAYING ... THAT USE TO BE A JOKE ...
WATCH THIS I KNOW HOW ... TO GET THEIR GOAT.
WHEN IT BECAME REALITY... IT CUT ME TO THE BONE ...
BECAUSE IT'S A SAD LIFE ... WHEN YOUR GOAT GETS GONE.

I WOULD LAY AWAKE ... ALMOST FROM DARK TO DAWN ...
PRAYING THAT MY GOAT ... WOULD FIND IT'S WAY HOME.
I WAS FEELING GOOD ONE MORNING ... AFTER I AWOKE ...
I LOOKED OUT MY WINDOW ... AND THERE STOOD MY GOAT.

MY HEART'S DONE AND GONE

VERSE ONE :

MY HEART HAS BEEN BROKEN ... SO MANY TIMES BEFORE ...
WE PROMISED NOT TO GO THERE ... AND DO THAT ANYMORE.

BUT MY EYES PULLED A TRICK ... AND MY HEART WAS DECIEVED ...
AND I FOUND MYSELF CAUGHT ... IN ANOTHER WEB THAT YOU
WEAVED.

VERSE TWO :

YOU WERE LIKE A SPIDER ... YOU BUILT A WEB AROUND ME ...
AND I WAS YOUR PREY ... I WAS HELPLESS AS COULD BE.

BUT I FINALLY GOT FREE ... AND ESCAPED FROM YOUR SNARE ...
I'M NO LONGER YOUR VICTOM ... SINCE I FOUND OUT YOU DON'T
CARE.

CHORUS :

I SAID I WOULD'NT GO BACK TO ... WHERE I'VE ALREADY BEEN ...
I SWORE I'D NEVER GET TANGLED UP ... LIKE I DID BACK THEN.

I WAS DOING ALRIGHT ... AND MY HEART WAS ON THE MEND ...
UH ! OH ! ... UH ! OH ! ... UH ! OH ! ... MY HEART'S DONE AND GONE
AND DONE IT AGAIN. .

VERSE THREE :

I MUST BE PLAIN STUPID ... AND DON'T KNOW WHAT I'M
THINKING OF ...
EVERYTIME I MEET SOMEONE NEW ... I SEEM TO FALL IN LOVE.

I'VE DONE THIS MANY TIMES ... AND IT'S COSTED ME A LOT ...
BUT ALL THE GIRLS OF MY PAST ... I SEEM TO HAVE FORGOT.

CHORUS :

I SAID I WOULD'NT GO BACK TO ... WHERE I'VE ALREADY BEEN ...
I SWORE I'D NEVER GET TANGLED UP ... LIKE I DID BACK THEN.

I WAS DOING ALRIGHT ... AND MY HEART WAS ON THE MEND ...
UH ! OH ! ... UH ! OH ! ... UH ! OH ! ... MY HEART'S DONE AND GONE
AND DONE IT AGAIN.

MY MOMMA SAID

CHORUS:
> MY MOMMA SAID SON ... TRY TO LIVE RIGHT ...
> BUT DON'T EVER RUN ... IF YOU HAVE TO FIGHT.
> DON'T LOOK FOR TROUBLE ... BUT IF IT COMES TO YOU ...
> YOU'RE ALWAYS OBLIGATED ... TO SEE IT THROUGH.

VERSE ONE:
> I GOT PUT IN JAIL ... FOR SOMETHING I DID'NT DO ...
> IT GOES TO SHOW YOU WHAT ... MY MOMMA SAID WAS TRUE.
> CAUSE WHEN I WENT TO COURT ... THE JUDGE DID'NT GRIN ...
> WHEN THEY FOUND OUT ... THEY HAD THE WRONG MAN.

VERSE TWO:
> MY MOMMA SAID SON ... I'M SO PROUD OF YOU ...
> FOR NOT DOING THE THINGS ... THAT THEY SAY YOU DO.
> YOU'RE GONNA FIND OUT ... THAT IN DUE TIME ...
> WHEN YOU'RE LIVING RIGHT ... YOU'LL WIN EVERYTIME.

VERSE THREE:
> ALWAYS BE HONEST ... STAND UP FOR WHAT'S RIGHT ...
> AND TRY NOT TO STAY OUT ... TOO LATE AT NIGHT.
> JUST LET FOLKS KNOW ... YOU'RE A VERY FIRM MAN ...
> AND YOU CAN HANDLE WHATEVER ... COMES HAND TO HAND.

VERSE FOUR:
> PEOPLE STOP AND THINK ... BEFORE YOU DO WHAT YOU DO ...
> THEN YOU'LL FIND OUT ... WHAT MY MOMMA SAID IS TRUE.
> THAT IF YOU DO WRONG ... YOU'LL HAVE TO EAT CROW ...
> I CAN STILL HEAR MY MOMMA SAY ... I TOLD YOU SO.

..... SING CHORUS .....

NORTH CAROLINA THAT IS

VERSE ONE:
   NOW I COME FROM THE NORTH ... NORTH CAROLINA THAT IS ...
AND NO STATE IN THE UNION ... IS AS WONDERFUL AS THIS.
   BORN IN RANDOLPH COUNTY ... THE CENTER OF THE STATE ...
IT WAS ALSO GOD GIVEN ... AND IT'S MY HOME PLACE.

VERSE TWO:
   AWAY OUT IN THE COUNTRY ... IS WHERE I COME FROM ...
AND THERE'S NOT VERY MUCH THERE ... THAT I HAVE'NT DONE.
   THERE'S PLENTY OF WORK ... AND THE STARS ARE BRIGHTER ...
THE TREES ARE TALLER ... AND THE GRASS IS GREENER.

VERSE THREE:
   THE NEIGHBORS KNOW EACH OTHER ... AND WILLING TO
   SHARE ...
YOU WILL FIND NO GREEDINESS ... IN THE PEOPLE THERE.
   THEY WOULD WALK FOR MILES ... IF THEY HAD TO ...
AND IF YOU NEEDED HELP ... THEY WOULD COME TO YOU.

VERSE FOUR:
   THERE IS NO PLACE ON EARTH ... AS IT IS IN THE NORTH ...
AND WE'RE NORTH CAROLINIANS ... SO DON'T CUT US SHORT.
   WE KNOW WHAT LOVE IS ... AND WE LOVE ONE ANOTHER ...
WE TREAT EACH OTHER CLOSER ...THAN SISTERS AND BROTHERS.

CHORUS:
   NORTH CAROLINA IS ... WHERE I'M GLAD TO CALL MY HOME ...
UNLESS YOU'RE LOOKING FOR TROUBLE ... BETTER LEAVE US ALONE.
   IF WE CAN'T HELP WE WON'T HURT... UNLESS YOU RUB IT IN ...
CAUSE WE'RE FROM THE NORTH ... NORTH CAROLINA THAT IS.

NOTHING TO DO

VERSE ONE:

SOMETIMES I SIT AROUND MY HOUSE ... WITH NOTHING TO DO ...

I GET SO BORED AT TIMES ... I CAN'T HELP FOR FEELING BLUE.

I GO AND SAT DOWN ON THE SOFA ... AND TURN ON MY TV ...

I CAN'T FIND ANYTHING ... THAT IS FITTING FOR ME TO SEE.

VERSE TWO:

I TURN THE TELESION OFF ... AND GET ON THE TELEPHONE ...

IT'S ANOTHER LET DOWN ... I CAN'T CATCH NO ONE AT HOME.

SOMETIMES IT GOES LIKE THIS ... THE WHOLE DAY THROUGH ...

I JUST SIT AND TWITTLE MY THUMBS ... WITH NOTHING TO DO.

CHORUS:

YOU MIGHT THINK IT WOULD BE FUN ... TO HAVE NOTHING TO DO ...

BUT IT WILL MAKE A TOTAL WRECK ... COMPLETELY OUT OF YOU.

IF YOU JUST LAY AROUND ... IT WILL WORK ON YOUR BRAIN ...

AND THE FIRST THING YOU KNOW ... IT WILL DRIVE YOU INSANE.

VERSE THREE:

I PICK UP MY GUITAR ... AND START PLAYING A SONG ...

THERE'S NO ONE TO LISTEN ... WHERE HAS EVERYONE GONE.

I SOON GET TIRED ... PUT MY GUITAR BACK IN THE CASE ...

WHEN YOU HAVE NOTHING TO DO ... IT'S A COMPLETE WASTE.

VERSE FOUR:

I GET TIRED OF MY GUITAR, TELEVSION AND TELEPHONE ...

SO I GO TO MY COMPUTER ... AND START TO WRITE ME A SONG.

JUST WHEN THINGS ARE GOING GOOD ... I GIVE YOU A CLUE ...

IT'S A VERY LONESOME LIFE ... WHEN YOU HAVE NOTHING TO DO.

CHORUS:
     YOU MIGHT THINK IT WOULD BE FUN ... TO HAVE NOTHING
     TO DO ...
BUT IT WILL MAKE A TOTAL WRECK ... COMPLETELY OUT OF YOU.
     IF YOU JUST LAY AROUND ... IT WILL WORK ON YOUR BRAIN ...
AND THE FIRST THING YOU KNOW ... IT WILL DRIVE YOU INSANE.

NOWHERE TO GO

VERSE ONE:

HE HEARD IT SO MANY TIMES ... IT WAS TOO MUCH TO INCLINE ...

OF HOW BAD LIFE WOULD GET ... BEFORE THE END OF TIME.

HE DID'NT KNOW WHAT TO DO ... AND HE HAD NO WHERE TO GO ...

AND SO HE FOUND HIMSELF A LIVING ... DOWN ON SKID ROW.

VERSE TWO:

SOMEONE GAVE HIM A GUITAR ... AND HE LOVED THAT OLD THING ...

AND HE LEARNED HOW TO PLAY ... AND HE LEARNED HOW TO SING.

HE PLAYED FOR EVERYONE ... HE PLANTED SEEDS THAT WOULD GROW ...

AND EVERYONE CALLED HIM ... THE KING OF SKID ROW.

CHORUS:

THEY CALLED HIM THE KING ... THE KING OF SKID ROW ...

YOU COULD HEAR HIM PLAYING... EVERYWHERE HE WOULD GO.

BUT FORTUNE AND FAME ... MADE HIM A TO WELL KNOWN JOE ...

AND SO HE WAS ALWAYS CONFUSED ... HE HAD NOWHERE TO GO.

VERSE THREE:

THEN HE STARTED PLAYING IN CLUBS ... AND HONKY TONKS AROUND ...

AND THE PEOPLE SEEMED TO LIKE ... HOW HIS MUSIC SOUND.

SO HE STARTED HIM A BAND ... AND THE REST OF IT YOU KNOW ...

HE WENT ALL THE WAY FROM SKID ROW ... TO NASHVILLE'S MUSIC ROW.

VERSE FOUR:

IT'S A LONG LONG WAYS ... FROM SKID ROW TO MUSIC ROW ...

THE LIGHTS ARE MORE BRIGHTER THERE .. WHERE THE GLAMOUR FLOWS.

NO ONE WOULD BELIEVE ... OR COULD EVER POSSIBLY
KNOW ...
HOW FAR THE KING OF SKID ROW WENT ... WITH NOWHERE TO GO.

CHORUS:
CHORUS:
THEY CALLED HIM THE KING ... THE KING OF SKID ROW ...
YOU COULD HEAR HIM PLAYING... EVERYWHERE HE WOULD GO.
BUT FORTUNE AND FAME ... MADE HIM A TOO WELL KNOWN
JOE ...
AND SO HE WAS ALWAYS CONFUSED ... HE HAD NOWHERE TO GO.

OH WHAT I'D GIVE TO GO

VERSE ONE:

OH WHAT I'D GIVE TO GO ... BACK ON THE ROAD AGAIN ... WHERE HARDSHIPS AND HAPPINESS ... NEVER HAS NO ENDS.

IT'S NEVER THE SAME TRIP ... NO MATTER WHERE YOU GO ... OH WHAT I'D GIVE TO GO ... BACK ON THE ROAD AGAIN ONCE MORE.

VERSE TWO:

I USED TO DRIVE A TRUCK ... WHEN I WAS IN MY PRIME ... AND I DID THE JOB RIGHT ... I DELIVERED THE LOADS ON TIME.

AND THERE'S NOT MANY PLACES ... THAT I HAVE'NT BEEN ... OH WHAT I'D GIVE TO GO ... BACK ON THE ROAD AGAIN.

CHORUS:

BACK ON THE ROAD AGAIN ... BACK ON THE ROAD AGAIN ... OH WHAT I'D GIVE TO GO ... BACK ON THE ROAD AGAIN.

VERSE THREE:

THE HIGHWAY WAS MY HOME ... TRUCKERS WAS MY FRIEND ... WHEN SOMEONE WAS IN NEED ... WE WOULD OFFER THEM A HAND.

WE WERE ALL ONE BIG FAMILY ... WE WERE JUST LIKE KIN ... AND OH WHAT I'D GIVE TO GO ... BACK ON THE ROAD AGAIN.

VERSE FOUR:

THE YEARS HAVE SLOWED ME DOWN ... AND I'M ALMOST BLIND... BUT I CAN STILL REMEMBER ... THE LIFE THAT ONCE WAS MINE.

I'LL ALWAYS HAVE THE MEMORIES... OF PLACES I HAVE BEEN ... BUT OH WHAT I'D GIVE TO GO ... BACK ON THE ROAD AGAIN.

CHORUS:

BACK ON THE ROAD AGAIN ... BACK ON THE ROAD AGAIN ... OH WHAT I'D GIVE TO GO ... BACK ON THE ROAD AGAIN

OLD AND WORN OUT

VERSE ONE:
     I'M JUST SITTING HERE ... IN THIS OLD AND WORN OUT CHAIR ...
THINKING ABOUT THE THINGS ... I HAVE DONE OVER THE YEARS.
     I NEVER HAD MUCH MONEY ... BUT MONEY AIN'T
EVERYTHING ...
BECAUSE I'VE STILL ENJOYED THE THINGS ... THAT LIFE HAS TO
BRING..

VERSE TWO:
     I'VE NEVER HAD THE LUXURY ... OF AN EASY GOING LIFE ...
AND IT SEEMS THINGS GOT EVEN WORSE ... AFTER I LOST MY WIFE.
     AND THE BED THAT I SLEEP IN ... IS GETTING OLD AND WORN
OUT ...
BUT IT STILL SLEEPS GOOD ... BECAUSE IT'S BUILT PRETTY STOUT.

SING CHORUS:

VERSE THREE:
     THAT OLD CAR THAT I DRIVE ... SOMETIMES SPITS AND SPOUT ...
BUT IT HAS BEEN A GOOD ONE ... BUT NOW IT'S OLD AND WORN OUT.
     THAT'S THE WAY IT GOES ... FOR EVERYTHING HERE ON
EARTH ...
IT'S A BATTLE YOU HAVE TO FIGHT ... UNTIL DEATH FROM YOUR
BIRTH.

VERSE FOUR:
     I WALKED INTO WORK ONE DAY ... THEY SAID THEY HAD TO
LET ME GO ...
YOU HAVE BEEN HERE A LONG TIME ... BUT NOW YOU'RE OLD AND
SLOW.
     I WONDER WHEN I DIE ... AND THEY PUT ME IN THE GROUND ...
WILL I BE TOO OLD AND WORN OUT ... FOR THE GROUND TO HOLD
ME DOWN.

VERSE FIVE:

NOW I'VE DONE A LOT OF CRAZY THINGS ... BEFORE I GOT
TOO OLD ...
AND THERE'S A LOT OF THOSE THINGS ... THAT HAS NEVER BEEN
TOLD.
BUT I'LL TAKE THEM WITH ME ... ALL THE WAY TO THE
GRAVE ...
CAUSE I'M TOO OLD AND WORN OUT ... FOR THEM TO MATTER
ANYWAY.

CHORUS:

I MAY BE GETTING OLD NOW ... THAT'S NOT WHAT IT'S ALL
ABOUT ...
IT'S HOW I LIVED MY LIFE ... WHILE STRUGGLING HERE WITHOUT.
SO DON'T LET ANYONE TELL YOU ... THAT YOU DONE GOT
TOO OLD ...
JUST GET UP THERE OUT OF THAT CHAIR ... AND LET YOURSELF GO.

OLD BUT SILL YOUNG

VERSE ONE:

    HE LOOKED SO YOUNG ... COMPARED TO HIS AGE ...

HE WAS THE QUITE TYPE ... NEVER HAD TOO MUCH TO SAY.

    HE WAS OLDER THAN ME ... BUT I CALLED HIM YOUNG FELLOW ...

AND HE CALLED ME OLD MAN ... WITH A VOICE SO MELLOW.

VERSE TWO:

    HE WAS A KIND MAN ... AND HIS NAME WAS BODENHIEMER ...

AND HE GOT AROUND REAL GOOD ... TO BE AN OLDTIMER.

    WE WOULD ALWAYS SPEAK ... AND SHAKE EACH OTHERS HAND ...

AND HE WOULD ALWAYS SAY ... WHAT 'LL YOU SAY OLD MAN.

CHORUS:

    HE WAS OLD BUT STILL YOUNG ... AND I BELIEVE HE'S HAD HIS FUN ...

HE DON'T SEEM TO REGRET ... MUCH OF THE STUFF THAT HE HAS DONE.

    I WOULD LIKE TO THINK ... THAT MY HEART WOULD BEAT LIKE A DRUM ...

AND I WOULD STILL FEEL ... THAT I AM OLD BUT STILL YOUNG.

VERSE THREE:

    HIS WIFE WAS IN THE REHAB CENTER ... AND SO WAS MINE ...

WE WOULD SEE EACH OTHER IN THE HALLWAY ... FROM TIME TO TIME.

    WE KNEW WHAT EACH OTHER ... WAS HAVING TO GO THROUGH ...

SO WE WOULD CHEER EACH OTHER UP ... IN WHATEVER WE COULD DO.

VERSE FOUR:

    HE MIGHT BE OLD IN HIS AGE ... BUT WAS YOUNG IN HIS HEART ...

WHEN IT CAME TO BEING HAPPY ... HE KNEW HOW TO PLAY THE PART.
    WHEN HE TALKED OF THE THINGS ... THAT HE HAD ONCE DONE ...
YOU COULD TELL BY THE WAY HE TALKED ... HE WAS OLD BUT STILL YOUNG.

CHORUS:
    HE WAS OLD BUT STILL YOUNG ... AND I BELIEVE HE'S HAD HIS FUN ...
HE DON'T SEEM TO REGRET ... MUCH OF THE STUFF THAT HE HAS DONE.
    I WOULD LIKE TO THINK ... THAT MY HEART WOULD BEAT LIKE A DRUM ...
AND I WOULD STILL FEEL ... THAT I AM OLD BUT STILL YOUNG.

OLD MEMORIES COMES ALIVE

VERSE ONE:

WHEN I SING THE PAST RINGS ... IT PUTS MY EMOTIONS IN DRIVE ...
I'LL NEVER FORGET THINGS I'VE DONE ... SINCE I WAS AROUND FIVE.
THINGS ARE NOT LIKE IT WAS THEN ... WHEN MOMMA TANNED MY HIDE ..
SOMETIMES I STILL RELIVE THE PAST ... OLD MEMORIES COMES ALIVE.

VERSE TWO:

WHEN MOMMA SAID TO DO THIS ... I KNEW I HAD BETTER DO THAT ...
CAUSE THE SWITCH THAT SHE WOULD USE ... FELT LIKE A BASEBALL BAT.
SHE DID'NT DO IT TO BE MEAN ... SHE TAUGHT ME TO BE DIGNIFIED ...
IT'S FUNNY NOW WHEN I THINK BACK ... AND OLD MEMORIES COMES ALIVE.

CHORUS:

OLD MEMORIES ARE A GOOD THING ... STORED UP IN YOUR MIND ...
WHEN YOU FACE PROBLEMS ... LET YOUR THOUGHTS GO BACK IN TIME.
DON'T DO THE THINGS YOU DID THEN ...YOU WERE LUCKY TO SURVIVE ...
IT'S NICE TO KNOW YOU LEARNED WHEN ... OLD MEMORIES COMES ALIVE

VERSE THREE:

WHEN OLD MEMORIES COMES ALIVE ... IT COMES AS NO SURPISE ...
BUT IT'S NOT LIKE IT WAS BACK THEN ... SOMETIMES I SIT AND CRY.

MY MOMMA HAD A HARD TIME ... AFTER MY DADDY HAD
DIED ...
SHE RAISED A HOUSE FULL OF KIDS ... SHE WORKED HARD TO
SURVIVE.

VERSE FOUR:
WHEN THE PRESENT SEEMS TO BE OVER ...THE PAST IS JUST
BEHIND ...
THE FUTURE CAN BE BRIGHTER ... IF YOU LOOK AT WHAT'S IN YOUR
MIND.
LET THE BAD THINGS STAY IN THE PAST ... GOOD THINGS
WILL ARRIVE ...
YOU'LL HAVE MORE TO LIVE FOR ... WHEN OLD MEMORIES COMES
ALIVE.

CHORUS:
OLD MEMORIES ARE A GOOD THING ... STORED UP IN YOUR
MIND ...
WHEN YOU FACE PROBLEMS ... LET YOUR THOUGHTS GO BACK IN
TIME.
DON'T DO THE THINGS YOU DID THEN ...YOU WERE LUCKY
TO SURVIVE ...
IT'S NICE TO KNOW YOU LEARNED WHEN ... OLD MEMORIES COMES
ALIVE.

OLDTIME SLIPPIN' AND SLIDIN' BLUES

VERSE ONE:
> EVERY MORNING WHEN I GET UP ... THE FIRST THING THAT I DO ...

IS SLIDE ON MY PANTS ... AND SLIP INTO MY SHOES.
> THEN I SLIP TO THE KITCHEN ... AND SLIDE THRU THE NEWS.

I ALWAYS HAVE THEM OLDTIME ... SLIPPING AND SLIDING BLUES.

VERSE TWO:
> THEN I SLIP ME A SIP ... OF SOME OLD ICE COLD DRINK ...

THEN I POUR IT OUT AND WATCH IT... SLIDE DOWN THE SINK.
> THEN I SLIP AWAY AND SLIDE ... INTO THE OTHER ROOM ...

AND I FEEL THEM OLDTIME ... SLIPPIN' AND SLIDIN' BLUES.

VERSE THREE:
> SOMETIMES MY MIND SLIPS BACK ...TO WHEN I WAS YOUNG ...

THEN I THINK ABOUT SOME ... OF THE THINGS THAT I HAVE DONE.
> SOMETHINGS SLIDES THRU MY MIND ... BUT IT'S NO USE ...

I'LL ALWAYS HAVE OLDTIME ... SLIPPIN' AND SLIDIN' BLUES.

VERSE FOUR:
> IF YOU THINK ABOUT SLIPPIN' AROUND ... DON'T GET CONFUSED...

ANYTIME YOU SLIP AND SLIDE ... MEMORIES WILL FOLLOW YOU.
> IF YOU TRY TO SLIDE BACK ... YOU'LL ONLY LIGHT THE FUSE ...

YOU'LL WIND UP WITH OLDTIME ... SLIPPIN' AND SLIDIN' BLUES.

CHORUS:
> WHEN YOU GET THEM OLDTIME ... SLIPPIN' AND SLIDIN' BLUES...

YOU MIGHT THINK YOU KNOW IT ALL ... BUT DON'T GET CONFUSED.
> YOU SHOULD SLOW DOWN AND LIVE ... AND WATCH WHAT YOU DO ...

THEN YOU CAN ENJOY THEM OLDTIME ... SLIPPIN' AND SLIDIN' BLUES.

ON AN OLD RUGGED CROSS

VERSE ONE:

HE WAS PUT ON MOUNT CALVARY ... ON AN OLD RUGGED CROSS ...

WHERE HE GAVE UP HIS EARTHLY LIFE ... FOR THEM THAT WAS LOST.

HE SAID IT IS FINISHED ... THE PLAN OF SALVATION WAS FULFILLED...

WHEN HE HUNG HIS HEAD IN SILENCE ... THERE ON CALVARY'S HILL.

VERSE TWO:

THEY CONDEMNED HIM FOR LOVE ... BEFORE THE PEOPLE THAT DAY ...

THEY HAD NO WAY OF KNOWING ... THAT HE WAS PREPARING THE WAY.

THE ONLY WAY TO SALVATION ... COULD ONLY BE BY HIS BLOOD ...

SO THEY CHOSE TO MOCK HIM ... AND THEY CRUCIFIED THE SON .

CHORUS:

THEY LOOKED AT HIM AND SAW ... THE EXPRESSION ON HIS FACE ...

HE SAID YOU MUST BELIEVE IN ... WHAT'S HAPPENING HERE TODAY.

AND IT IS ALL BECAUSE OF ... MY FATHER'S AMAZING GRACE ...

THAT ON AN OLD RUGGED CROSS ... GOD'S SON TOOK YOUR PLACE.

VERSE THREE:

THEY DID'NT TAKE HIS LIFE ... BUT HE GAVE IT ON HIS OWN ...

SO THAT THROUGH HIS PRECIOUS BLOOD ... WE COULD BE REBORN.

THEY LAUGHED AT HIM ... WHEN HE CLAIMED TO BE GOD'S SON ...

WHEN IT WAS OVER THEY WERE SORRY ... FOR WHAT THEY HAD DONE.

VERSE FOUR:

    THEY TOOK HIM FROM THE CROSS ... AND PUT HIM IN A TOMB ...

MANY OF THEM HEARD HIM SAYING ... HE WOULD RETURN TO THEM SOON.

    THEN AFTER THREE DAYS ... HE WAS SEEN BY MANY WHERE HE TROD ...

AND ALL THE PEOPLE KNEW ... THAT HE REALLY WAS THE SON OF GOD.

CHORUS:

    CHORUS:

    THEY LOOKED AT HIM AND SAW... THE EXPRESSION ON HIS FACE ...

HE SAID YOU MUST BELIEVE IN ... WHAT'S HAPPENING HERE TODAY.

    AND IT IS ALL BECAUSE OF ... MY FATHER'S AMAZING GRACE ...

THAT ON AN OLD RUGGED CROSS... GOD'S SON TOOK YOUR PLACE.

ONE DAY IN OUR SHOES

VERSE ONE:
>THINGS ARE SO DIFFERENT ... COMPARED TO DAYS OF OLD ...
WHEN KIDS WOULD LISTEN ... TO WHAT THEY WERE TOLD.
>NOW THEY DO AS THEY PLEASE ... GETTING EVERYTHING NEW ...
THESE KIDS WOULD'NT LAST ... ONE DAY IN OUR SHOES.

VERSE TWO:
>IF THEY DON'T GET WHAT THEY WANT ...THEY THROW A FIT ...
BUT IF WE GOT ANYTHING ... WE HAD TO WORK FOR IT.
>AND NOW THEY TELL ... THEIR PARENTS WHAT TO DO ...
THEY SURE WOULD'NT LAST ... ONE DAY IN OUR SHOES.

VERSE THREE:
>THE THINGS THAT WE GOT ... WAS'NT EASY TO COME BY ...
WE WORKED ALL DAY IN THE FIELDS ... AND WE DID'NT CRY.
>OF COURSE DAYS ARE NOT ... LIKE THEY WERE BEFORE ...
IT WOULD KILL THESE KIDS TO WEAR ...THE SHOES THAT WE WORE.

VERSE FOUR:
>WE WERE PROUD TO WORK ... FOR THE FOOD ON OUR TABLE ...
BUT THE KIDS TODAY THINKS ... IT WAS SOME KIND OF A FABLE.
>THEY THINK THAT EVERYTHING ...THEY GET HAS TO BE NEW...
THEY SURE WOULD'NT HAVE LASTED ... ONE DAY IN OUR SHOES.

CHORUS:
>I'VE THOUGHT MANY TIMES ... OF THE SHOES THAT I WORE ...
AND THE THINGS I HAD TO GO THRU... WHEN MY FEET GOT SORE.
>WALKING MILES TO SEE ... A SICK FRIEND WITH THE FLU ...
THE KIDS OF TODAY WOULD'NT LAST ... ONE DAY IN OUR SHOES.

OPEN UP YOUR HEART

VERSE ONE:
  I ONCE HEARD OF A MAN ... THAT MADE A SACRIFICE ...
THAT THRU HIS BLOOD ... WE COULD HAVE ETERNAL LIFE.
  BUT YOU MUST BELIEVE ... AND THEN REPENT ...
AND OPEN UP YOUR HEART ... AND LET HIM COME IN.

VERSE TWO:
  HIS SPIRIT WILL NOT ALWAYS ... STRIVE WITH MAN ...
THOSE ARE THE WORDS ... OF A VERY PRECIOUS FRIEND.
  SO COME TO HIM NOW ... WHILE YOU STILL CAN ...
JUST OPEN UP YOUR HEART ... AND LET HIM COME IN.

CHORUS:
  OPEN UP YOUR HEART ... AND LET HIM COME IN ...
DON'T MAKE HIM WAIT ... HE MAY NOT KNOCK AGAIN.
  NOW IS THE TIME ... TO MAKE YOUR AMENDS ...
SO OPEN UP YOUR HEART ... AND LET HIM COME IN.

VERSE THREE:
  DRINK FROM THIS FOUNTAIN ... YOU WILL SURELY WIN...
BECAUSE YOU WILL NEVER ... EVER THRIST AGAIN.
  HE WILL CLEANSE YOUR SOUL ... TAKE AWAY YOUR SIN ...
IF YOU'LL OPEN UP YOUR HEART ... AND LET HIM COME IN.

VERSE FOUR:
  DON'T HARDEN YOUR HEART... TO NOT LET HIM COME IN ...
YOU'LL FIND ALL THAT HE ASK ... IS FOR ALL TO REPENT.
  DON'T TURN HIM AWAY ... BECAUSE HE IS YOUR FRIEND ...
JUST OPEN UP YOUR HEART ... AND LET HIM COME IN.

PICKIN' UP PICK UPS

VERSE ONE:

I PICKED UP MY GUITAR ... WHEN I PICKED UP THE BLUES ...
IN THE MIDDLE OF THE MORNING ... THINKING OF YOU.
I PICKED A SAD SONG ... THAT HAD A SLOW BEAT ...
AND WHEN I PICKED UP THE SOUND ... IT PUT ME ON MY FEET.

VERSE TWO:

I THOUGHT I WAS ALRIGHT ... DRIVING MY PICK UP TRUCK ...
UNTIL ONE DAY I PICKED UP ... A LITTLE BIT OF BAD LUCK.
I WONDERED WHY BAD TIMES ... ALWAYS PICKED ON ME ...
WHEN I PICKED UP MY GUITAR ... AND WENT TO TENNESSEE.

VERSE THREE:

I PICKED THE WRONG TIME ... TO GO TO MUSIC CITY ...
CAUSE WHEN I GOT THERE ... THE SIGHT WAS'NT PRETTY.
THERE WAS RIP RAFT ... IN THE MUSIC HALL OF FAME ...
IT SHOULD'NT BE THERE ... BUT WAS THERE JUST THE SAME.

VERSE FOUR:

THEIR TYPE OF MUSIC ... DID'NT MATCH WITH MINE ...
THAT'S WHEN I KNEW ... I HAD PICKED THE WRONG TIME.
SO I PICKED UP MY GUITAR ... AND WALKED TO THE DOOR.
AND I WAS HEADED BACK TO WHERE ... I HAD BEEN BEFORE.

CHORUS:

I PICKED UP A HITCH HIKER ... THAT WAS GOING MY WAY ...
SHE LOOKED PRETTY GOOD ... BUT IT WAS'NT MY DAY.
SAID SHE WAS IN TROUBLE ... WHEN SHE GOT IN MY TRUCK ...
I KNEW I'VE DONE IT AGAIN ... BY PICKIN' UP PICK UPS.

ROBERT RO- BEARD-Y

CHORUS:
     IF WE COULD TURN BACK TIME ... AS IT WAS THEN ...
AND WE COULD GO BACK ... TO WHERE IT ALL BEGAN.
     WE WOULD'NT DO THE THINGS ... THAT WE DID THEN ...
IF WE COULD LIVE OUR LIVES ... ALL OVER AGAIN.

VERSE ONE:
     I WOULD EAT IN A RESTURANT ... EVERY NOW AND THEN ...
THERE WAS THIS GUY ... I WOULD SEE TIME AND TIME AGAIN.
     HE ALWAYS HAD A BEARD ... AND A NAME THAT FIT'IM.
AND EVERYBODY CALLED HIM ... ROBERT RO- BEARD-Y.

VERSE: TWO
     HE WORKED DAY AND NIGHT... AND NEVER HAD NOTHING ...
HE WOULD NEVER SAVE HIS MONEY... HE SPENT IT IN A HURRY.
     HE ALWAYS STAYED BUSY ... GETTING NOTHING DONE ...
AND WHEN IT CAME TO MONEY ... HE NEVER DID HAVE NONE.

VERSE THREE:
     ROBERT RO- BEARD-Y ... WHY MUST YOU ALWAYS HURRY ...
SLOW DOWN AND LIVE ... SEE WHAT LIFE HAS TO GIVE.
     YOU PASS THE TIME AWAY... THINKING ABOUT TODAY...
NEVER TAKING TIME TO SEE ... WHAT'S COMING YOUR WAY.

CHORUS:
     IF WE COULD TURN BACK TIME ... AS IT WAS THEN ...
AND WE COULD GO BACK ... TO WHERE IT ALL BEGAN.
     WE WOULD'NT DO THE THINGS ... THAT WE DID THEN ...
IF WE COULD LIVE OUR LIVES ... ALL OVER AGAIN.

ROCKY ROADS TO REGRET

VERSE ONE:

    MY LIFE HAS NOT ALWAYS GONE GOOD ... THINGS DID'NT GO MY WAY ...

AND I'VE MADE A LOT OF BAD MISTAKES ... AND FOR THIS I HAD TO PAY.

    I THOUGHT THINGS WOULD CHANGE ... BUT SO FAR THEY HAVE'NT YET ...

IT'S BEEN ROUGH TIMES GOING DOWN ... THE ROCKY ROADS TO REGRET.

VERSE TWO:

    THERE WERE TIMES IN MY LIFE ... THAT I JUST SIMPLY HATED ...

BUT I STILL DID THINGS MY WAY ... AND FOR THIS I HAVE REGRETED.

    IT SEEMED THEY WENT WRONG ... AND DID'NT GO LIKE I PL;ANNED ...

BUT THE ROCKY ROADS TO REGRET ...IS WAITING FOR ANY MAN.

CHORUS:

    ROUGH ROADS OR SMOOTH ROADS ... WHICH ONE WILL YOU TAKE ...

THAT IS YOUR DECISION ... SO THINK ABOUT WHAT YOU HAVE AT STAKE.

    IF YOU SEE ROCKS IN THE ROAD ... DETOUR AWAY FROM ALL THAT ...

AND DON'T GO TRAVELING DOWN ... THE ROCKY ROADS TO REGRET.

VERSE THREE:

    IF YOU'RE SMART TAKE MY ADVICE ... AND DON'T WALK ON THIN ICE ...

WHEN YOU MAKE A MISTAKE ... DON'T MAKE THE SAME MISTAKE TWICE.

    ALWAYS DO IT RIGHT THE FIRST TIME ... THEN GOOD THINGS WILL GROW ...

YOU CAN BELIEVE THAT ROCKY ROADS TO REGRET ... IS NOT THE WAY TO GO.

VERSE FOUR:

GOING DOWN THE ROCKY ROADS TO REGRET ... WILL DRIVE YOU INSANE ...

NOT ONLY DOING DAMAGE TO YOUR BODY ... IT WILL DESTROY YOUR BRAIN.

SO BEFORE YOU DO SOMETHING WRONG ... STOP AND THINK IT OVER ...

BECAUSE THE ROCKY ROADS TO REGRET ... IS NOT A BED OF CLOVER.

CHORUS:

ROUGH ROADS OR SMOOTH ROADS ... WHICH ONE WILL YOU TAKE ...

THAT IS YOUR DECISION ... SO THINK ABOUT WHAT YOU HAVE AT STAKE.

IF YOU SEE ROCKS IN THE ROAD ... DETOUR AWAY FROM ALL THAT ...

AND DON'T GO TRAVELING DOWN ... THE ROCKY ROADS TO REGRET.

RODEO JOE

VERSE ONE:
>JOE USED TO ROPE STEERS ... AT A LOT OF RODEO'S ...
AND HE RODE A LOT OF BULLS ... AND TOOK A LOT OF THROWS.
>BUT HE NEVER GAVE UP ... HE WOULD GET UP AGAIN ...
THEY ALL CALLED HIM THE BULL ... RIDING RODEO MAN.

VERSE TWO:
>WHEN THE ANNOUNCER WOULD SAY ... HERE COMES JOE ...
THE PEOPLE WOULD STAND UP AND SHOUT ... AT THE RODEO.
>HE WOULD GIVE THEM A THRILL ... EVEN IF HE TOOK A SPILL ...
AND SOME TIMES HE CAME CLOSE ... TO ALMOST BEING KILLED.

VERSE THREE:
>ONCE JOE GOT THROWED ... AND WHILE HE WAS DOWN ..
HIS LIFE WAS SAVED ... BY THE RODEO CLOWNS.
>IT CAUSED HIM TO HAVE ... LOTS OF ACHES AND PAINS ...
BUT JOE WISHES HE STILL ... COULD DO IT ALL AGAIN.

VERSE FOUR:
>HERE COMES RODEO JOE ... HE'S WALKING REAL SLOW ...
HE NEVER TOOK ANY PILLS ... SINCE A LONG TIME AGO.
>HE HAS BEEN AROUND ... FOR A LONG LONG TIME ...
HE RODE ALL THE RODEO'S ... UP AND DOWN THE LINE.

CHORUS:
>HE'S HAD BROKEN BONES ... AND A SKINNED UP HEAD ...
BUT HE'S STILL ALIVE ... BECAUSE HE SURE AIN'T DEAD.
>I LEARNED LOTS LESSONS ... FROM A LONG TIME AGO...
FROM A BULL RIDING COWBOY ... CALLED RODEO JOE .

ROLL THAT GRAVE STONE AWAY

VERSE ONE:

 THEY CRUCIFIED OUR LORD ... FOR THINGS HE WAS'NT GUILTY FOR ...

HE DIED FOR THE WORLDS SIN ... SO IN VICTORY WE WOULD WIN.

 THEY LAID HIM IN A GRAVE ... THINKING THAT HE WOULD STAY ...

BUT HE ROSE UP LIKE HE SAID ... AND HE CAME BACK IN THREE DAYS.

VERSE TWO:

 ROLL THAT GRAVE STONE AWAY... ANGELS HEARD THE MASTER SAY ...

MAYBE THEN THEY'LL BELIEVE ... IF THEY SEE HE'S STILL ALIVE TODAY.

 WHEN JESUS APPEARED BEFORE THEM ...THEY KNEW HE WAS GOD'S SON ...

WHEN THEY SAW ALL THE MIRACLES ... THAT GOD THE FATHER HAD DONE.

 CHORUS:

 ROLL THAT STONE AWAY BOYS... ROLL THAT STONE AWAY ...

GOD WILL SURELY REMOVE IT... IF WE WILL FALL ON OUR KNEE'S AND PRAY.

 IF WE ARE READY FOR SALVATION ... JUST BELIEVE IN WHAT GOD SAYS ...

AND IF WE WILL ONLY ASK HIM ... HE WILL ROLL THAT STONE AWAY.

VERSE THREE:

 THE GRAVE STONE WAS ROLLED AWAY ... AND HE WAS'NT IN THE GRAVE ...

HE SAID THAT HE WAS COMING BACK ... HE DID'NT GO THERE TO STAY.

 THEY LOOKED EVERYWHERE ... HIS SWADLING WAS ALL THEY FOUND ...

HE WAS RAISED FROM THE DEAD ... THE GRAVE COULD'NT HOLD HIM DOWN.

VERSE FOUR:

WE ALL HAVE SOME KIND OF STONE ... THAT HENDERS OUR WAYS ...

WE CAN'T UNDERSTAND WHY LIFE ... GETS SO ROUGH SO MANY DAYS.

SOME THINGS WE DON'T WANT TO GIVE UP ... WE KEEP THEM AT BAY ...

BUT IN ORDER TO REALLY LIVE ... WE MUST ROLL THAT STONE AWAY.

CHORUS:

ROLL THAT STONE AWAY BOYS ... ROLL THAT STONE AWAY ...

GOD WILL SURELY REMOVE IT... IF WE WILL FALL ON OUR KNEE'S AND PRAY.

IF WE ARE READY FOR SALVATION ... JUST BELIEVE IN WHAT GOD SAYS ...

AND IF WE WILL ONLY ASK HIM ... HE WILL ROLL THAT STONE AWAY.

RUNNING THE ROADS

CHORUS:
     RUNNING THE ROADS ... WILL NEVER GET OLD ...
YOU WILL MAKE MEMORIES ... NO MATTER WHERE YOU GO.
       YOU WILL HAVE GOOD TRIPS ... ALL WITHOUT MEASURE ...
AND YOU WILL HAVE GOOD TIMES ... THAT YOU WILL TREASURE.

VERSE ONE:
     RUNNING THE ROADS ... I HAVE HAD A LOT OF GOOD TIMES ...
AND YOU CAN BELIEVE ME ... I HAVE HAD A LOT OF BAD.
     I CAN REMEMBER SOME OF THE TIMES ... THAT I HAVE HAD ...
WHILE RUNNING THE ROADS ... THAT WAS REALLY BAD.

VERSE TWO:
     DON'T GET DISGUSTED ... WHEN THINGS AIN'T YOUR WAY ...
BECAUSE EVEN A BAD TRIP ... YOU WILL STILL GET PAID.
     SO PUT IT ALL BEHIND YOU ... AND KEEP MOVING ON ..
AND RUNNING THE ROADS ... CAN BE A HAPPY SONG.

CHORUS:
     RUNNING THE ROADS ... WILL NEVER GET OLD ...
YOU WILL MAKE MEMORIES ... NO MATTER WHERE YOU GO.
       YOU WILL HAVE GOOD TRIPS ... ALL WITHOUT MEASURE ...
AND YOU WILL HAVE GOOD TIMES ... THAT YOU WILL TREASURE.

SANTA CLAUS THIS YEAR

VERSE ONE:

I HOPE I'VE BEEN GOOD ENOUGH ... FOR SANTA CLAUS THIS YEAR ...

MAYBE HE WILL TAKE ME FOR A RIDE ... ON RUDOLPH THE REINDEER.

IF HE DON'T IT'LL BREAK MY HEART ... AND I'LL PROBALY SHED A TEAR ...

BUT I CAN'T WAIT TIL CHRISTMAS DAY ... TO SEE SANTA CLAUS THIS YEAR.

VERSE TWO:

EXPECT SANTA CLAUS THIS YEAR ... TO BRING IN A LOT OF CHEER ...

HE'LL BRING TOYS FOR GIRLS AND BOYS ... WITH HAPPINESS EVERYWHERE.

ALWAYS KEEP A SMILE ON YOUR FACE ... BECAUSE HE IS VERY NEAR ...

BE SURE TO WATCH OUT DAY AND NIGHT ... FOR SANTA CLAUS THIS YEAR.

CHORUS:

DEAR OLD SANTA CLAUS ... THERE'S SOMETHING WE WANT YOU TO HEAR ...

YOU ALWAYS MAKE US FEEL SO GLAD ... WHEN YOU WIPE AWAY OUR TEARS.

CHRISTMAS IS ALWAYS ABOUT HAPPINESS ... SHARED WITHOUT FEAR ...

SO THE WHOLE WORLD IS WAITING FOR ... SANTA CLAUS THIS YER.

VERSE THREE:

CHRISTMAS IS ALWAYS ...THE MOST WONDERFUL TIME OF YEAR ...

WITH CHILDREN EXPECTING TOYS ... MOM AND DAD WATCHING WITH CHEER.

IT FILLS OUR HEARTS WITH JOY ... WITH PEOPLE WE LOVE SO DEAR ...

AND THE TIME IS GETTING CLOSE ... FOR SANTA CLAUS THIS YEAR.

VERSE FOUR:
  WHEN YOU HAVE BURDENS WITH SOMETHING ... BOTHERING
  YOU INSIDE ...
REMEMBER WHAT CHRISTMAS DAY REALLY IS ... AND WHY THE
SAVIOR DIED.
  HE CAME TO EARTH WITH LOVE ... AND HE GAVE HIS LIFE
  FOR US ...
THAT'S WHY WE CELEBRATE CHRISTMAS DAY ... THE BIRTHDAY OF
JESUS.

CHORUS:
  DEAR OLD SANTA CLAUS ...THERE'S SOMETHING WE WANT
  YOU TO HEAR ...
YOU ALWAYS MAKE US FEEL SO GLAD ... WHEN YOU WIPE AWAY OUR
FEARS.
  CHRISTMAS IS ALWAYS ABOUT HAPPINESS ... SHARED WITHOUT
  TEARS ...
SO THE WHOLE WORLD IS WAITING FOR ... SANTA CLAUS THIS YER.

SCARED TO DEATH

VERSE ONE:
    WNEN I WAS A BOY ... I WAS SCARED TO DEATH ...
SCARED TO FIGHT ... SCARED OF WHAT I MIGHT GET.
    MOMMA WOULD WHIP ME ... IF I GOT OUT OF THE WAY ...
SCARED OF DARKNESS ... AND SCARED OF THE DAY.

VERSE TWO:
    WNEN I GOT OLD ENOUGH ... TO GO TO SCHOOL ...
I WOULD RUN AND HIDE .. IF ANYONE SAID BOO.
    MANY YEARS LATER ... AFTER MY DADDY HAD DIED ...
I WAS SCARED OF HURTING ... MY FAMILY'S PRIDE.

VERSE THREE:
    AS I WAS A WALKING ... DOWN THE STREET ONE DAY ...
I SAW A GIRL I'D LIKE TO DATE... COMIN' MY WAY.
    BUT I WAS SCAREDTO DEATH ... SHE MIGHT SAY NO ...
SO I HUNG MY HEAD DOWN ... AND AWAY I DID GO.

VERSE FOUR:
    SCARED TO DEATH TO BE ... SOMEONE I KNOW I'M NOT...
I HAD TO FREE MY PAST ... OF THAT ONE DARK BLOT.
    I FINALLY REALIZED ... WHO I WANTED TO BE ...
AND NOW I AM HAPPY ... OF JUST BEING ME.

CHORUS:
    DON'T WASTE YOUR LIFE ... TRYING TO BE SOMEONE ELSE...
WHEN YOU CAN BE HAPPY ... JUST BEING YOURSELF.
    LIFE IS WHAT YOU MAKE OF IT... HOLD ON TO YOUR PRIDE...
AND DON'T BE SCARED TO DEATH ...TO SAY THAT YOU TRIED.

SICK AS A DOG

VERSE ONE:

    MY DOG'S BEEN SICK ... WITH THE WHOOPING COUGH ...
AND THERE IS NOTHING ... THAT I CAN DO ...
    CAUSE I HAVE'NT FELT GOOD ... IN OVER A WEEK ...
AND I THINK I'M COMING DOWN ... WITH THE FLU.

VERSE TWO:

    I KNOW EVERYONE ... HAS PROBLEMS OF THEIR OWN ...
BUT I SURE WILL BE GLAD ... WHEN SOME OF MINE ARE GONE,
    IT'S MORE THAN I CAN TAKE ... I FEEL SO ALL ALONE ...
BUT I'LL STILL HAVE PROBLEMS ... UNTIL THE COWS COME HOME.

CHORUS:

    THE BIRDS DON'T SING ... OR EVEN TWEET NO MORE ...
AND THE SUN DON'T SHINE ... LIKE IT DID BEFORE.
    BUT I'LL BEAR MY BURDENS ... TILL A WREATH IS ON MY DOOR ...
THEN I WON'T BE AROUND ... TO CARE ANYMORE.

VERSE THREE:

    THE ONLY MAIL THAT I GET ... IS BILLS THAT AIN'T BEEN PAID ...
OR A BUNCH OF ADVERTISEMENTS ... THAT'S NO GOOD ANYWAY.
    I DON'T KNOW HOW I LIVED ... TO BE ABLE GET THIS OLD ...
BUT I CAN TELL YOU MORE TROUBLES ... THAN HAS EVER BEEN TOLD.

VERSE FOUR:

    SO THE NEXT TIME YOU THINK ... THAT YOU HAVE TROUBLES ...
JUST REMEMBER THAT SOMEWHERE ... SOMEONE HAS DOUBLES.
    SO WHEN YOU WAKE UP IN THE MORNING ... JUST THANK THE
LORD ...
IF YOU HAVE A PLACE YOU CAN ... PUT YOUR FEET ON THE FLOOR.

VERSE FIVE:

    DON'T SPEND YOUR TIME ... SITTIN' AROUND COMPLAINING ...
JUST BE THANKFUL TO BE UNDER A ROOF ... WHEN IT'S RAINING.
    LET THOSE POOR ANIMALS ... MAKE IT ON THEIR OWN ...
AND MIND YOUR OWN BUSSINESS ... AND STAY IN YOUR HOME.

SING A HAPPY BIRTHDAY SONG

VERSE ONE:
> NOBODY WILL EVER SING ... HAPPY BIRTHDAY TO ME ...
I MUST NOT BE EVERYTHING ... THAT THEY WANT ME TO BE.
> BUT I HAVE MY OWN WAYS ... AND SO DO THEY ...
BUT WHAT'S SO HARD TO SAY ... HAVE A HAPPY BIRTHDAY.

VERSE TWO:
> SINGING HAPPY BIRTHDAY ... COULD DO SO MUCH ...
IT COULD PICK SOMEONE UP ... WHEN THEY'RE DOWN ON THEIR
LUCK.
> IT COULD BRING A SMILE TO THEIR FACE ... TO KNOW
> SOMEONE CARES ...
SO SING THEM HAPPY BIRTHDAY ... AND HOPE THEY LIVE MANY
YEARS.

CHORUS:
> SOME PEOPLE ARE LONELY ... ESPECIALLY ON THEIR
> BIRTHDAY ...
WHEN THERE IS NO ONE THERE ... TO SHARE THEIR BIRTHDAY
CAKE.
> SO IF YOU CAN'T VISIT THEM ... THEN CALL THEM ON THE
> PHONE ...
TELL THEM YOU WERE THINKING OF THEM ... AND SING A HAPPY
BIRTHDAY SONG.

VERSE THREE:
> SINGING HAPPY BIRTHDAY ... IS ABOUT AS OLD AS IT GETS ...
IT MAKES PEOPLE HAPPY ... AND IT'S NEVER GOT TOO OLD YET.
> SO IF YOU KNOW SOMEONE ... THAT'S HAVING A BIRTHDAY ...
TELL THEM HAPPY BIRTHDAY ... AND LIGHTEN UP THEIR WAY.

CHORUS:

 SOME PEOPLE ARE LONELY ... ESPECIALLY ON THEIR BIRTHDAY ...
WHEN THERE IS NO ONE THERE ... TO SHARE THEIR BIRTHDAY
CAKE.

 SO IF YOU CAN'T VISIT THEM ... THEN CALL THEM ON THE
 PHONE ...
TELL THEM YOU WERE THINKING OF THEM ... AND SING A HAPPY
BIRTHDAY SONG.

SING ME A LOVE SONG

VERSE ONE:

    SING ME A LOVE SONG ... BUT NOT OF SOMEONE WHO IS GONE ... TELL ME OF SOMEONE WHO WILL STAY ... AND BE HERE FROM NOW ON.

    LET THE WORDS BE SO TRUE ... AND SING THEM FROM YOUR HEART ...

AND TELL ME THAT YOU LOVE ME ... AND WILL NEVER EVER PART.

CHORUS:

    DON'T SING ABOUT SOME COWBOY ... WHO RIDES THE TRAIL ALONE ...

OR SOMEONE WHO IS HOMESICK ... AND WANTS TO GO HOME.

    DON'T SING ABOUT SOME SUICIDE ... OF SOMEONE'S LIFE THAT'S GONE ...

BUT MAKE IT SWEET AND CHARMING ... AND SING ME A LOVE SONG.

VERSE TWO:

    THERE IS NOTHING ANY STRONGER ... THAN A BEAUTIFUL LOVE SONG ...

TO PUT YOU BACK ON YOUR FEET ... WHEN THINGS SEEMS TO GO WRONG.

    LOVE IS THE BEST THING ... WHEN TWO HEARTS BEAT AS ONE ...

SO PUT YOUR ARMS AROUND ME ... AND SING ME A LOVE SONG.

VERSE THREE:

    SING ME A LOVE SONG ... OF SOMEONE WHO'S LOVE IS TRUE ...

AND LET THAT SWEET LOVE SONG ... BE ABOUT ME AND YOU.

    THE MEMORIES WILL ALWAYS ... STAY PICTURED IN OUR MINDS ...

SO KEEP A SONG IN YOUR HEART ... UNTIL THE END OF TIME.

COURSE:

    DON'T SING ABOUT SOME COWBOY ... WHO RIDES THE TRAIL ALONE ...

OR SOMEONE WHO IS HOMESICK ... AND WANTS TO GO HOME.

DON'T SING ABOUT SOME SUICIDE ... OF SOMEONE'S LIFE THAT IS GONE ...

BUT MAKE IT SWEET AND CHARMING ... AND SING ME A LOVE SONG.

REPEAT CHORUS AGAIN:

DON'T SING ABOUT SOME COWBOY ... WHO RIDES THE TRAIL ALONE ...

OR SOMEONE WHO IS HOMESICK ... AND WANTS TO GO HOME.

DON'T SING ABOUT SUICIDE ... OR SOMEONE WHOSE LIFE'S GONE ...

BUT MAKE IT SWEET AND CHARMING ... AND SING ME A LOVE SONG.

SING ME A MERRY CHRISTMAS SONG

CHORUS:
    SING ME A MERRY ... CHRISTMAS SONG ...
I CAN FEEL THE SPIRIT ... A'COMIN' ON.
    PEOPLE ARE SINGING ... AND BELLS ARE A'RINGING ...
SO SING ME A MERRY ... CHRISTMAS SONG.

 VERSE ONE:
    I LOVE TO GO TO TOWN ... TO SEE ALL THE LIGHTS ...
WHEN EVERYTHING IS ALL ... LIT UP AT NIGHT.
    SINGING AND LAUGHTER ... AND CARRYING ON ...
JUST SINGING THEIR ... MERRY CHRISTMAS SONGS.

 VERSE TWO:
    PEOPLE ARE HAPPY ... GOING HERE AND THERE ...
RUNNING TO AND FRO ... GOING EVERYWHERE.
    BUYING SOME PRESENTS ... TO GIVE SOMEONE ...
AND SINGING THEIR MERRY ... CHRISTMAS SONGS.
        SING CHORUS AND THEN BREAK:
VERSE THREE:
    PEOPLE ARE WALKING ... DOWN MEMORY LANE ...
HOPING IT WILL SOON ... SNOW AGAIN.
    THINKING OF TIMES ... WHEN THEY WERE YOUNG ...
AND SINGING THEIR MERRY ... CHRISTMAS SONGS.

VERSE FOUR:
    LET THE BELLS JINGLE ... LET THE MUSIC RING ...
IF YOU FEEL THE SPIRIT ... STAND UP AND SING.
    IF YOU CAN'T SING ...WAVE YOUR HANDS AND SHOUT...
THAT'S WHAT THE JOY OF CHRISTMAS ... IS ALL ABOUT.
        SING CHORUS TWICE:

SNOW IS ON THE WAY

I HEARD ... THE WEATHER MAN TODAY ...
AND I LIKED ... WHAT HE HAD TO SAY.
    HE SAID FOLKS ... GET IN YOUR HOUSE AND STAY...
BECAUSE SNOW ... IS ON THE WAY.

    TRY TO MAKE THE BEST OF... WHATEVER IS TO COME ...
MAKE YOURSELF SOME SNOW CREAM ... AND ENJOY SOME.
    TURN YOUR TV ON ... AND CUDDLE UP BY THE FIRE ...
SNOW IS ON THE WAY ... SO DON'T PLAN TO GO NOWHERE.

    THERE IS NOTHING LIKE ... AN OLD FASHION SNOW ...
ESPECIALY IF YOU HAVE ... NOWHERE TO GO.
    IT'S ALL YOU MAKE OF IT ... SO ENJOY IT WHILE YOU CAN ...
AND IF YOU ARE ABLE ... GO AND BUILD A SNOWMAN.

    WHEN YOU HAVE ALL SNOW ... WITH NO SLEET OR ICE ...
AND THE GROUND TURNS WHITE ... IT'S A BEAUTIFUL SIGHT.
    MAKE A SNOWBALL ... AND HAVE A SNOWBALL FIGHT ...
GET READY FOR A SNOWY DAY ... CAUSE SNOW IS ON THE WAY.

SO LONG MY FRIENDS

VERSE ONE:
    HE WOULD WALK OUT ... ONTO THE STAGE ...
WITH THE MICROPHONE ... IN HIS HAND.
    HE WOULD SAY ... I HAVE REALLY MISSED YOU ...
BECAUSE YOU ARE ... MY DEAREST FRIENDS.

VERSE TWO:
    THEN HE'D SAY ... I'M LIKE GEORGE STRAIT ...
I COULD'NT EVEN ... HARDLY WAIT.
    NOW I'VE GOT A SHOW ... I'VE GOT TO DO ...
BUT I COULD'NT DO IT ... WITHOUT YOU.

VERSE THREE:
    HAVE YAWL MISSED ME ... LIKE I'VE MISSED YOU ...
I AIN'T GONNA TELL YOU ... WHAT I'VE BEEN THRU.
    DON'T REMEMBER ALL ... THE THINGS I'VE DONE ...
JUST REMEMBER ... THE SONGS I'VE SUNG.

VERSE FOUR:
    HE WOULD SING SOME SONGS ... SWEET AND LOW ...
THEY WOULD REACH ... ALL THE WAY TO YOUR SOUL.
    HE WOULD SING SAD SONGS ... FROM HIS HEART ...
THAT WOULD TEAR ... YOUR WHOLE WORLD APART.

CHORUS:
    HE'D SAY DEAR FRIENDS ... IT'S THAT TIME AGAIN ...
THEY SAY ALL GOOD THINGS ... MUST COME TO AN END ...
    SO I'LL HAVE TO SAY ... SO LONG MY FRIENDS ...
UNTIL SOMEDAY ... WHEN WE MEET AGAIN.

SOMEDAY PAYDAY

CHORUS:
      SOMEDAY I'M GONNA GET ... SOME KIND OF A REWARD ...
I'LL GET ALL THE THINGS ... THAT I'VE BEEN WORKING FOR.
      I KNOW THINGS WILL BE BETTER ... FOR ME SOMEDAY ...
WHEN I GET THAT BIG OLD ... SOMEDAY PAYDAY.

VERSE ONE:
      THINGS THAT ARE SLOW ... WILL GET BETTER SOMEDAY ...
BUT MY BILLS KEEP PILING UP ... THEY DON'T GO AWAY.
      MY BOSSMAN SAID ... WE WERE GOING ON THREE DAYS ...
BUT I REALLY DON'T WORRY ... IT'S JUST NOT MY WAY.

VERSE TWO:
      I TOLD THE BOSSMAN ... I HAD TO HAVE ME A RAISE ...
HE SAID MAYBE I'LL GIVE YOU ONE ... ONE OF THESE DAYS.
      GETTIN' MORE MONEY IS LIKE ... A NEEDLE IN A STACK OF HAY ...
BUT I'LL KEEP ON WORKING ... FOR MY SOMEDAY PAYDAY.

CHORUS:
      SOMEDAY I'M GONNA GET ... SOME KIND OF A REWARD ...
I'LL GET ALL THE THINGS ... THAT I'VE BEEN WORKING FOR.
      I KNOW THINGS WILL BE BETTER ... FOR ME SOMEDAY ...
WHEN I GET THAT BIG OLD ... SOMEDAY PAYDAY.

VERSE THREE:
      THE BIBLE SAYS TO BE READY ... FOR THE JUDGEMENT DAY ...
I'LL GET MY REWARD WHEN ... THE DEATH ANGEL TAKES ME AWAY.
      BUT I SURE DO HOPE ... IT WON'T BE PUT ON DELAY ...
LIKE THE PROMISES AT WORK ... FOR MY SOMEDAY PAYDAY.

CHORUS:
      SOMEDAY I'M GONNA GET ... SOME KIND OF A REWARD ...
I'LL GET ALL THE THINGS ... THAT I'VE BEEN WORKING FOR.
      I KNOW THINGS WILL BE BETTER ... FOR ME SOMEDAY ...
WHEN I GET THAT BIG OLD ... SOMEDAY PAYDAY.

SOMETHING GOOD IS ON IT'S WAY

CHORUS:

    I HEARD SOMEONE SAY ... SOMETHING GOOD IS ON IT'S WAY ...
AND I DO HOPE THAT THIS TIME ... IT WILL BE HERE TO STAY.

    I WANT TO KNOW TODAY ... WHAT'S ABOUT TO TAKE PLACE ...
I'VE GOT A GOOD FEELING ... SOMETHING GOOD IS ON IT'S WAY.

VERSE ONE:

    THE WEATHERMAN SAYS ... THERE'S A CHANGE ON THE WAY...
THAT TODAY WILL BE WARMER ... THAN IT WAS YESTERDAY.

    BUT TOMORROW WILL BE HOTTER ...THAN IT WILL BE TODAY...
SO GET IT TOGETHER NOW ... SOMETHING GOOD IS ON IT'S WAY.

VERSE TWO:

    THE NATIONS ECONOMY ... IS LOOKING BETTER EVERYDAY...
THE FUTURE LOOKS BRIGHTER ... AS IT CHANGES DAY BY DAY.

    IT REMINDS ME OF WORDS ... MY MOTHER USED TO SAY ...
DON'T WORRY ABOUT IT ... SOMETHING GOOD IS ON IT'S WAY.

    ... SING CHORUS AND THEN INSTRUMENTAL BREAK ....

VERSE THREE:

    AND OH YES, GOD SAID ... YOU BETTER SING A NEW SONG ...
BECAUSE YOU'VE HAD YOUR WAY NOW ... FOR MUCH TOO LONG.

    HE IS COMING BACK AGAIN ... AND IT COULD BE TODAY...
SO KEEP YOUR EYES OPEN ... SOMETHING GOOD IS ON IT'S WAY.

    ... SING CHORUS AGAIN ....

SOMEWHERE COULD BE ANYWHERE

VERSE ONE:
I WALKED IN A RESTURANT ... TO GET SOMETHING TO EAT ...
HOW ARE YOU DOING ... SOMEONE ASK ME.
AND JOKINGLY I REPLIED ... I'M JUST GLAD TO BE HERE ...
CAUSE IF I WAS'NT HERE ... I WOULD HAVE TO BE SOMEWHERE.

VERSE TWO:
AND IF I WAS SOMEWHERE ... I WOULD HAVE TO BE THERE ...
AND IF I WAS THERE ... I COULD BE ANYWHERE.
IT COULD BE AT A PARTY ... AND HAVING LOTS OF FUN ...
OR IN TROUBLE WITH THE LAW ... AND ALWAYS ON THE RUN.

VERSE THREE:
IT COULD BE SOMEWHERE IN MISERY ... SICK IN THE BED ...
OR IT COULD BE IN A HOSPITAL ... SOMEWHERE ALMOST DEAD.
IT COULD EVEN BE IN HEAVEN ... JUST PRAISING THE LORD...
OR MAYBE EVEN IN HELL ... BEING PUNISHED FOREVER MORE.

VERSE FOUR:
NO MATTER WHERE YOU ARE ... BE THANKFUL TO BE ALIVE...
CAUSE TIME GOES SO FAST ... THE YEARS JUST FLY ON BY.
THOUGH THINGS ARE BAD HERE ...THEY ARE BAD EVERYWHERE ...
AND EVERYWHERE IS SOMEWHERE ...THAT COULD BE ANYWHERE.

SOON I WILL BE GONE

VERSE ONE:

    I HAVE BEEN LONGING TO GO ... ON A FAR AWAY JOURNEY ...
TO A PLACE CALLED HEAVEN ... WHERE I HAVE BEEN YEARNING.
    SOON I WILL BE GONE ... I AM LEAVING THIS OLD WORLD ...
GOING WHERE STREETS ARE GOLD ... AND GATES MADE OF PEARL.

CHORUS:

    I NEVER WAS ONE FOR WISHING ... BUT I WISH THAT I WAS
GONE ...
TO A PLACE THAT'S CALLED GOD'S CITY ... TO MY BRAND NEW
HOME.
    IT'S BEEN IN PREPARATION ... AND SOON I WILL BE GONE.
I CAN HEAR THE FATHER CALLING ME ... SON COME ON HOME.

VERSE TWO:

    IF I DON'T SHOW UP ... AND YOU CAN'T FIND ME AROUND ...
YOU'LL KNOW THAT I HAVE MOVED ... TO A MUCH HIGHER GROUND.
    SOMEDAY I'M GONNA MOVE ... LIKE A ROLLING STONE ...
YOU MIGHT CALL MY NAME ... BUT SOON I WILL BE GONE.

VERSE THREE:

    THIS OLD WORLD HAS BEEN TOO MUCH ... FOR MUCH TOO
LONG ...
AND I AIN'T HANGING AROUND ... BECAUSE SOON I WILL BE GONE.
    I'M GOING FAR AWAY ... FARTHER THAN EYES CAN SEE ...
WHEN I GET THERE IT WILL BE MINE ... FOR ALL ETERNITY.

VERSE FOUR:

    A PLACE THAT'S CALLED HEAVEN ... I WAS PROMISED LONG
AGO ...
AND SOMEDAY I'LL FLY AWAY ... BUT I WON'T BE FLYING TOO LOW.
    I KNOW YOU'VE HEARD ME SAYING ... THAT FOR MUCH TOO
LONG ...
BUT ONE DAY YOU WILL FIND OUT ... BECAUSE SOON I WILL BE
GONE.

CHORUS:
> I NEVER WAS ONE FOR WISHING ... BUT I WISH THAT I WAS
> GONE ...

TO A PLACE THAT'S CALLED GOD'S CITY ... TO MY BRAND NEW HOME.

> IT'S BEEN IN PREPARATION ... AND SOON I WILL BE GONE.

I CAN HEAR THE FATHER CALLING ME ... SON COME ON HOME.

STAY OUT OF THE WAY

VERSE ONE:
    TRUCK DRIVERS ARE THE BEST PEOPLE ... THERE IS ON THE ROAD ...
BUT THEY CAN GET MEAN ... IF YOU TRY TO MESS WITH THEIR LOAD.
    THEY HAVE A JOB TO DO ... SO STAY OUT OF THE WAY ...
BECAUSE GETTING THEIR LOAD OFF ... IS HOW THEY MAKE THEIR PAY.

VERSE TWO:
    DRIVING DAY AND NIGHT ... JUST TO GET THE JOB DONE ...
AND WHEN THINGS DON'T GO RIGHT ... IT SURE AIN'T NO FUN.
    IF ONE OF THEM NEEDS HELP ... SOMEWHERE ALONG THE WAY ...
STOP AND LEND A HELPING HAND ... YOU'LL BE PAID BACK SOMEDAY.

CHORUS:
    WHEN YOU SEE A TRUCK ... THAT IS COMING DOWN THE ROAD ...
REMEMBER THEY ARE CARRYING ... THE WORLDS GOODS IN THEIR LOAD.
    WITHOUT TRUCK DRIVERS ... THE WORLD WOULD STAND STILL ...
SO STAY OUT OF THE WAY ... OF THAT DRIVER BEHIND THE WHEEL.

VERSE THREE:
    SOMETIME YOU MIGHT BREAK DOWN ... THIS YOU NEVER KNOW ...
AND IT MAY BE A TRUCK DRIVER ... THAT GETS YOU BACK ON THE ROAD.
    BUT IF YOU CAN'T BE NICE ...THEN JUST LISTEN TO WHAT I SAY ...
GET BACK IN YOUR VEHICLE ... AND JUST STAY OUT OF THE WAY..

VERSE FOUR:
    STAY OUT OF THE WAY ... AND DON'T GET INVOLVED IN THEIR
    WORK ...
BECAUSE IF YOU CAUSE A PROBLEM ... YOU MIGHT GET HURT.
    THEY TOO HAVE TO GO THROUGH ... A LOT OF HARD TIMES ...
SO JUST STAY OUT OF THE WAY ... AND EVERYTHING WILL BE FINE.

CHORUS:
    WHEN YOU SEE A TRUCK ... THAT IS COMING DOWN THE
    ROAD ...
REMEMBER THEY ARE CARRYING ... THE WORLDS GOODS IN THEIR
LOAD.
    WITHOUT TRUCK DRIVERS ... THE WORLD WOULD STAND
    STILL ...
SO STAY OUT OF THE WAY ... OF THAT DRIVER BEHIND THE WHEEL.

STOP AND THINK

CHORUS:
>STOP AND THINK ... BEFORE YOU DO WHAT YOU DO ...
STOP AND THINK ... WHAT IS THE BEST THING FOR YOU.
>STOP BEFORE YOUR WHOLE LIFE ... GOES ON A BLINK ...
THE BEST THING YOU CAN DO ... IS STOP AND THINK.

VERSE ONE:
>WHEN I STOP AND THINK ... SOMETIMES ABOUT TOMORROW ...
I WONDER IF IT WILL BE FULL OF JOY ... OR WILL IT BE SORROW.
>I EVEN WONDER IF IT WILL ... EVEN COME MY WAY ...
WILL IT BRING SUNSHINE ... OR WILL ALL THE SKY BE GRAY.

VERSE TWO:
>WE WAS NEVER PROMISED ... THERE WOULD BE ANOTHER DAY ...
BUT WE SHOULD BE PREPARED ... IN CASE ONE COMES OUR WAY.
>WE COULD MAKE THINGS MUCH BETTER ... IF ONLY WE WOULD ...
WE COULD TURN OUR BAD TIMES ... INTO SOMETHING GOOD.

CHORUS:
>STOP AND THINK ... BEFORE YOU DO WHAT YOU DO ...
STOP AND THINK ... WHAT IS THE BEST THING FOR YOU.
>STOP BEFORE YOUR WHOLE LIFE ... GOES ON A BLINK ...
THE BEST THING YOU CAN DO ... IS STOP AND THINK.

VERSE THREE:
>WE USUALLY CREATE ... ALL THE BAD TIMES WE GO THRU ...
THEN WE OFTEN WONDER ... WHAT ON EARTH DID WE DO.
>BUT IF WE STOP AND THINK ... WHAT MAKES US SO BLUE ...
MAYBE WE WOULD REALIZE ... THE THINGS WE SHOULD'NT DO.

CHORUS:
>STOP AND THINK ... BEFORE YOU DO WHAT YOU DO ...
STOP AND THINK ... WHAT IS THE BEST THING FOR YOU.
>STOP BEFORE YOUR WHOLE LIFE ... GOES ON A BLINK ...
THE BEST THING YOU CAN DO ... IS STOP AND THINK.

STOP ... WHAT YOU'RE DOING

VERSE ONE:
STOP ... WHAT YOU'RE DOING ... IF YOU KNOW IT'S WRONG ...
STOP ... GOING TO PLACES ... THAT YOU DON'T BELONG.
STOP ... LOOKING FOR WAYS ... TO DO IT ON YOUR OWN ...
STOP ... WHAT YOU'RE DOING ... SOON YOU WILL BE GONE.

VERSE TWO:
WHEN YOUR TIME COMES ... TO GO ON THATJOURNEY ...
THAT YOU'VE BEEN PLANNING ON ... FOR SO LONG.
STOP ... WHAT YOU'RE DOING ... AND PLAN TO BE GONE ...
CAUSE ST. PETER IS A CALLIN' ... FOR YOU TO COME HOME.

CHORUS:
STOP ... WHAT YOU'RE DOING ... ST. PETER IS A CALLIN' ...
HE'S CALLIN' ... FOR YOU TO COME HOME.
HE'S STANDING AT THE GATE ... WITH ARMS OPENED WIDE ...
SO GET READY NOW ... HE WANTS TO WELCOME YOU INSIDE.

VERSE THREE:
YOU'RE ONE HEART BEAT AWAY ... FROM JUDGEMENT DAY ...
YOU WILL LEAVE THIS OLD BODY ... OF FLESH AND CLAY.
YOU'LL TAKE NOTHING WITH YOU ... AS YOU TRAVEL ON ...
SO STOP ... WHAT YOU'RE DOING ... BEFORE IT'S TIME TO GO HOME.

VERSE FOUR:
WHEN YOUR NAME IS CALLED ... YOU WILL ANSWER HERE
AM I ...
AND BELIEVE ME ... YOU WILL HEAR IT IN THE SWEET BYE AND BYE.
SO WHILE YOU'RE ON EARTH ... ALWAYS BE IN THE KNOWING ...
IF YOU KNOW IT IS WRONG ... THEN STOP ... WHAT YOU'RE DOING.

CHORUS:
STOP ... WHAT YOU'RE DOING ... ST. PETER IS A CALLIN' ...
HE'S CALLIN' ... FOR YOU TO COME HOME.
HE'S STANDING AT THE GATE ... WITH ARMS OPENED WIDE ...
SO GET READY NOW ... HE WANTS TO WELCOME YOU INSIDE.

STUFF AND THINGS

VERSE ONE:
    I ONCE MET A MAN ... WHO SAID HE HAD EVERYTHING ...
I WALKED IN HIS HOUSE ... IT LOOKED LIKE A CIRCUS RING.
    I ASK HIM ABOUT SOME THINGS ... HE HAD ON A SHELF ...
HE SAID JUST STUFF AND THINGS ... AND EVERYTHING ELSE.

VERSE TWO:
    I ASKED WHAT IN THE WORLD ... ARE YOU GONNA DO? ...
BECAUSE WHEN YOU DIE ... YOU CAN'T TAKE IT WITH YOU.
    HE SAID I'VE GATHERED UP STUFF... ALL OF MY LIFE ...
AND TO GET RID OF IT NOW ... JUST WOULD'NT BE RIGHT.

VERSE THREE:
    HE SAID HE FEELS LIKE ... HE'S ACCOMPLISHED SOMETHING...
AS LONG AS HE'S GOT ... A LITTLE BIT OF EVERYTHING.
    WHEN HE DON'T WANT TO HEAR ... HE ACTS REAL DEAF ...
AND WON'T SELL HIS STUFF AND THINGS... AND EVERYTHING ELSE.

chorus:
    NOW ONE MAN'S TRASH ... IS ANOTHER MAN'S TREASURE ...
EVEN IF IT CAUSE'S HIM ... TO HAVE A HIGH FEVER.
    IF IT MAKES YOU FEEL GOOD... AS A RICH MAN YOURSELF...
THEN GET YOU SOME STUFF AND THINGS ... AND EVERYTHING
ELSE.

VERSE FOUR:
    WOULD YOU HAVE SOLD YOUR SOUL ... FOR A PRICE YOURSELF...
OR SETTLE FOR SOME STUFF AND THINGS... AND EVERYTHING ELSE.
    BEFORE YOU CONDEMN HIM ... PUT YOURSELF IN HIS SHOES...
IF A BUNCH OF JUNK WAS ALL YOU HAD ... WHAT WOULD YOU DO?

TIME KEEPS MARCHING ON

VERSE ONE:

IT'S GOOD TO KNOW THAT SOMEDAY ... WE ALL WILL BE GONE ...
FROM THE EVERYDAY PROBLEMS ... WE'VE CARRIED FOR SO LONG.
THINGS KEEPS ON HAPPENING ... EACH DAY THAT COMES ALONG.
BUT SOMEDAY WE'LL ALL BE FREE ... AS TIME KEEPS MARCHING ON.

CHORUS:

YES TIME KEEPS MARCHING ON ... IT'S HEADED FOR THE MARK ...
WHEN ALL OF OUR TROUBLES ... WILL BE LEFT OUT IN THE DARK.
LIFE IS SLOWLY CLOSING ... AND THE FUTURE IS ALMOST BLIND ...
EVERYTHING WILL BE REMEMBERED ... BY THE PAST WE LEAVE BEHIND.

VERSE TWO:

NOW HAVE YOU EVER WONDERED ... JUST WHAT PEOPLE MIGHT SAY ...
WHEN YOUR TIME COMES TO DIE ... AND YOU HAVE PASSED AWAY.
WILL YOUR MEMORIES LIVE ON ... LIKE THE WORDS OF A LOVE SONG ...
OR WILL YOU SOON BE FORGOTTEN ... AS TIME KEEPS MARCHING ON.

VERSE THREE:

SOMETIMES LIFE IS COMPLICATED ... BUT WE MAKE IT THAT WAY...
IT IS WHATEVER WE MAKE OF IT ... AS WE LIVE FROM DAY TO DAY.
DON'T JUST THINK OF YOURSELF ... THINK OF OTHERS TOO ...
THEN AS TIME KEEPS MARCHING ON ... THERE'LL BE REWARDS FOR YOU.

VERSE FOUR;

WHATEVER LIFE HAS TO OFFER ... ALWAYS GIVE BACK IN RETURN ...

LET PEOPLE THINK OF THINGS ... THAT WAS YOUR GREATEST CONCERN.

YOU DON'T WANT TO BE JUST SOMEONE ... WHO IS FINALLY GONE ...

BE REMEMBERED FOR GOOD THINGS... AS TIME KEEPS MARCHING ON.

THAT BIG OLD TRUCK

VERSE ONE:

I DRIVE A BIG OLD TRUCK ... I'M A TRUCK DRIVIN' MAN ...
I DELIVER MY LOADS ... ALL OVER THIS LAND.
I HAVE BEEN OVER HERE ... I HAVE BEEN OVER THERE ...
I THINK I HAVE TRAVELED ... ALMOST EVERYWHERE.

CHORUS:

SO NOW COME ON BOYS ... MAKE THEM BIG WHEELS ROLL ...
YOU'VE GOT THAT FEELING ... DOWN DEEP IN YOUR SOUL.
JUST KEEP ON A DRIVING ... DON'T EVER GIVE UP ...
AND KEEP ON A WHEELIN' ... THAT BIG OLD TRUCK.

VERSE TWO:

BUT THERE WAS A TIME ... THINGS DID'NT GO SO WELL ...
I GOT MYSELF LOCKED UP ... IN A COUNTY JAIL.
AND NEVER HAVE I SEEN A PLACE ... LIKE IT WAS THERE ...
WHEN A MAN GETS LOCKED UP ... JUST FOR DRINKING A BEER.

VERSE THREE:

BUT THAT'S WHAT IT'S LIKE ... WHEN YOU RUN THE ROADS ...
YOU NEVER KNOW WHERE ... YOU'LL GO THE NEXT LOAD.
JUST KEEP YOUR FAITH ... AND TRUST IN YOUR LUCK ...
AND KEEP ON A DRIVIN' ... THAT BIG OLD TRUCK.

CHORUS:

SO NOW COME ON BOYS ... MAKE THEM BIG WHEELS ROLL ...
YOU'VE GOT THAT FEELING ... DOWN DEEP IN YOUR SOUL.
JUST KEEP ON A DRIVING ... DON'T EVER GIVE UP ...
AND KEEP ON A WHEELIN' ... THAT BIG OLD TRUCK.

THAT DANGED OLD TRUCK

VERSE ONE:

    I DID'NT KNOW WHAT I WANTED TO DO ... WHEN I GREW UP ... BUT I GOT ME A JOB ... DRIVING A DANGED OLD TRUCK.

    I WOULD DRIVE DAY AND NIGHT ... AROUND THE CLOCK ... THE ONLY TIME I STOPPED ... WAS WHEN I GOT TO THE LOADING DOCK.

VERSE TWO:

    ALL MY FRIENDS WOULD TELL ME ... THAT I HAD BETTER QUIT ...
THAT DANGED OLD TRUCK ... WOULD BE THE DEATH OF ME YET.

    BUT I LOVED TO TRAVEL ... AND I ENJOYED BEING GONE ... AND SO THAT DANGED OLD TRUCK ... BECAME MY HOME.

CHORUS:

    SO COME ON BOYS ... BEFORE YOU DECIDE TO HANG IT UP ... LET'S PUT A FEW MORE MILES ... ON OUR OVER THE ROAD LUCK.

    SOME PEOPLE SITS AROUND ... LIKE AN OLD LAME DUCK ... BUT IT SEEMS LIKE I'M STUCK ... IN THAT DANGED OLD TRUCK.

VERSE THREE:

    I MET A LOT OF DRIVERS ... ALL UP AND DOWN THE LINE ... I WAS PROUD TO TELL THEM ... THAT DANGED OLD TRUCK WAS MINE.

    I DROVE IT SO LONG ...THAT I FELT IT WAS A BIG PART OF ME ... AND SITTING BEHIND THAT WHEEL ... WAS WHERE I WANTED TO BE.

VERSE FOUR:

    I KEPT IT SHINEY AND CLEAN ... AND ALWAYS TUNED UP ... THERE WAS'NT A PRETTIER SIGHT ... THAT THAT DANGED OLD TRUCK.

    SOME PEOPLE DON'T UNDERSTAND ... LIFE ON THE ROAD ... BUT WHEN MY TIME COMES ... THAT'S THE WAY I WANT TO GO.

CHORUS:
   SO COME ON BOYS ... BEFORE YOU DECIDE TO HANG IT UP ...
LET'S PUT A FEW MORE MILES ... ON OUR OVER THE ROAD LUCK.
   SOME PEOPLE SITS AROUND ... LIKE AN OLD LAME DUCK ...
BUT IT SEEMS LIKE I'M STUCK ... IN THAT DANGED OLD TRUCCK.

THAT HOMEMADE WINE

VERSE ONE:

    I'VE HEARD THAT OLD SONG ... SO MANY TIMES ...
ABOUT GOING OUT AND MAKING ... SOME HOMEMADE WINE.
    IT MAY BE STRAWBERRY... BLUEBERRY OR MUSCADINE ...
BUT THERE'S NOTHING LIKE ...THAT OLD HOMEMADE WINE.

VERSE TWO:

    IF YOU WANT'A GET UP ... AND COME FROM BEHIND ...
JUST GET YOU A BOTTLE ... OF THAT HOMEMADE WINE.
    IT WILL MAKE YOU TINGLE ... AND FEEL REAL FINE ...
WHEN YOU DRINK A LITTLE ... OF THAT HOMEMADE WINE.

VERSE THREE:

    IF YOU DRINK TOO MUCH ... YOUR EYES WILL SHINE ...
THERE'S NOTHING ELSE LIKE ... THAT HOMEMADE WINE .
    IT WILL PICK YOU UP ... AND THEN PUT YOU DOWN ...
AT TIMES IT WILL MAKE ... YOUR HEAD SPIN AROUND.

VERSE FOUR:

    SO GET YOU A JUG ... OF THAT OLD HOMEMADE WINE ...
BUT DON'T LET IT TAKE YOU ... TO THE END OF THE LINE.
    IF YOU ASK ME ... THE FAVORITE DRINK OF MINE ...
I WILL HAVE YO SAY ... IT'S THAT GOOD HOMEMADE WINE.

THAT SOFT WARM SMILE

VERSE ONE:
SITTIN' IN A RESTURANT ... JUST LOOKING OUT ...
WATCHING HOW THE WORLD ... JUST STIRS ABOUT.
PEOPLE WALKING BY ... AND CARS GOING THERE ...
EVERYBODY IS TRYING ... TO GET SOMEWHERE.

VERSE TWO:
THEN I SAW YOU ... AS YOU WALKED IN STYLE ...
WITH A WALK OF GRACE ... AND A SOFT WARM SMILE.
IT DID'NT TAKE LONG ... BECAUSE SOON I KNEW ...
THAT YOU ARE THE ONE I WANT ... I'VE GOT HAVE YOU.

CHORUS:
I WANT YOU I NEED YOU ... I LIKE YOUR STYLE ...
I LOVE THE WAY YOU LOOK ... WITH THAT SOFT WARM SMILE.
AND NOW THAT I FOUND YOU ... TELL ME WHAT TO DO ...
BECAUSE I WANT YOU I NEED YOU ... I'VE GOT TO HAVE YOU.

VERSE THREE:
THAT MOMENT MY WORLD ... TURNED UPSIDE DOWN ...
AND I NEED YOU TO HELP ME ... TURN IT BACK AROUND.
YOU WALKED INTO MY LIFE ... AT THE RESTURANT ...
AND NOW YOU ARE ALL ... THAT I EVER WANT.

CHORUS:
I WANT YOU I NEED YOU ... I LIKE YOUR STYLE ...
I LOVE THE WAY YOU LOOK ... WITH THAT SOFT WARM SMILE.
AND NOW THAT I FOUND YOU ... TELL ME WHAT TO DO ...
BECAUSE I WANT YOU I NEED YOU ... I'VE GOT TO HAVE YOU.

THAT SQUEAKY OLD SWING

VERSE ONE:
> I REMEMBER ONE NIGHT ... AS I WAS A SWINGING ...
> ON MY FRONT PORCH ... WHILE I WAS A SINGING.
> WHEN I MOVED MY FEET ... THE SWING WOULD SQUEAK ...
> AND THE FASTER I WOULD MOVE ... THE FASTER THE BEAT.

VERSE TWO:
> THEN I NOTICED THAT ... THAT SQUEAKY OLD SWING ...
> WAS REALLY RELYING ON ... TWO RUSTY OLD CHAINS.
> BUT THE MOVING MOTION ... WAS STILL THERE ...
> LIKE A BALD HEADED MAN ... WITHOUT ANY HAIR.

VERSE THREE:
> THEN I WONDERED IF MAYBE ... IT WAS HAVING ANY PAIN ...
> FROM THE SCRILLS I HEARD ... IN THAT SQUEAKY OLD THING.
> I THOUGHT NOTHING MADE ... SUCH A BEAUTIFUL SCREAM ...
> AS THE SCREECH THAT I HEARD ... FROM THAT OLD SWING..

VERSE FOUR:
> THAT SQUEAKY OLD SWING ... WAS GETTING PRETTY WEAK ...
> BUT IT SEEMED TO KEEP RHYTHM ... WHEN I MOVED MY FEET.
> EVERY NOTE THAT I PICKED ... ON MY GUITAR STRINGS.
> STAYED IN MOTION WITH ... THAT SQUEAKY OLD SWING.

CHORUS:
> THAT SQUEAKY OLD SWING ... IS NOT THERE ANYMORE ...
> IT'S ONLY A THING OF THE PAST ... THAT I USED TO LIVE FOR.
> MEMORIES COME BACK ... LIKE FLOWERS IN THE SPRING ...
> OF THE TIMES THAT I HAD ... IN THAT SQUEAKY OLD SWING.

THAT WORN OUT ROCKIN' CHAIR

CHORUS:
   SHE WOULD READ FROM THE BIBLE ... THEN TAKE TIME OUT
   TO PRAY ...
WHILE WAITING FOR THE ANGELS ... COMING TO TAKE HER AWAY.
   SHE ALWAYS SEEMED CONTENT ... WHILE SHE WAS SITTING
   THERE ...
SHE WOULD JUST ROCK AWAY ... IN THAT WORN OUT ROCKING
CHAIR.

VERSE ONE:
   GRANDMA SAT FOR YEARS... IN THAT WORN OUT ROCKIN'
   CHAIR ...
SHE NEVER HAD NO WORRIES ... AND SHE SEEMED TO LIKE IT
THERE.
   SOMETIMES SHE WOULD SING ... ONE OF HER FAVORITE SONGS ...
I'LL SOON BE LEAVING YOU ... THIS OLD WORLD IS NOT MY HOME.

VERSE TWO:
   SHE SAID SHE HAD A MANSION ... JUST OVER THE HILLTOP ...
WHERE SHE WAS A GOING ... AND SHE TALKED ABOUT IT A LOT.
   SHE SAID SHE SURE HATED ... TO HAVE TO LEAVE IT HERE ...
SHE THOUHT SHE WOULD MISS ... THAT WORN OUT ROCKIN' CHAIR.

CHORUS:
   SHE WOULD READ FROM THE BIBLE ... THEN TAKE TIME OUT
   TO PRAY ...
WHILE WAITING FOR THE ANGELS ... COMING TO TAKE HER AWAY.
   SHE ALWAYS SEEMED CONTENT ... WHILE SHE WAS SITTING
   THERE ...
SHE WOULD JUST ROCK AWAY ... IN THAT WORN OUT ROCKIN'
CHAIR.

VERSE THREE:
   SHE SAID SHE WAS LEAVING ... AND SHE SAID IT WITH PRIDE ...
SHE WAS GOING OVER THAT MOUTAIN ... TO THE OTHER SIDE.

SHE HAD ENOUGH FAITH ... NOTHING COULD HOLD HER
HERE ...
NOT EVEN HER MOST PECIOUS ... WORN OUT ROCKIN' CHAIR.

CHORUS:
SHE WOULD READ FROM THE BIBLE ... THEN TAKE TIME OUT
TO PRAY ...
WHILE WAITING FOR THE ANGELS ... COMING TO TAKE HER AWAY.
SHE ALWAYS SEEMED CONTENT ... WHILE SHE WAS SITTING
THERE ...
SHE WOULD JUST ROCK AWAY ...IN THAT WORN OUT ROCKIN'
CHAIR.

VERSE FOUR:
MANY YEARS HAVE COME AND GONE ... I KNOW SHE'S HAPPY
NOW ...
SHE'S GONE ON TO HEAVEN ... BUT I'LL SEE HER AGAIN SOMEHOW.
I CAN JUST IMAGINE SEEING HER ... JUST SITTING THERE ...
IN THAT BRAND NEW ... SOLID GOLD ROCKIN' CHAIR.

THAT'S HOW IT WAS

VERSE ONE:
    MY MOTHER CRIED ... WHEN I CALLED HER ...
AND TOLD HER AGAIN ... THAT I WAS IN JAIL ...
    EVEN THOUGH ... SHE WOULD'NT ASK WHY ...
SHE WOULD COME UP ... AND SIGN MY BAIL.

VERSE TWO:
    BUT THAT'S HOW IT WAS...WHEN I NEEDED HELP...
SHE WAS THERE ... WHEN I COULD'NT HELP MYSELF.
    SHE WAS A BLESSING ... PERHAPS IN DISGUISE ...
BUT THAT'S HOW IT WAS ... WHEN MY MOTHER CRIED.

CHORUS:
    YES! THAT'S HOW IT WAS ... WHEN I LIVED IN SIN ...
I HAD NO HOPE FOR TOMORROW ... NO PEACE WITHIN.
    THEN IT ALL HAPPENED... MY WHOLE LIFE CHANGED ...
I MET THE MASTER ... AND HE CHANGED EVERYTHING.

VERSE THREE:
    I NO LONGER LIVED ... IN THE DARKNESS OF NIGHT ...
AND IT'S ALL BECAUSE ... I KNOW WRONG FROM RIGHT.
    I REGRET THE PAIN ... I CAUSED MY MOTHER INSIDE ...
I WILL NEVER FORGET ... HOW MUCH MOTHER CRIED.

CHORUS:
    YES! THAT'S HOW IT WAS ... WHEN I LIVED IN SIN ...
I HAD NO HOPE FOR TOMORROW ... NO PEACE WITHIN.
    THEN IT ALL HAPPENED ... MY WHOLE LIFE CHANGED ...
I MET THE MASTER ... AND HE CHANGED EVERYTHING.

THE AMERICAN MAN

CHORUS:
    WELL IF I CAN ... THEN YOU CAN ...
AND IF YOU CAN ... THEN HE CAN.
    IF HE CAN ... THEN THEY CAN ...
LIVE LIKE ... THE AMERICAN MAN.

VERSE ONE:
    NOW WE CAN DO ... WHAT WE WANT TO ...
IF WE DON'T QUIT ... BEFORE WE'RE THRU.
    WE ALL WANT DREAMS ... TO EXPAND ...
THAT'S THE WAY ... OF THE AMERICAN MAN.

VERSE TWO:
    WE'VE SEEN GOOD TIMES ... AND WE'VE SEEN BAD ...
SOME HAVE LOST ... EVERYTHING THEY HAD.
    BUT WE ARE PROUD ... TO BE AN AMERICAN.
BECAUSE IF ANYBODY CAN ... WE CAN.

CHORUS:
    WELL IF I CAN ... THEN YOU CAN ...
AND IF YOU CAN ... THEN HE CAN.
    IF HE CAN ... THEN THEY CAN ...
LIVE LIKE ... THE AMERICAN MAN.

VERSE THREE:
    WE LOVE EACH OTHER ... NO MATTER WHAT COLOR ...
WHETHER IT'S A FOREIGNER ... SISTER OR BROTHER.
    WE SHOW OUR LOVE ... IN EVERY WAY WE CAN ...
THAT'S THE WAY ... OF THE AMERICAN MAN.

THE CAROLINA COUNTRY SIDE

VERSE ONE:

    FROM THE COUNTRY SIDE ... OF NORTH CAROLINA ...
IS WHERE MY FOLKS ... ALL COME FROM.
    I WAS BORN WAY DOWN ... IN RANDOLPH COUNTY ...
THAT'S THE PLACE ... I CALLED MY HOME.

VERSE TWO:

    WHEN MY DADDY DIED ... MY MOMMA CRIED ...
AND TOOK US CHILDREN ... ALL TO TOWN.
    BUT I NEVER WAS ... FULLY SATISFIED ...
CAUSE BAD LUCK ... WAS ALL THAT I FOUND.

VERSE THREE:

    I FELT LIKE A FOOL ... WHEN I STARTED TO SCHOOL ...
WITH PEOPLE PUSHING ME ... ALL AROUND.
    I WOULD RUN AND HIDE ... AND SOMETIMES I CRIED ...
CAUSE I MISSED THAT CAROLINA ... COUNTRY SIDE.

VERSE FOUR:

    IN MY EARLY TEENS ... I HAD ME A DREAM ...
ABOUT SWIMMING IN A STREAM ... SO WIDE.
    I BOUGHT ME A HOME ... WHERE I FELT I BELONGED ...
IN THE CAROLINA ... COUNTRY SIDE.

CHORUS:

    IT WAS IN ... THE CAROLINA COUNTRY SIDE ...
I COULD LEAVE MY WINDOWS ... OPENED WIDE.
    AND I KNOW THIS IS WHERE ... I WILL ABIDE ...
IN THE CAROLINA ... COUNTRY SIDE.

THE CURTAINS WILL COME DOWN

VERSE ONE:

THE CURTAINS OPENED ... HE WAS STANDING ON STAGE ...
YOU COULD PLAINLY SEE ... HE WAS GETTING UP IN AGE.
BUT HE WAS STILL ABLE ... TO DO HIS THING ...
AND THE PEOPLE STILL LOVED ... TO HEAR HIM SING.

VERSE TWO:

HE HAD GRAY HAIR ... AND WRINKLES ON HIS FACE ...
HE DRESSED REAL NICE ... AND HAD A CLEAN SHAVE.
EVEN THOUGH HE WAS OLD ... AND MOVED REAL SLOW ...
HE WAS STILL ABLE TO PUT ON ... A REAL GOOD SHOW.

VERSE THREE:

BUT SO MUCH TIME ... HAS COME AND GONE ...
AND HE HAS SUNG SO MANY ... OF HIS BEST SONGS.
ALL THROUGH THE YEARS ... YOU WERE HIS FANS ...
BUT YOU MAY NOT BE ABLE ... TO HEAR HIM AGAIN.

CHORUS:

THE CURTAINS WILL COME DOWN ... FOR HIS LAST TIME ...
THEY SAY THAT THE SUN ... WILL NOT ALWAYS SHINE.
BUT I BELIEVE HIS NAME ... WILL BE ETCHED IN STONE ...
BECAUSE HIS KIND OF MUSIC ... WILL LIVE ON AND ON.

THE DAY MY MOMMA DIED

VERSE ONE:

  I NEVER WILL FORGET ... ONE OF MY SADDEST TIMES ...
THAT REALLY DID HURT ME ... AND I ALMOST LOST MY MIND.
  MY HEART WENT WITH HER ... I FELT EMPTY INSIDE ...
I LOST A BIG PART OF ME ... THE DAY MY MOMMA DIED.

VERSE TWO:

  MY MOTHER WAS A PERSON ... THAT I COULD COUNT ON ...
AND I REALLY DO MISS HER ... NOW THAT SHE IS GONE.
  SHE WAS ALWAYS THERE FOR ME ... WITH ARMS OPENED
WIDE ...
AND THE ANGELS WELCOMED HER ... THE DAY MY MOMMA DIED.

CHORUS:

  MOMMA ... I MISS YOU ... BUT I KNOW THAT YOU'RE OKAY ...
ST. PETER CALLED YOUR NAME ... IT WAS ON THE ROLL THAT DAY.
  SOON I'LL COME TO JOIN YOU ... BUT FIRST I MUST WAIT ...
THEN WE WILL LIVE FOREVER ... INSIDE THE PEARLY GATES.

VERSE THREE:

  SHE WILL BE GLAD TO SEE ME ... WHEN MY TIME COMES TO
DIE ...
WE WILL NEVER PART AGAIN ... THERE IS NO SUCH THING AS TIME.
  I DON'T THINK ABOUT YARD SALES ... OR THINGS I USED TO
BUY ...
MY THOUGHTS HAVE BEEN IN HEAVEN ... SINCE THE DAY MY
MOMMA DIED.

VERSE FOUR:

  THE STREETS ARE PURE GOLD ... WITH MANSIONS BUILT SO
HIGH ...
AND THERE WILL BE NO TEARS ... WITH NO REASONS THERE TO CRY.
  THERE IS A RIVER FLOWING ... BESIDE THE TREE OF LIFE...
AND I KNOW SHE IS ENJOYING ... SINCE THE DAY MY MOMMA DIED.

CHORUS:

     MOMMA ... I MISS YOU ... BUT I KNOW THAT YOU'RE OKAY ...
ST. PETER CALLED YOUR NAME ... IT WAS ON THE ROLL THAT DAY.
     SOON I'LL COME TO JOIN YOU ... BUT FIRST I MUST WAIT ...
THEN WE WILL LIVE FOREVER ... INSIDE THE PEARLY GATES.
     YES ... WE WILL LIVE FOREVER ... INSIDE THE PEARLY GATES.

THE DAY THAT JESUS DIED

VERSE ONE:
    IT WAS A VERY SAD DAY ... THE DAY THAT JESUS DIED ...
ALL HOPE SEEMED TO BE GONE ... AND THE WHOLE WORLD CRIED.
    BUT THEN SOMETHING HAPPENED ... HE ROSE UP FROM THE
    GRAVE ...
JUST THE WAY HE SAID HE WOULD ... AFTER ONLY THREE DAYS.

VERSE TWO:
    THE PEOPLE STARTED REJOICING ... THEIR HOPE WAS
    RENEWED ...
BECAUSE THEY KNEW THAT THEN ... WHAT HE SAID WAS TRUE.
    THE DEVIL WAS DEFEATED ... THERE WAS NOWHERE FOR HIM
    TO HIDE ...
GOD'S SON HAD CONQUERED DEATH ... THE DAY THAT JESUS DIED.

CHORUS:
    THAT DAY WILL NEVER BE FORGOTTEN ... THE DAY THAT JESUS
    DIED ...
WHEN THEY PUT THORNS ON HIS HEAD ... AND PIERCED HIM IN
HIS SIDE.
    THEY DROVE NAILS THRU HIS HANDS AND FEET ... OPENED
    GASHES WIDE ...
BUT THAT MADE HIS LIFE COMPLETE ... THE DAY THAT JESUS DIED.

VERSE THREE:
    HE WAS HUNG ON THE CROSS ... HE LET THEM TORCHER HIM ...
HE SUFFERED AND HE DIED ... TO FREE THE WORLD FROM SIN.
    HE SHOWED HIS LOVE THAT DAY ... FOR THEM THAT WOULD
    ABIDE ...
IT'S NEVER BEEN A LOVE LIKE THIS ... SINCE THE DAY THAT JESUS
DIED.

VERSE FOUR:
    THEY COULD'NT HAVE TAKEN HIS LIFE ... FOR HE WAS GOD'S
    OWN SON ...

BUT HE WILLINGLY LET THEM DO IT ... SO SALVATION COULD BE WON

HE COULD HAVE STOPPED THEM ... IF ONLY HE HAD TRIED ... THE PLAN OF SALVATION WAS FULFILLED ... THE DAY THAT JESUS DIED..

CHORUS:

THAT DAY WILL NEVER BE FORGOTTEN ... THE DAY THAT JESUS DIED ...
WHEN THEY PUT THORNS ON HIS HEAD ... AND PIERCED HIM IN HIS SIDE.

THEY DROVE NAILS THRU HIS HANDS AND FEET ... OPENED GASHES WIDE ...
BUT THAT MADE HIS LIFE COMPLETE ... THE DAY THAT JESUS DIED.

THE GOOD OLD USA

I WENT TO A SHOPPING CENTER ... TO TAKE MY DAILY WALK ...
I GOT TIRED AND SAT DOWN ... TO LISTEN TO SOME PEOPLE TALK.
I COULD'NT BELIEVE THE WORDS ... OF THE THINGS THAT I
HEARD...
THE WAY THEY RAN OUR COUNTRY DOWN ... WAS JUST PLAIN
ABSURB.

IT WAS ABOUT HOW HIGH ... THE COST OF LIVING HAD
GOTTEN ...
THEY DID'NT SEEM TO CARE ... ABOUT THE THREATS OF BEN LADEN.
ALL THEY WANTED TO DO WAS ... JUST SIT THERE AND
COMPLAIN...
THEY WAS'NT EVEN THANKFUL FOR ... GETTING RID OF SADDEM
HUSIAN.

THIS COUNTRY IS NOT PERFECT... BUT IT'S THE BEST IN THE
WORLD...
IF YOU'RE NOT SATISFIED HERE ... LOCK YOURSELF UP IN A BARREL.
AND DON'T EVEN THINK ABOUT ... EVER TRYING TO GET OUT ...
BECAUSE WE ARE AMERICANS ... WE DON'T NEED TO HEAR YOUR
MOUTH.

SOME COUNTRYS PEOPLE ARE BEGGING ... TO GET SOMETHING
TO EAT...
THEY HAVE NO DOCTOR'S THERE ... AND PEOPLE ARE DYING IN THE
STREET.
HERE IF ANYONE IS HUNGRY ... THEY CAN GET SOME FOOD
STAMPS ...
THE STATE GIVES THEM VOUCHERS ... TO HAVE A PLACE TO LAY
DOWN.

WE ARE AMERICANS AND PROUD ... OF THE OLD RED WHITE
AND BLUE ...
AND IF YOU DON'T PLEDGE OUR FLAG ... WE WANT NO PART OF YOU.

LET'S FIGHT FOR OUR FREEDOM ... TO WORSHIP IN OUR OWN WAY ...

AND PLEDGE TO THE STARS AND STRIPES ... OF THE GOOD OLD USA.

LET'S MAKE IT WORK FOR ALL PEOPLE ... THE RICH AND POOR ALIKE ...

AND HELP CHANGE EACH OTHERS FUTURE ... FROM DARKNESS INTO LIGHT.

LET'S ALL LOVE ONE ANOTHER ... AND MAKE THE SORROWS GO AWAY ...

AND JUST BE PROUD TO BE A PART OF ... THE NEW USA.

THE HERE AFTER

VERSE ONE:

     I'VE HEARD A LOT OF TALK ... ABOUT THE HERE AFTER ...

BUT WHEN IT COMES TO LIVING ... THERE IS ANOTHER CHAPTER.

     IT'S ABOUT LIVING LIFE NOW ... AND THINGS HAPPENING TODAY ...

AND WONDERING WHAT DID YOU ... COME HERE AFTER ANYWAY.

VERSE TWO:

     IT'S GOOD TO GET OLD ... BUT YOU MUST PAY A PRICE THOUGH ...

YOU DON'T GET AROUND AS FAST ... AND YOUR MEMORY GETS SLOW.

     SOMETIMES I GO TO THE STORE ... FOR WHAT I CAN'T REMEMBER ...

I ASK WITH A LITTLE LAUGHTER ... WHAT DID I COME HERE AFTER.

CHORUS:

     NOW PEOPLE THINKS THAT HERE AFTER ... IS A LONG WAYS OFF ...

BUT IT'S KNOCKING ON YOUR BACK DOOR ... IT MAY BE IN YOUR LOFT.

     SO WHEN YOUR MEMORY FAILS YOU ... DON'T LOOK THE OTHER WAY ...

JUST HAVE HOPE FOR TOMORROW ... THAT'S HERE AFTER TODAY.

VERSE THREE:

     I WAS DOING SOME REPAIR WORK ... FOOLING AROUND MY HOME ...

WHEN I NEEDED SOME THINGS ... THAT WAS IN THE OTHER ROOM.

     I DECIDED TO GO TO THE WORKSHOP ... TO GET ME A LADDER ...

AND WHEN I GOT THERE I ASK ... WHAT DID I COME HERE AFTER.

VERSE FOUR:

     THE HERE AFTER IS TODAY ... THAT YOU WORRIED ABOUT YESTERDAY.

YOU THINK ABOUT SOME THINGS ... THAT DID'NT GO YOUR WAY.

YOU ALWAYS GET CONFUSED ... AND DON'T KNOW WHAT TO SAY ...

YOU GET MIXED UP AND WONDER ... WHAT YOU'RE HERE AFTER ANYWAY.

CHORUS:

NOW PEOPLE THINKS THAT HERE AFTER ... IS A LONG WAYS OFF ...

BUT IT'S KNOCKING ON YOUR BACK DOOR ... IT MAY BE IN YOUR LOFT.

SO WHEN YOUR MEMORY FAILS YOU ... DON'T LOOK THE OTHER WAY ...

JUST HAVE HOPE FOR TOMORROW ... THAT'S HERE AFTER TODAY.

THE HIGH POINT CITY JAIL

VERSE ONE:

     IF I'M NOT AT HOME ... WHEN YOU CALL ME ON THE PHONE...
YOU CAN WRITE ME ... A LINE OR TWO.
     AND THEN I'LL KNOW ... YOU ARE THINKING OF ME ...
AND I'LL BE ... A THINKING OF YOU.

VERSE TWO:

     I WILL NEVER FORGET ... THE DAY THAT YOU LEFT ...
AND I KNEW ... YOU WAS'NT GOING TO STAY.
     BUT I MISSED YOU SO MUCH ...I WENT AND GOT DRUNK ...
AND THEY LOCKED ME UP ... TODAY.

CHORUS:

     BUT YOU CAN STILL ... WRITE ME A LETTER ...
BUT BE SURE ... TO DROP IT IN THE MAIL.
     AND DON'T FORGET ... TO SEND IT IN CARE ...
OF THE HIGH POINT ... CITY JAIL.

VERSE THREE:

    I STUMBLED AND FELL ... AND BROKE A FINGER NAIL ...
AND I WAS TRIMMING IT ... WITH MY KNIFE.

    BUT A WOMAN THOUGHT ... IT WAS AN ASSAULT ...
AND THAT WOMAN ... WAS THE JUDGE'S WIFE.

CHORUS:

    BUT YOU CAN STILL ... WRITE ME A LETTER ...
BUT BE SURE ... TO DROP IT IN THE MAIL.

    AND DON'T FORGET ... TO SEND IT IN CARE ...
OF THE HIGH POINT ... CITY JAIL.

THE KING OF SKID ROW

VERSE ONE:
HE HEARD IT SO MANY TIMES ... IT WAS TOO MUCH TO
INCLINE ...
OF HOW BAD LIFE WOULD GET ... BEFORE THE END OF TIME.
HE DID'NT KNOW WHAT TO DO ... AND HE DID'NT KNOW
WHERE TO GO ...
AND SO HE FOUND HIMSELF A LIVING ... DOWN ON SKID ROW.

VERSE TWO:
SOMEONE GAVE HIM A GUITAR ... AND HE LOVED THAT OLD
THING ...
AND HE LEARNED HOW TO PLAY ... AND HE LEARNED HOW TO SING.
HE PLAYED FOR EVERYONE ... HE PLANTED SEEDS THAT WOULD
GROW ...
AND EVERYONE CALLED HIM ... THE KING OF SKID ROW.

CHORUS:
THEY CALLED HIM THE KING ... THE KING OF SKID ROW ...
YOU COULD HEAR HIM PLAYING ... EVERYWHERE HE WOULD GO.
BUT FAME AND FORTUNE MADE HIM ... A TOO WELL KNOWN
JOE ...
AND SO HE WENT BACK TO BEING ... JUST A BUM ON SKID ROW.

VERSE THREE:
THEN HE STARTED PLAYING IN CLUBS ... AND HONKY TONKS
AROUND ...
AND THE PEOPLE SEEMED TO LIKE ... HOW HIS MUSIC WOULD
SOUND.
SO HE STARTED HIM A BAND ... AND THE REST OF IT YOU
KNOW ...
HE WENT ALL THE WAY FROM SKID ROW ... TO NASHVILLE'S
MUSIC ROW.

VERSE FOUR:
IT'S A LONG LONG WAYS ... FROM SKID ROW TO MUSIC ROW ...

THE LIGHTS ARE MORE BRIGHTER THERE .. WHERE THE GLAMOUR FLOWS.

NO ONE WOULD BELIEVE ... OR COULD EVER POSSIBLY KNOW ...

HOW FAR THE KING OF SKID ROW WENT ... TO NASHVILLE'S MUSIC ROW.

CHORUS:

THEY CALLED HIM THE KING ... THE KING OF SKID ROW ...

YOU COULD HEAR HIM PLYING ... EVERYWHERE YOU WOULD GO.

BUT FORTUNE AND FAME ... MADE HIM A TOO WELL KNOWN JOE ...

AND SO HE WENT BACK TO BEING ... JUST A BUM ON SKID ROW.

THE LAST COWBOYS SONG

VERSE ONE:
A COWBOYS LIFE IS RUGGED AND ROUGH ... BUT STILL IT MUST GO ON ...
THEY CAN'T GET ENOUGH SO THEY KEEP IT UP ... SINGING ALL NIGHT LONG.
COOKING THEIR FOOD ON AN OLD CAMPFIRE ... WORKING AS TIME GOES ON ...
LAUGHING AND JOKING AND SINGING ... AND LOVING THEIR COWBOYS SONGS .

VERSE TWO:
THEY SING ABOUT THEIR WOMEN ... OR SOMETHING THAT WENT WRONG ...
THEY SING WITH THE RYTHM AND BEAT ... OF TIME THAT IS GONE.
AS THE CAMPFIRE SPARKLES ... IT KEEPS A GOOD RYTHM AT NIGHT ...
THEY SING IN THE MIDNIGHT MOONLIGHT ... TO KEEP THE CATTLE QUIET.

VERSE THREE:
IT'S GOOD TO HEAR THE COWBOYS ... AS THEY SING THEIR SONGS ...
IT FILLS THEIR HEARTS WITH JOY ... AS THEY SING ALL NIGHT LONG.
THEY HAVE A SEAT RESERVED ... JUST SITTING IN THEIR SADDLE ...
WITH A SONG IN THEIR HEART ... AND WATCHING OVER THE CATTLE.

CHORUS:
YODELING OVER AN OLD CAMPFIRE ... LONG NIGHTS UNTIL DAWN ...
AND SLEEPING IN A SLEEPING BAG ... THAT IS A COWBOYS HOME.
IT WILL BE A SAD TIME ... WHEN ALL THE COWBOYS ARE GONE ...
THE PRAIRE WILL BE QUIET... WHEN THEY SING THE LAST COWBOYS SONG.

VERSE FOUR:

    A COWBOYS SONG IS HIS PRIDE AND JOY ... AS HE RIDES
    ALONG ...
IT TELLS OF THINGS IN HIS LIFE ... WHETHER IT WAS RIGHT OR
WRONG.
    HE LOVES RIDING THE RANGE ... WHERE THE SADDLE IS HIS
    HOME ...
THEY PUT THEIR PAST IN A CRADDLE ... AS THEY SING A COWBOYS
SONG.

VERSE FIVE:

    THEY LOVE TO KEEP ON SINGING ... IT KEEPS THEIR SPIRIT
    STRONG ...
THERE WILL ALWAYS BE YODELING ... UNTIL ALL THE COWBOYS
ARE GONE.
    A COWBOY DOES WHAT HE LIKES ... HE KNOWS WHERE HE
    BELONGS ...
IT WILL GO DOWN IN HISTORY WHEN THEY SING ...THE LAST
COWBOYS SONG.

"THE LETTER"

VERSE ONE:

    I DREAMED I GOT A LETTER ... POST MARKED FROM HEAVEN ... IT WAS THE STRANGEST GIFT ... I HAD EVER BEEN GIVEN.

    I THOUGHT AT FIRST ... IT WAS SOME KIND OF A JOKE ... UNTIL I BEGAN TO READ ... THE WORDS THAT WAS WROTE.

    IT SAID I KNOW YOU DO THINGS ... YOU SHOULD'NT DO ... AND I KNOW ALL THE HARD TIMES ... YOU ARE GOING THROUGH.

    SOMETIMES I SEE YOU TALKING ... TO SOME OF YOUR FRIENDS ... THE CONVERSATIONS ARE NOT PLEASANT ... BUT I'LL WAIT AGAIN.

VERSE THREE:

    I WAIT BECAUSE I WANT YOU ... TO TALK BACK WITH ME TOO ... I WANT YOU TO KNOW ... THAT I MADE THIS DAY FOR YOU.

    I'LL WAIT AND I'LL WAIT ... EVEN UNTIL THE JOURNEY'S END ... BECAUSE I JUST WANT YOU TO KNOW ... THAT I AM YOUR FRIEND.

VERSE FOUR:

    BUT YOU WON'T EVEN LISTEN ... WHEN I TELL YOU I LOVE YOU. BUT IF YOU LOOK YOU CAN SEE IT ... IN THE SKIES SO BLUE.

    SOMETIMES I EVEN WHISPER IT ... ALL THROUGH THE TREES ... AND I EVEN BREATH IT ... ALL THROUGH THE EVENING BREEZE.

VERSE FIVE:

    I LET THE WATERS FLOW ... DOWN THE MOUNTAIN STREAMS ... I GIVE ALL THE BIRDS ... BEAUTIFUL LOVE SONGS TO SING.

    SO IF YOU'LL TALK TO ME ... YOU'LL FIND I'M FAIR AND JUST ... AND IT WAS SIGNED BY YOUR FRIEND ... JESUS.

THE MAN HE USED TO BE

VERSE ONE:

    I NEVER GOT TO KNOW HIM ... CAUSE HE DIED WHEN I WAS ONE ...

BUT IN MY HEART I FELT HE WAS WITH ME ... BECAUSE I WAS HIS SON.

    I'LL NEVER UNDERSTAND WHY GOD ... TOOK HIM AWAY FROM ME ...

BUT I BELIEVE HE IS IN HEAVEN BECAUSE ... OF THE MAN HE USED TO BE.

VERSE TWO:

    HE WORKED HIMSELF TO DEATH ... AT A VERY YOUNG AGE ...

BUT HE LEFT A GOOD LEGACY ... TO BE WRITTEN ON THE FAMILY PAGE.

    HE WAS A VERY GOOD FATHER ... TO A VERY LARGE FAMILY ...

AND NOT MANY MEN CAN HOLD A LIGHT ... TO THE MAN HE USED TO BE.

CHORUS:

    I WISH I HAD KNOWN MY DAD ... ALL I KNOW IS WHAT I'VE HEARD ...

THEY SAY HE WAS A VERY GOOD MAN ... AND I BELIEVE EVERY WORD.

    THEY SAY THEY CAN SEE HIM IN ME ... IF SO I EARNED IT FREE ...

BUT I KNOW THAT I WILL NEVER BE ... THE MAN HE USED TO BE.

VERSE THREE:

    WE LIVED ON A FARM ... IN THE MIDDLE OF NORTH CAROLINA ...

THE LAND WAS RICH AND TREE'S WAS TALL ... AND GRASS WAS GREENER.

    HE KEPT FOOD ON THE TABLE ... AND SHOE'S ON OUR FEET ...

NO ONE CAN COMPLAIN ABOUT ... THE MAN HE USED TO BE.

VERSE FOUR:

    IT'S HARD GROWING UP WITHOUT A DAD ... BUT IT'S BEEN HANDED DOWN ...

HE WAS A HARD WORKING MAN ... AND A BETTER ONE COULD'NT BE FOUND.

WHEN I LEAVE THIS EARTH ... I HOPE THEY'LL SAY THE SAME ABOUT ME ...
WHEN THEY TALK AND SPEAK ABOUT... THE MAN HE USED TO BE.

CHORUS:
I WISH I HAD KNOWN MY DAD ... ALL I KNOW IS WHAT I'VE HEARD ...
THEY SAY HE WAS A VERY GOOD MAN ... AND I BELIEVE EVERY WORD.
THEY SAY THEY CAN SEE HIM IN ME ... IF SO I EARNED IT FREE ...
BUT I KNOW THAT I WILL NEVER BE ... THE MAN HE USED TO BE.

THE NIGHT JESUS WAS BORN

VERSE ONE:

I WAS IN SIN BARELY LIVIN' ... AND DOING ALL KINDS OF DRUGS ... BUT WHEN I HEARD ABOUT THE BIRTH OF JESUS ... IT GAVE ME A NUDGE.

IT OPENED MY EYES AND I COULD SEE ... WHAT IT WAS DOING TO ME ...

THEN I COULD'NT RUN ANYMORE ... SO I FELL DOWN ON MY KNEE'S.

VERSE TWO:

MY DAYS WERE SO WEARY ... AND MY LIFE WAS SO TORN ... UNTIL THE DAY I HEARD ABOUT ... THE NIGHT JESUS WAS BORN.

I FELT A NEW BEGINNING COMING ON ... BECAUSE I BELIEVED ... I OPENED MY HEART AND INVITED HUM IN ... AND HIS LOVE I RECIEVED.

VERSE THREE:

NOW MY LIFE HAS A MEANING ... SINCE I HAVE ACCEPTED HIM ...

AND NOW I AM SO MUCH HAPPIER ... SINCE I LET HIM IN.

HE HELPS ME FIGHT THE BATTLES ... WHEN I GO THRU THE STORMS ...

THE FUTURE IS SO MUCH BRIGHTER ... SINCE THE NIGHT JESUS WAS BORN.

CHORUS:

THE NIGHT JESUS WAS BORN ... WAS SPREAD AROUND THE WORLD ...

HE CAME TO SAVE THOSE THAT ARE LOST ... INCLUDING BOYS AND GIRLS.

ALL THE ANGELS WERE SINGING ... WITH SOUNDS OF A HORN ... NOW THE WHOLE WORLD KNOWS ABOUT ... THE NIGHT JESUS WAS BORN.

VERSE FOUR:

NOW WHEN I SEE ALL THE FLASHES ... OF THE CHRISTMAS LIGHTS ...

I CAN SEE ALL THE TWINKLES ... I KNOW HE HAS IN HIS EYES.
CHRISTMAS DAY IS A SPECIAL DAY ... THAT SHOULD BE ADORED ...
BECAUSE IT CELEBRATES THE BIRTH OF ... THE NIGHT JESUS WAS BORN.

CHORUS:
THE NIGHT JESUS WAS BORN ... WAS SPREAD AROUND THE WORLD ...
HE CAME TO SAVE THOSE THAT ARE LOST ... INCLUDING BOYS AND GIRLS.
ALL THE ANGELS WERE SINGING ... WITH SOUNDS OF A HORN ...
NOW THE WHOLE WORLD KNOWS ABOUT ... THE NIGHT JESUS WAS BORN.

THE NIGHT THE SNOW FELL

VERSE ONE:
> STANDING ON THE CORNER ... THE NIGHT THE SNOW FELL DOWN ...

IT LOOKED SO SOFT ... AS IT STUCK TO THE GROUND.
> I WATCHED IT GLITTER ... AS IT FELL FROM THE SKY ...

LIKE THE TWINKLE THAT I SAW ... WHEN I LOOKED INTO HER EYES.

VERSE TWO:
> I WILL NEVER FORGET ... THE NIGHT THAT WE MET ...

SHE WAS STANDING THERE ... SNOW WAS FLAKING IN HER HAIR.
> SHE LOOKED AROUND AT ME ... AND THEN I SAW HER SMILE ...

I JUST STOOD THERE A'LOOKING ... AT HER FOR A WHILE.

CHORUS:
> THE NIGHT THE SNOW FELL ... THE FASTER MY HEART BEAT ...

WHEN I WALKED CLOSE TO HER ... MY HEART FELL AT HER FEET.
> I COULD HARDLY STAND STILL ... AND I COULD BARELY SPEAK ...

MY KNEE'S STARTED KNOCKING ... AND I GOT SO WEAK.

VERSE THREE:
> THAT'S ONE TIME I'LL NEVER FORGET ... IT WAS LATE IN DECEMBER ...

THE NIGHT THE SNOW WAS FALLING ... I WILL ALWAYS REMEMBER.
> IT WAS ALMOST CHRISTMAS TIME ... AND I WAS FEELING LOW ...

BUT THEN SOMETHING HAPPENED ... GOD SENT DOWN THE SNOW.

VERSE FOUR:
> I ASK HER FOR A DATE ... SHE SAID I DON'T KNOW YOU ...

I SAID MAYBE IF YOU TRIED ... YOU COULD LEARN A THING OR TWO.
> SHE LOOKED AT ME AND GRINNED ... AND SAID I GUESS SO ...

WE BEGIN TO WALK DOWN THE STREET ... A KICKING AT THE SNOW.

VERSE FIVE:

THE NIGHT SNOW WAS FALLING DOWN ... WE WALKED ALL
OVER TOWN ...
WE WERE LAUGHING AND SINGING ... PEOPLE STANDING ALL
AROUND.
BUT THEN ALL OF A SUDDEN ... I NOTICED SHE WAS GONE ...
BUT I HAD ENOUGH MEMMORIES ... TO LAST ME FROM NOW ON.

CHORUS:

THE NIGHT THE SNOW FELL ... THE FASTER MY HEART BEAT ...
WHEN I WALKED CLOSE TO HER ... MY HEART FELL AT HER FEET.
I COULD HARDLY STAND STILL ... AND I COULD BARELY
SPEAK ...
MY KNEE'S STARTED KNOCKING ... AND I FELT SO WEAK.

THE OBITUARY

VERSE ONE:

    THE OBITUARY TELLS THE STORY ... OF A PERSON AFTER THEY DIE ...

IT MOSTLY SPEAKS OF GOOD THINGS ... THEY DID WHILE THEY WERE ALIVE.

    IT SPEAKS OF WHAT THEY DID ... AND WHO THEIR FAMILIES ARE ...

SOMETIMES IT SAYS THEY'VE GONE SOMEWHERE ... FAR BEYOND THE STARS.

VERSE TWO:

    I READ ABOUT A CERTAIN WOMAN ... WHO HAD JUST PASSED AWAY ...

WHO FELL IN LOVE WITH A CERTAIN MAN ... WHO IS STILL LIVING TODAY.

    THEY WERE HAPPILY MARRIED ... AND MOVED INTO THEIR NEW HOME ...

BUT THINGS WILL BE DIFFERANT NOW ... BECAUSE HE HAS TO LIVE ALONE.

CHORUS:

    HER OBITUARY SAID THAT SHE HAD RETIRED ... IN HER LATER YEARS ...

AND AS I READ A LITTLE FURTHER ... I COULD'NT HOLD BACK THE TEARS.

    SHE WAS A VERY LOVING PERSON ... AND HAD A LOT OF FRIENDS ...

BUT TO TELL THE WHOLE STORY ... I WOULD'NT KNOW WHERE TO BEGIN.

VERSE THREE:

    YOU COULD WRITE A WHOLE BOOK ... WITH LOVE ON EVERY PAGE ...

SHE HAD SO MUCH LOVE TO GIVE ... AND IT GOT BETTER WITH OLD AGE.

I KNOW SHE WILL BE MISSED ... BY THOSE WHO LOVED HER SO
DEAR ...
SHE LEFT A LOT OF GOOD MEMORIES ... WHILE SHE WAS LIVING
DOWN HERE.

VERSE FOUR:
I DON'T KNOW WHY WE HAVE TO LOSE ... THE ONES WE
DEARLY LOVE ...
BUT THAT'S HOW THIS LIFE IS ... AND THAT'S HOW IT ALWAYS WAS.
THE OBITUARY COULD'NT TELL ... EVERYTHING GOOD ABOUT
HER LIFE ...
I KNOW SHE WAS A GOOD PERSON ... BECAUSE THAT WOMAN WAS
MY WIFE.

THE OLD MAN

I ONCE KNEW A PERSON ... KNOWN ALL OVER THE LAND ...
NO ONE KNEW HIS NAME ... THEY CALLED HIM THE OLD MAN.
HE DID'NT HAVE NO ENEMIES ... JUST A LOT OF FRIENDS ...
HE MADE YOU LAUGH ... EVEN IF FATE HAD THE UPPER HAND.

HE ALWAYS HAD A SMILE ... AND HE WORE A BIG BLACK HAT ..
YOU COULD'NT HELP BUT TO LIKE HIM ... WHERE EVER HE WAS AT.
HE WOULD BRING HAPPINESS ... WHEN EVER HE CAME TO
BAT ...
BECAUSE THE OLD MAN HAD SOMETHING ... NO ONE ELSE HAD.

NO ONE NEVER ASKED ... WHERE HE REALLY CAME FROM ...
AND NO ONE EVER KNEW ... ALL THE THINGS HE HAD DONE.
THERE WAS NO WAY OF KNOWING ...THE PLACES HE HAD
BEEN ...
WHEN YOU NEEDED HELP ... THE OLD MAN WOULD DO IT AGAIN.

HE WAS GETTING UP IN AGE ... BUT THE MAN WOULD CONFESS ...
THROUGHOUT HIS WHOLE LIFE ... HE HAD REALLY BEEN BLESSED.
HE WOULD'NT TALK MUCH ... ABOUT THE PAST HE HAD
LIVED ...
HE WOULD SAY HE'S THANKFUL ... FOR WHAT LIFE HAD TO GIVE.

HIS FACE WOULD LIGHT UP ... EVERY TIME HE SMILED ...
SOMETIMES HE HAD THE APPEARANCE ... OF A LITTLE CHILD.
NO MATTER WHAT THE PROBLEM ... WHEN EVER HE CAME IN ...
THE LEGEND STILL HAS IT ... THE OLD MAN HAS DONE IT AGAIN.

THE SEASONS OF LIFE

VERSE ONE:

LIFE BEGINS TO FLURISH ... THE MOMENT YOU COME ALIVE ...
AND THERE ARE DIFFERENT SEASONS ... TO LIVE BEFORE YOU DIE.
THE FIRST IS THE SPRINGTIME ... WHEN A NEW BORN BABY
SMILES ...
BUT THE SEASON IS TOO SHORT ... IT ONLY LAST FOR A LITTLE
WHILE.

VERSE TWO:

THEN COMES THE SUMMER ... WHEN YOU'RE IN THE UPPER
TEENS ...
YOU'RE FULL OF LIFE SO YOU LOOK FOR ... THE GIRL OF YOUR
DREAMS.
YOU GET MARRIED AND HAVE KIDS ... WHILE YOU ARE IN YOUR
PRIME ...
AND THAT MAKES LIFE SO BEAUTIFUL ... AND THAT IS THE
SUMMERTIME.

VERSE THREE:

AND THEN COMES THE FALL ... YOU WATCH THE GRAND KIDS
PLAY ...
SUDDENLY THEY ARE ALL GONE ... LIKE THE LEAVES THAT ARE
BLOWN AWAY.
THEN LIFE SEEMS SO EMPTY ... LIKE THE TREE JUST STANDING
THERE ...
LIFE BEGINS TO TAKE IT'S TOLL ... AND YOU WONDER IF ANYONE
CARES.

VERSE FOUR:

AND THEN IT FINALLY GETS HERE ... THE WINTER TIME AND
THE COLD ...
YOUR HAIR HAS TURNED WHITE ... LIKE THE GROUND COVERED
WITH SNOW.

YOUR BODY IS GETTING WEAK NOW ... THE SEASONS OF LIFE
ARE ALL GONE ...
SO THEY PUT YOU IN THE GRAVE ... WHERE YOU BEEN HEADED ALL
ALONG.

CHORUS:
THE SEASONS OF LIFE ARE OVER ... IT'S TIME TO REAP WHAT
YOU SOWED ...
YOU CAME FROM THE DUST OF THE EARTH ... BACK TO THE DUST
YOU'LL GO.
IT'S BEEN A LONG HARD BATTLE ... SINCE THE DAY THAT YOU
WERE BORN ...
YOU'RE GOING TO A NEW DIMENSION ... FROMM A BODY THAT'S
WEAK AND WORN.

THE VERY BEST

VERSE ONE:

     MY FRIENDS TRIED TO TELL ME ... IT COULD'NT BE DONE ...
BUT I WAS STILL DETERMINED ... TO HAVE MY FUN.
     I WAS KIND OF STUBBURN ... AND HARD HEADED TOO ...
THINKING THERE WAS NOTHING ... THAT I COULD'NT DO.

VERSE TWO:

     IF THEY SAID I COULD'NT DO IT ... I WOULD DO IT ANYWAY...
SOMETIMES MY HEART WOULD BREAK ... LIKE A PIECE OF CLAY.
     BUT I WOULD GET RIGHT UP ... AND DO IT ALL AGAIN ...
KNOWING THERE WAS NO WAY ... I WAS GOING TO WIN.

VERSE THREE:

     I FOUGHT MANY BATTLES ... OF WHICH MOST I WON ...
BUT WHAT DID I WIN ... ONCE IT WAS OVER AND DONE.
     I HAD TO PROVE SOMETHING ... ONLY TO MYSELF ...
I CERTAINLY DID'NT HAVE TO PROVE IT ... TO ANYONE ELSE.

VERSE FOUR:

     BY DOING STUPID THINGS ... I WASTED MY LIFE AWAY ...
NOT THINKING THAT SOMEDAY ... I WOULD HAVE TO PAY.
     I HEARD IT SAID ... THAT YOU REAP JUST WHAT YOU SOW ...
BUT I WAS SO MIXED UP ... I DID'NT KNOW WHICH WAY TO GO.

VERSE FIVE:

     WATCH HOW YOU LIVE ... BE SURE YOU LIVE IT RIGHT ...
DON'T LET IT MAKE YOU ... TO LOSE ANY SLEEP AT NIGHT.
     LET PEOPLE SAY ... THAT YOU WAS DOING GOOD ...
AND YOU DID THE VERY BEST ... THAT YOU COULD DO.

THE WAY I LIVED BACK THEN

CHORUS:
I TOOK MY WHOLE LIFE ... AND I PUT IT IN A SONG ...
I SPOKE ABOUT THE RIGHT ... AND I SUNG ABOUT THE WRONG.
I TOLD OF HOW IT WAS ... NOT HOW IT SHOULD HAVE BEEN ...
I WONDER HOW I MADE IT ... THE WAY I LIVED BACK THEN.

VERSE ONE:
SOMETHINGS I KNEW NOT TO DO ... I DID THEM ANYWAY ...
BUT I WON'T APOLOGIZE ... I CAN'T TURN BACK YESTERDAY.
THERE'S NOTHING I CAN DO ... I CAN'T CHANGE ONE MINUTE ...
WHY WORRY ABOUT THE PAST ... I'LL HAVE TO LIVE WITH IT.

VERSE TWO:
PEOPLE TALKS ABOUT THE PAST ... THAT'S ALL OVER NOW ...
SO LIVE FOR TODAY ... THAT'S ALL WE HAVE ANYHOW.
WE DON'T HAVE THE POWER ... TO CHANGE YESTERDAY ...
THIS MOMENT RIGHT NOW ... IS ALL WE HAVE ANYWAY.

VERSE THREE:
NOW JUST LIVE YOUR LIFE ... AND BE GLAD YOU'RE LIVING ...
AND ENJOY EVERY MOMENT ... THAT YOU ARE GIVEN.
YOU ONLY HAVE ONE LIFE ... SO DON'T LIVE IT IN FEAR ...
AND DON'T BE ASHAMED OF WHAT ... YOU DID WHILE HERE.

VERSE FOUR:
I HAVE HEARD PEOPLE SAY... THEIR LIFE HAS BEEN WASTED ...
AND IF TOMORROW GETS HERE ... THEY ARE AFRAID TO FACE IT.
BUT ALWAYS WEAR A SMILE ... AND DO THE BEST YOU CAN ...
THEN IF TOMORROW GETS HERE ...YOU'LL HAVE THE UPPER HAND.

THE WAY OF THE AMERICAN

CHORUS:
>WELL IF I CAN ... THEN YOU CAN ...
AND IF YOU CAN ... THEN HE CAN.
>AND IF HE CAN ... THEN THEY CAN ...
AND THAT'S THE WAY ... OF THE AMERICAN.

VERSE ONE:
>NOW WE CAN DO ... WHAT WE WANT TO ...
IF WE DON'T QUIT ... BEFORE WE ARE THRU.
>WE ALL WANT DREAMS ... TO EXPAND ...
THAT'S THE WAY ... OF THE AMERICAN.

VERSE TWO:
>WE'VE SEEN GOOD TIMES ... AND WE'VE SEEN BAD ...
SOME HAVE LOST ... EVERYTHING THEY HAD.
>BUT WE'RE PROUD TO BE ... AN AMERICAN.
CAUSE IF ANYBODY CAN ... WE CAN.

CHORUS:
>WELL IF I CAN ... THEN YOU CAN ...
AND IF YOU CAN ... THEN HE CAN.
>AND IF HE CAN ... THEN THEY CAN ...
AND THAT'S THE WAY ... OF THE AMERICAN.

VERSE THREE:
>WE LOVE EACH OTHER ... NO MATTER WHAT COLOR ...
WHETHER IT'S FOREIGNER'S ... OR SISTER AND BROTHER.
>WE SHOW OUR LOVE ... IN EVERY WAY WE CAN ...
THAT'S THE WAY ... OF THE AMERICAN.

THE WEATHER HAS BEEN TOO COLD

CHORUS:
    THE WEATHER HAS BEEN ... TOO COLD FOR ME ...
THE WEATHER HAS BEEN ... TOO COLD.
    THE ONLY THING ... THAT I KNOW ...
IS THE WEATHER ... HAS BEEN TOO COLD.

VERSE ONE:
    THE WEATHERMAN SAID ... IT'S GONNA GET COLD ...
AND MAYBE ... DOWN TO ZERO.
    THAT'S THE ONLY THING ... WE HAVE TOLD ...
THE WEATHER ... IS GONNA GET COLD.

VERSE TWO:
    THE WEATHER HAS BEEN ... TOO COLD FOR ME ...
THE WEATHER ... HAS BEEN TOO COLD.
    AND WHEN I TRY ... TO GO TO SLEEP ...
I HAVE NOBODY ... TO HOLD.

CHORUS:
    THE WEATHER HAS BEEN ... TOO COLD FOR ME ...
THE WEATHER HAS BEEN ... TOO COLD.
    THAT'S THE ONLY THING ... THAT I KNOW ...
THE WEATHER ... HAS BEEN TOO COLD.

VERSE THREE:
    THE TEMPATURE GOT SO BAD ... MY WATER PIPES ARE FROZE ...
THE ONLY WATER IN MY HOME ... IS THE DRIPPING OF MY NOSE.
    I'M FREEZIMG TO DEATH FROM ... MY HEAD DOWN TO MY
TOE'S ...
ONE THING I KNOW FOR SURE IS ...THE WEATHER HAS BEEN TOO
COLD.

VERSE FOUR:
    I TRY TO BE A SIMPLE MAN ... DOING THE BEST I CAN ...
BUT I CAN'T BEAT THE WEATHER ... IT HAS THE UPPER HAND.

I HATE TO COMPLAIN ... BUT THAT'S THE WAY IT GOES ...
WHEN ALL I CAN SAY IS ... THE WEATHER HAS BEEN TOO COLD.

CHORUS:
THE WEATHER HAS BEEN ... TOO COLD FOR ME ...
THE WEATHER HAS BEEN ... TOO COLD.
THAT'S THE ONLY THING ...THAT I KNOW ...
THE WEATHER ... HAS BEEN TOO COLD.

THERE AIN'T NO USE

COURSE:

    I'M GONNA CHEW CHEW CHEW MY TOBACCO ...
I'M GONNA SPIT SPIT SPIT MY JUICE.
    AND I BELIEVE YOU REALLY LOVE ME ...
BUT BABY THERE AIN'T NO USE.

VERSE ONE:

    MY LIFE IS ONLY A GAMBLE ...
AND I'VE ALWAYS LIVED THAT A WAY.
    WHEN I GET THE URGE TO RAMBLE ...
I GO SOMEWHERE FAR AWAY.

VERSE TWO:

    I DON'T KNOW WHERE I'LL BE TOMORROW ...
I'M LUCKY TO BE HERE TODAY.
    I'VE SHARED LOTS OF OTHER'S SORROW ...
BUT I GUESS THAT'S JUST MY WAY.

VERSE THREE:

    YOU SAY YOU'VE SEEN PEOPLE LIKE ME ...
BUT NO ONE EVER KNOWS THE TIME OF DAY.
    SO HOW CAN YOU BE SO LUCKY ...
WHEN YOU DON'T EVEN KNOW YOUR OWN WAY.

VERSE FOUR:

    SOMEDAY I MIGHT DECIDE TO SLOW DOWN ...
BUT UNTIL THAT DAY DOES COME AROUND.
    DON'T WASTE YOUR TIME TELLING ME WHAT TO DO...
TO EVEN THINK ABOUT IT THERE AIN'T NO USE.

THERE REALLY IS A GOD

I KNOW THERE IS A GOD ... THE BIBLE TELLS ME SO ...
MY MOMMA TOLD ME BY THE TIME ... I WAS FOURS YEARS OLD..
 THE EARTH WAS WITHOUT FORM ... DARKNESS EVERYWHERE ...
GOD SAID LET THERE BE LIGHT ... THEN LIGHT FILLED THE AIR.

 GOD CREATED EARTH ... AND GAVE US PRETTY FLOWERS ...
THEN HE GAVE US TIME ... EACH DAY HAS TWENTY FOUR HOURS.
 HE MADE THE SKY SO BLUE ... AND PUT CLOUDS UP ABOVE ...
THEN HE SAID I'VE GOT TO ADD ... A LITTLE MORE OF MY LOVE.

 HE MADE MAN FROM DUST ... SAID HE MUST BE MADE WHOLE ...
HE BREATHED INTO MAN'S NOSTRILS ... AND GAVE HIM A SOUL.
 HE SAW THAT THIS MAN ... WAS THE LONELIEST ON EARTH ...
HE MADE THE MAN A WOMAN ... TO SHARE LOVE AND GIVE BIRTH.

 THEN AS TIME WENT ON ... THE HUMAN RACE MULTIPLIED ...
SIN SNEEKED INTO THE WORLD... AND GOD WAS NOT SATISFIED.
 HE SAID I'LL DESTROY THE EARTH ... WITH A WATER FLOOD ...
IT'LL BE TOO LATE BUT THEY"LL KNOW ... THERE REALLY IS A GOD.

 THEN HE TOLD NOAH TO BUILD ... HIM A VERY LARGE ARK ...
HE SAID I'LL DESTROY THE EARTH ... WE'LL MAKE ANOTHER START.
 NOAH DID AS HE WAS TOLD ... AND GOD SENT DOWN THE
RAIN ...
THEN THEY KNEW THERE IS A GOD ... BUT THEY ALL DIED IN VAIN.

THINGS OF THE PAST

VERSE ONE:

ONE NIGHT I WENT TO BED ... THINKING OF THINGS OF THE PAST ..

OF THINGS WE LOVED TO DO ... THAT WE WISHED FOREVER WOULD LAST.

WE WOULD SPEND LOTS OF NIGHTS ... SLEEPING IN OUR CARS ...

WITH OUR GIRLS IN THE SEATS ... AND WHITE LIQUER IN A JAR.

VERSE TWO:

WE WOULD GO TO THE CREEK ... AND TAKE OUR WOMEN ...

THEN PULL OFF ALL OUR CLOTHES ... AND WE WOULD GO SWIMMIN'.

SOMETIMES WE WOULD LAY DOWN ... ON A BLANKET ON THE GROUND ...

THESE WERE THINGS OF THE PAST ... WE USED FOR HAND ME DOWNS.

VERSE THREE:

WE WERE ALL HAPPY FRIENDS ... AND FULL OF LIFE BACK THEN ...

AND OH WHAT WE'D GIVE ... TO LIVE THE THINGS OF THE PAST AGAIN.

IT'S A SHAME TO GET OLD ... AND MISS OUT ON ALL THE FUN ...

JUST SIT AROUND AND THINK ABOUT ... THINGS OF THE PAST WE'VE DONE.

VERSE FOUR:

THE THINGS OF THE PAST ... WE DID'NT REALIZE BACK THEN ...

WOULD REMAIN IN OUR MINDS ... UNTIL OUR JOURNEY'S END.

BE CAREFUL OF WHAT YOU DO ... BUT GO AHEAD AND HAVE YOUR FUN ...

BUT REMEMBER THINGS OF THE PAST ... IS LIKE A HOT DOG ON A BUN.

VERSE FIVE:

    NOW A HOT DOG CAN BE GOOD ... OR A HOT DOG CAN ALSO
    BE BAD ...
THAT'S THE WAY THAT IT IS ... ABOUT THE THINGS OF THE PAST.
    WHEN THEY SPEAK OF SOMEONE HIGHLY ... YOU'D LIKE TO
    BE THE ONE ...
WHEN YOU GET OLD AND LOOK BACK ... OF THINGS IN THE PAST
YOU'VE DONE.

CHORUS:

    THERE ARE THINGS OF THE PAST ... WE'D LIKE TO HOLD ON
    TO BUT YET ...
THERE ARE A LOT OF THINGS WE HAVE DONE ... WE WOULD LIKE
TO FORGET.
    SO KEEP YOUR SPIRITS UP ... AND MAKE MEMORIES THAT
    WILL LAST ...
AND DON'T BE AFRAID TO LOOK BACK ... AT THE THINGS OF THE
PAST.

THINGS THAT YOU DO

VERSE ONE:
    I KNOW THAT YOU KNOW ... THAT I KNOW IT TOO ...
THE PLACES YOU'RE GOING ... THE THINGS THAT YOU DO.
    SOMEDAY YOUR PAST WILL ... CATCH UP WITH YOU ...
IF YOU DON'T STOP DOING ... THE THINGS THAT YOU DO.

VERSE TWO:
    EVERYONE IS TALKING ... ABOUT WHAT PEOPLE DO ...
THEY HAVE ALWAYS TALKED ... THAT IS NOTHING NEW.
    THEY LOOK TO SEE WHO ... THEY CAN RUN DOWN ...
YOU DON'T WANT TO BECOME ... THE TALK OF THE TOWN.

CHORUS:
    YOU WILL BE REMEMBERED ... BY THE THINGS YOU DO...
YOU WANT TO BE RESPECTED ... WHEN THEY THINK OF YOU.
    LEAVE A LOT OF MEMORIES ... MORE THAN JUST A FEW ...
KEEP YOUR LIFE RIGHT ... BY THE THINGS THAT YOU DO.

VERSE THREE:
    DON'T BE ASHAMED OF... THE THINGS THAT YOU DO...
DON'T GET THEM ALL MIXED UP ... LIKE A WITCH'S BREW.
    IF YOU HAVE TO START OVER ... START YOUR LIFE ANEW...
AND TRY TO HELP OTHERS ... BY THE THINGS THAT YOU DO.

CHORUS:
    YOU WILL BE REMEMBERED ... BY THE THINGS YOU DO...
YOU WANT TO BE RESPECTED ... WHEN THEY THINK OF YOU.
    LEAVE A LOT OF MEMORIES ... MORE THAN JUST A FEW ...
KEEP YOUR LIFE RIGHT ... BY THE THINGS THAT YOU DO.

THINK OF ME

CHORUS:
>THINK OF ME ... WHEN YOU ARE FEELING LONELY ...
THINK OF ME ... WHEN YOU ARE FEELING BLUE.
>ANYTIME ... YOU NEED SOMEONE TO TALK TO ...
THINK OF ME ... CAUSE I'LL BE THINKING OF YOU.

VERSE ONE:
>ANYTIME ... IT COMES TO BEING LONESOME ...
AND YOU NEED SOMEONE ... TO COMFORT YOU.
>JUST REMEMBER ... I STILL LOVE YOU ONLY ...
THINK OF ME ... CAUSE I'LL BE THINKING OF YOU.

VERSE TWO:
>THINK OF ME ... AND THINGS WE USED TO DO ...
THINK OF WHEN ... WE SAID OUR LOVE WAS TRUE.
>THINK OF ME ... WHEN YOUR DAY IS THRU ...
THINK OF ME ... CAUSE I'LL BE THINKING OF YOU.

CHORUS:
>THINK OF ME ... WHEN YOU ARE FEELING LONELY ...
THINK OF ME ... WHEN YOU ARE FEELING BLUE.
>ANYTIME ... YOU NEED SOMEONE TO TALK TO ...
THINK OF ME ... CAUSE I'LL BE THINKING OF YOU.

VERSE THREE:
>THINK OF ME ... WHEN YOU TURN OUT THE LIGHTS ...
THINK OF ME ... WHEN YOU LAY DOWN AT NIGHT.
>THINK OF ME ... WHEN NO ONE ELSE WILL DO ...
THINK OF ME ... CAUSE I'LL BE THINKING OF YOU.

CHORUS:
>THINK OF ME ... WHEN YOU ARE FEELING LONELY ...
THINK OF ME ... WHEN YOU ARE FEELING BLUE.
>ANYTIME ... YOU NEED SOMEONE TO TALK TO ...
THINK OF ME ... CAUSE I'LL BE THINKING OF YOU.

THIS IS THE CHILD

CHORUS:
>MY MOMMA SAID ... WHEN I WAS BORN ...
THIS IS THE CHILD ... I BEEN LOOKIN' FOR.
>HE'S GOT BLUE EYES ... I SURE ADORE ...
SO THIS IS THE CHILD ... I BEEN LOOKIN' FOR.

VERSE ONE:
>SHE TRIED HER BEST ... TO RAISE ME RIGHT ...
KEPT ME UNDER HER THUMB ... BOTH DAY AND NIGHT.
>BUT THINGS WOULD CHANGE ... WHEN I WENT TO SCHOOL ..
BECAUSE I WOULD SOON LEARN ... HOW TO BE COOL.

VERSE TWO:
>THEN MY FRIENDS WOULD SAY ... YOU ARE OKAY ...
AND YOU CAN COUNT ON US ... ANY OLE DAY.
>THEN WE MET SOME GIRLS ... AND WENT ON A DATE ...
I GUESS THAT'S WHEN ... I LOST MY CHILDHOOD DAYS.

VERSE THREE:
>I LEARNED HOW TO DRINK ... AND I LEARNED TO FIGHT ...
AND I WOULD STAY OUT ... TO REAL LATE AT NIGHT.
>MY MOMMA WOULD ASK ME ... WHERE HAVE I BEEN ...
AND I WOULD TELL HER ... I BEEN OUT WITH MY FRIENDS.

VERSE FOUR:
>THEN I GOT INTO TROUBLE ... AND THEY PUT ME IN JAIL ...
AND I WOULD CALL MY MOMMA ... TO GO ON MY BAIL.
>MY MOMMA ALWAYS SAID ... MANY TIMES BEFORE ...
THIS IS THE CHILD ... I BEEN LOOKIN' FOR.

THIS OLD MAN AND ME

CHORUS:
    I'M NOT LOOKING FOR PITY ... I JUST NEED SOME RELIEF ...
SOMETIMES I CAN'T EVEN STAND ... ON MY OWN TWO FEET.
    TAKE AWAY THESE ACHES AND PAINS ... AND SET ME FREE...
PLEASE LORD HAVE MERCY ... ON THIS OLD MAN AND ME.

VERSE ONE:
    WHEN I WAS A JUST A BOY ... I WAS SO FULL OF ENERGY ...
WHEN IT CAME DOWN TO SICKNESS ... I WAS ALMOST PAIN FREE.
    BUT AS TIME WENT ON ... ALL MY FRIENDS HAD TO LEAVE ...
AND NOW THERE IS NO ONE ... BUT THIS OLD MAN AND ME.

VERSE TWO:
    WHEN I WAS A YOUNG MAN ... I DID'NT JUST PLAY AROUND ...
SAY SOMETHING I DID'NT LIKE ... AND I WOULD KNOCK YOU DOWN.
    BUT NOW I HAVE CHANGED ... I AM NOT LIKE I USED TO BE ...
BECAUSE OLD FATHER TIME ... MADE AN OLD MAN OUT OF ME.

VERSE THREE:
    THE OLDER I WOULD GET ... THE WEAKER I GOT ...
AND THAT IS THE TRUTH ... YOU CAN BELIEVE IT OR NOT.
    BECAUSE TIME DID'NT STOP ... IT JUST KEPT TICKING ON ...
NOW THIS OLD MAN AND ME ... ARE JUST ABOUT GONE.

VERSE FOUR:
    MY EYE'S ARE ALMOST BLIND ... I CAN'T HARDLY SEE ...
DON'T FEEL SORRY FOR ME ... I DON'T NEED YOUR SYMPATHY.
    THE ONLY THING I ASK OF YOU ... IS LISTEN TO MY PLEA ...
AND PLEASE DON'T LOOK DOWN ON ... THIS OLD MAN AND ME.

THIS TIME I'M A LEAVIN'

CHORUS:
> I'VE BEEN SAYING THIS ... FOR MUCH TOO LONG ...
THIS TIME I'M A'LEAVIN' ... I'LL SOON BE GONE.

VERSE ONE:
> ALL WE EVER DO ... IS FIGHT FIGHT FIGHT ...
I NEVER HAVE NO PEACE ... NEITHER DAY OR NIGHT.
> I HAVE TRIED MY BEST ... TO GET ALONG WITH YOU ...
THIS TIME I'M A LEAVIN' ... CAUSE WE'RE REALLY THRU.

VERSE TWO:
> THE DAY OF OUR MARRIAGE ... WE BOTH FELT GREAT ...
BUT NOW THAT I'M LEAVIN' ... I CAN HARDLY WAIT.
> YOU PUSHED ME AROUND ... LIKE A DOG WITHOUT A BONE ...
BUT THIS TIME I'M A LEAVIN' ... I'LL SOON BE GONE.

VERSE THREE:
> NOW DON'T TELL ME THOSE LIES ... LIKE YOU DID BEFORE ...
AND DON'T STAND IN MY WAY ... WHEN I WALK TO THE DOOR.
> I CAN'T TAKE IT ANYMORE ... IT'S EATING UP MY INSIDES ...
SO THIS TIME I'M A LEAVIN' ... EVEN IF YOU CRY.

VERSE FOUR:
> I WILL NEVER LOOK BACK ... I'LL LEAVE THE PAST BEHIND ...
I'M A'GONNA DO SOMETHING ... WITH THIS LIFE OF MINE.
> I WON'T BE HERE NO MORE ... WHEN THE MORNINGS DAWN ...
CAUSE THIS TIME I'M A LEAVIN' ... I'LL SOON BE GONE.

TODAY IS THE DAY

VERSE ONE:
TODAY IS THE DAY ... THAT THE EAGLE'S FLY ...
MUCH TOO LONG ... MY THROAT HAS BEEN DRY.
TODAY WHEN I PUNCH OUT ... I''LL SAY GOODBYE ...
CAUSE TODAY IS THE DAY ... THAT THE EAGLE'S FLY.

VERSE TWO:
TODAY WHEN I GET PAID ... I'LL WALK OUTSIDE ...
AND LOOK UP AT THE CLOUDS ... FAR AND WIDE.
I'LL BE AS FREE AS THE BIRDS ... UP IN THE SKY ...
CAUSE TODAY IS THE DAY ... THAT THE EAGLE'S FLY.

VERSE THREE:
I'LL BE LIKE A BIRD ... THAT HAS LEFT IT'S NEST ...
BE BLOWING IN THE BREEZE ... YOU KNOW THE REST.
I MAY NOT HAVE A BALL ... BUT I'M SURE GONNA TRY ...
CAUSE TODAY IS THE DAY ... THAT THE EAGLE'S FLY.

VERSE FOUR:
I'LL HAVE MONEY ... WITH NOTHING TO TIE ME DOWN ...
I'LL HAVE ME A BLAST ... CAUSE I AIN'T FOOLIN' AROUND.
THERE CAN'T NOBODY SAY ... THAT I DID'NT TRY ...
CAUSE TODAY IS THE DAY ... THAT THE EAGLE'S FLY.

VERSE FIVE:
SOME THINKS I'M CRAZY ... BUT THEY DON'T KNOW ME ...
CAUSE I LIKE TO BE FOOT LOOSE ... AND FANCY FREE.
YOU MAY NOT UNDERSTAND ... BUT DON'T ASK ME WHY ...
CAUSE TODAY IS THE DAY ... THAT THE EAGLE'S FLY.

TODAYS HERE AFTER

VERSE ONE:

I'VE HEARD A LOT OF TALK ... ABOUT THE HERE AFTER ...

BUT WHEN IT COMES TO LIVING ... THERE IS ANOTHER CHAPTER.

IT'S ABOUT LIVING LIFE NOW ... AND THINGS HAPPENING TODAY ...

AND WONDERING WHAT DID YOU ... COME HERE AFTER ANYWAY.

VERSE TWO:

IT'S GOOD TO GET OLD ... BUT IT COMES WITH A PRICE THOUGH ...

YOU DON'T GET AROUND AS FAST ... AND YOUR MEMORY GETS SLOW.

SOMETIMES I GO TO THE STORE ... FOR WHAT I CAN'T REMEMBER ...

I ASK WITH A LITTLE LAUGHTER ... WHAT DID I COME HERE AFTER.

CHORUS:

NOW PEOPLE THINKS THAT HERE AFTER ... IS A LONG WAYS OFF ...

BUT IT'S KNOCKING ON YOUR BACK DOOR ... IT MAY BE IN YOUR LOFT.

SO WHEN YOUR MEMORY FAILS YOU ... DON'T LOOK THE OTHER WAY ...

JUST HAVE HOPE FOR TOMORROW ... THAT'S HERE AFTER TODAY.

VERSE THREE:

I WAS DOING SOME REPAIR WORK ... FOOLING AROUND MY HOME ...

WHEN I NEEDED SOME THINGS ... THAT WAS IN THE OTHER ROOM.

I DECIDED TO GO TO THE WORKSHOP ... TO GET ME A LADDER ...

AND WHEN I GOT THERE I ASK ... WHAT DID I COME HERE AFTER.

VERSE FOUR:

THE HERE AFTER IS TODAY ... THAT YOU WORRIED ABOUT YESTERDAY.

YOU THINK ABOUT SOME THINGS ... THAT DID'NT GO YOUR WAY.

YOU ALWAYS GET CONFUSED ... AND DON'T KNOW WHAT TO
SAY ...
YOU GET MIXED UP AND WONDER ... WHAT YOU'RE HERE AFTER
ANYWAY.

CHORUS:
NOW PEOPLE THINKS THAT HERE AFTER ... IS A LONG WAYS
OFF ...
BUT IT'S KNOCKING ON YOUR BACK DOOR ... IT MAY BE IN YOUR
LOFT.
SO WHEN YOUR MEMORY FAILS YOU ... DON'T LOOK THE OTHER
WAY ...
JUST HAVE HOPE FOR TOMORROW ... THAT'S HERE AFTER TODAY.

TWO OLD MEN

VERSE ONE:

 I CAME BY A RESTURANT ... I STOPPED AND WALKED IN ...
THE ONLY CUSTOMERS THERE ... WAS THESE TWO OLD MEN.

 I ORDERED ME A DRINK ... AND SAT DOWN NEAR THEM ...
AND THEN I STARTED TALKING ... TO THESE TWO OLD MEN.

VERSE TWO:

 THEY DID'NT KNOW ME ... BUT THAT WAS'NT MY FAULT ...
THEY KNEW MY FAMILY ... SO WE WERE CLOSER THAN WE THOUGHT.

 AFTER WE TALKED AWHILE ... WE BECAME GOOD FRIENDS ...
AND I STILL BLESS THE DAY ... I MET THESE TWO OLD MEN.

VERSE THREE:

 THE ONLY TIME I WOULD SEE THEM ... WAS ON SATURDAY
NIGHT ...

IF THEY DID'NT SHOW UP ... I WAS AFRAID SOMETHING WAS'NT
RIGHT.

BUT WHEN THEY DID WE WOULD TALK ... ABOUT THINGS BACK THEN ...
AND THEY ALWAYS SEEMED GLAD TO SEE ME ... THESE TWO OLD MEN.

VERSE FOUR:
WE ALWAYS TRIED TO BE THERE ... EVERY SATURDAY NIGHT ... WE LOOKED FORWARD TO MEETING EACH OTHER ... IN THE EVENING LIGHT.
I DON'T THINK I COULD EVER ... MEET TWO PEOPLE AGAIN ... THAT I ENJOYED TALKING WITH ... AS THESE TWO OLD MEN.

VERSE FIVE:
I BELIEVE WHEN THEIR TIME COME ... FOR ONE OF THEM TO DIE ...
THERE IS SOMETHING WAITING FOR THEM ... AWAY UP IN THE SKY.
BUT I WOULD SURE MISS ... THE LAUGHTER AND THE GRIN'S ... THAT I WAS ALWAYS GLAD TO SHARE ... WITH THESE TWO OLD MEN.

UNFORGIVEN

VERSE ONE:

IF I HAD MY WHOLE LIFE ... TO LIVE ALL OVER ...
I TELL YOU THE FIRST THING ... THAT I WOULD DO.
I WOULD PAY MORE ATTENTION ... TO MY TEACHERS ...
AND TRY TO LEARN MORE ... WHILE GOING TO SCHOOL.

VERSE TWO:

I WAS JUST A HARD HEADED ... LITTLE YOUNG'UN ...
WHO WAS TOO STUBBORN ... TO LISTEN TO ANYONE.
NOT REALIZING ... WHAT I WAS REALLY DOING ...
AND NOT KNOWING ... JUST WHAT I WOULD BECOME.

VERSE THREE:

MY PARENTS DID'NT REALLY KNOW ... HOW I ACTED ...
AND SOME OF THE WILD THINGS ... THAT I DID AS A KID.
HAD THEY KNOWN ... I WOULD HAVE BEEN CORRECTED ...
AND I WOULD HAVE DONE ... MUCH BETTER THAT I DID.

VERSE FOUR:

I REMEMBER BY THE TIME ... I WAS A TEENAGER ...
YOU COULD'NT TELL ME ... I ALREADY KNEW EVERYTHING.
MY LAST YEAR IN SCHOOL ... I GOT INTO TROUBLE ...
THE PRINCIPAL EXPELLED ME ... BEFORE I WAS SIXTEEN.

CHORUS:

I HAD TO WORK MANY JOBS ...TO MAKE A LIVING ...
NOT KNOWING HOW LONG ... MY NEXT JOB WOULD LAST.
I FELT THE STUPID THINGS I DID ... WAS UNFORGIVEN ...
AND IT CAUSED ME TO LIVE ... MY LIFE IN THE PAST.

WAITIN' FOR THE SNOW

VERSE ONE:
> WELL THE WEATHER MAN SAID ... IT WAS GOING TO SNOW ...
AND PEOPLE ARE A WAITIN' ... FOR THE FLAKES TO FLOW.
> THEY JUST CAN'T WAIT ... FOR THE GROUND TO BE FROZE ...
SO THERE WILL BE NOWHERE ... FOR THEM TO GO.

VERSE TWO:
> THEY RUSH TO THE STORE ... TO GET MILK EGGS AND BREAD,,,
THEY BELIEVE EVERY WORD ... THAT THE WEATHER MAN SAID.
> WHEN THEY GET BACK HOME ... THEY JUST SIT AROUND ...
AND WAIT FOR THE SNOW ... TO START COMING DOWN.

VERSE THREE:
> THE KIDS ARE ALL EXCITED ... JUST WAITIN' FOR THE SNOW ...
SO THEY CAN GO OUTSIDE ... AND CATCH THEM A COLD.
> THEY JUST WANT TO PLAY... AND NOT THINK ABOUT SCHOOL ...
NOT REALIZING THE SICKNESS ... THEY MIGHT GO THROUGH.

VERSE FOUR:
> WELL HERE IT COMES ... GET READY FOR THE BLOW ...
CAUSE AFTER ALL ... YOU BEEN WAITIN' FOR THE SNOW.
> NOW GET YOU A BOWL ... AND MAKE SOME SNOW CREAM ...
AND MAKE THIS THE HAPPIEST SNOW ... YOU HAVE EVER SEEN.

VERSE FIVE:
> NOW YOU MUST REMEMBER ... YOU REAP WHAT YOU SOW ...
SO WHEN THE ROADS GET SLICK ... DON'T TRY TO GO.
> JUST STAY AT HOME ... AND WATCH THE CHILDREN GROW ...
AND LOVE YOUR FAMILY ... WHILE WAITIN' FOR THE SNOW.

WALKING BAREFOOTED

VERSE ONE:

DOWN HERE I HAVE TO WEAR SHOES ... I HAVE TENDER FEET ...
AND I ALSO WEAR SOCKS ... HALF WAY UP TO MY KNEES.
I CAN'T WALK ON HOT CEMENT ... GRAVEL OR DIRT ...
MY FEET STARTS TO BLEEDING ... AND THEY BEGIN TO HURT.

VERSE TWO:

BUT I HAVE HEARD OF A PLACE ... SOMEWHERE IN THE SKY ...
WHERE I CAN WALK BAREFOOTED ... IN HEAVEN AFTER I DIE.
THERE I WILL NEED NO BUS ... NO AIRPLANE OR NO CAR ...
I'LL BE WALKING BAREFOOTED ... SOMEWHERE BEYOND THE STARS.

CHORUS:

I'LL BE WALKING BAREFOOTED ... WEARING A ROBE OF
WHITE ...
TOURING ALL OF HEAVEN ... AND VIEWING ALL THE SITES.
I'LL BE WALKING WITH JESUS ... AND LOVED ONES I KNOW ...
BUT I'LL BE WALKING BAREFOOTED ... EVERYWHERE I GO.

VERSE THREE:

I'LL BE WALKING BAREFOOTED ... DOWN THE STREETS OF
GOLD ...
THERE I'LL NEVER GET TIRED ... AND I'LL NEVER GET OLD.
NOW WHEN MY NAME IS CALLED ... I WILL SHED THESE
SHOES ...
AND I'LL BE WALKING BAREFOOED ... SOMEWHERE BEYOND THE
BLUE.

VERSE FOUR:

I CAN'T WAIT TO GET LOOSE ... AND COME OUT OF THESE
SHOES ...
I NEVER WANT TO GO BACK ... TO DOING THE THINGS I USED TO DO.
THERE ARE BETTER THINGS TO DO ... IN HEAVEN I KNOW ...
AND I'LL BE WALKING BAREFOOTED ... EVERYWHERE I GO.

CHORUS:

    I'LL BE WALKING BAREFOOTED ... WEARING A ROBE OF WHITE ...

I'LL BE TOURING ALL OF HEAVEN ... AND VIEWING ALL THE SITES.

    I'LL BE WALKING WITH JESUS ... AND THE LOVED ONES I KNOW ...

BUT I'LL BE WALKING BAREFOOTED ... EVERYWHERE I GO.

WASHINGTON STREET POOLROOM BRAWL

VERSE ONE:

MY BROTHER AND MY BROTHER-IN-LAW ... AND MYSELF ONE NIGHT...

WE ALL GOT TO DRINKING ... AND DECIDED TO GO AND LOOK FOR A FIGHT.

WE WENT INTO A POOLROOM ... WHERE THE BLACK PEOPLE WENT ...

THE PLACE WAS PACKED FULL ... WITH SMOKE AND ALCOHOL SCENT.

VERSE TWO:

I ORDERED A BUD IN A BOTTLE ... HE SAID WE DON'T SELL BUD HERE ...

HE SAID THE ONLY THING HE SERVED ... WAS THE DRAFT BEER.

MY BROTHER AND MY BROTHER-IN-LAW ... ORDERD THEM ONE ...

I SAID IF I CAN'T HAVE WHAT I WANT ... I DON'T WANT NONE.

VERSE THREE:

I WENT TO THE POOL TABLE ... TO WATCH THEM SHOOT THE BALL...

I PROPED MY FOOT UP BEHIND ME ... AND LEANED AGAINST THE WALL.

THE BARTENDER SAID ... I CAN SEE WHERE YOUR FOOT HAS BEEN ...

I SAID IT AIN'T THERE NOW IS IT ... HE SAID DON'T PUT IT THERE AGAIN.

VERSE FOUR:

I JUMPED UP ON THE POOL TABLE ... THE BRAWL REALLY BEGAN ...

THERE WAS POOL BALLS FLYING EVERYWHERE ... I HAD A KNIFE IN EACH HAND.

THEY THREW ME OUT THREE TIMES ... I DID'NT GO BACK NO MORE ...

SOMEONE ON THE OUTSIDE TURNED MY LIGHTS OUT .. WITH A TWO BY FOUR.

VERSE FIVE:

I WOKE UP IN THE HOSPITAL ... THEY WERE SEWING MY FACE UP ...
I STARTED LAUGHING ... THE NURSE ASKED AIN'T YOU HAD ENOUGH.
I LOOKED ACROSS THE ROOM ... THERE WERE OTHERS GETTING SEWED ...
I LOST TWO OF MY POCKET KNIVES ... BUT NOT BEFORE THE BLOOD FLOWED.

VERSE SIX:

THE MORAL TO THIS STORY ... IS JUST LIKE ALWAYS BEFORE ...
IF YOU GO LOOKING FOR TROUBLE ... YOU'LL GET MORE THAN YOU BARGAIN FOR.
I'M LUCKY TO STILL BE ALIVE ... BUT I'M GLAD I CAN STILL RECALL ...
THE NIGHT HISTORY WAS WRITTEN .... AT THE WASHINGTON ST. POOLROOM BRAWL.

WELCOME HOME

VERSE ONE:

    IT WAS A SAD DAY ... WHEN YOU HAD TO GO AWAY ...
WE WANT YOU TO KNOW ... WE MISSED YOU EVERYDAY.
    NOW THAT YOU ARE BACK ... THE SADDNESS IS GONE ...
AND ALL WE CAN SAY IS ... YOU ARE WELCOME HOME.

VERSE TWO:

    THERE HAVE BEEN TIMES ... WE DID'NT KNOW WHAT TO DO...
JUST SITTING AROUND ... AND THINKING ABOUT YOU.
    WE SURE DID MISS YOU ... WHILE YOU WERE GONE ...
AND IT'S GOOD TO HAVE YOU BACK ... SO WELCOME HOME.

VERSE THREE:

    WE'LL NEVER FORGET THE HARDSHIPS ... YOU WENT THRU ...
JUST DOING SOME OF THE THINGS ... THAT YOU HAD TO DO.
    WORRYING ABOUT YOU ... REALLY CUT US TO THE BONE ...
BUT THOSE DAYS ARE OVER NOW ... SO WELCOME HOME.

VERSE FOUR:

    WE WORRIED A LOT ... WHILE WATCHING THE NEWS ...
THE THINGS WE WOULD HEAR ABOUT... MADE US THINK OF YOU.
    THERE WAS A LOT OF TIMES ... WE WOKE UP AT DAWN ...
WISHING YOU WERE HERE ... SO WE COULD SAY WELCOME HOME.

VERSE FIVE:

    YOU KNOW WE LOVE YOU ... AND YOU KNOW OUR LOVE IS
REAL ...
SO DON'T EVER THINK ... ABOUT GOING BACK OVER THE HILL.
    LET THIS GOOD ENDING ... BE THE END OF A SAD SONG ...
AND DON'T YOU EVER FORGET ... YOU ARE WELCOME HOME.

WELCOME TO BURGER KING

CHORUS:
>WELCOME TO BURGER KING ... WHERE THE TASTE TELLS THE TALE ..

YOU SURE ARE LOOKING GOOD ... AND WE HOPE YOU'RE FEELING WELL.
>WE HAVE A LOT OF SPECIALS ... WITH VERY GOOD FOOD ON SALE ...

SO WELCOME TO BURGER KING ... WHERE THE TASTE TELLS THE TALE.

VERSE ONE:
>SOMETIMES YOU MAY GO TO TOWN ... LOOKING ALL AROUND ...

AND STILL NOT BE HAPPY... AT WHAT YOU HAVE FOUND.
>BURGER KING IS WHERE ... THE TASTE TELLS THE TALE ...

SO BRING THE COUPONS IN ... THAT YOU RECIEVE IN THE MAIL.

VERSE TWO:
>YOU WILL ALWAYS LEAVE HERE HAPPY ... NOW THERE IS NO DOUBT ...

BECAUSE GOOG FOOD IS WHAT ... LIFE IS REALLY ALL ABOUT.
>THEY SAY WHAT YOU EAT IS WHAT ... MAKES YOU FEEL SO WELL.

SO WELCOME TO BURGER KING ... WHERE THE TASTE TELLS THE TALE

CHORUS:
>WELCOME TO BURGER KING ... WHERE THE TASTE TELLS THE TALE ..

YOU SURE ARE LOOKING GOOD ... AND WE HOPE YOU'RE FEELING WELL.
>WE HAVE A LOT OF SPECIALS ... WITH VERY GOOD FOOD ON SALE ...

SO WELCOME TO BURGER KING ... WHERE THE TASTE TELLS THE TALE.

VERSE THREE:

WHEN YOU EAT HERE WITH US ... YOU WILL JUST WANT TO SHOUT ...

BECAUSE THE MEALS ARE SO GOOD ... LIKE RIDING ON A CLOUD.

WE WANT YOU TO KNOW .. YOUR MEAL IS REALLY SWELL ...

SO WELCOME TO BURGER KING ... WHERE THE TASTE TELLS THE TALE ...

CHORUS:

WELCOME TO BURGER KING ... WHERE THE TASTE TELLS THE TALE ..

YOU SURE ARE LOOKING GOOD ... AND WE HOPE YOU'RE FEELING WELL.

WE HAVE A LOT OF SPECIALS ... WITH VERY GOOD MEALS ON SALE ...

SO WELCOME TO BURGER KING ... WHERE THE TASTE TELLS THE TALE.

WHAT ABOUT ME

CHORUS:
    YOU SAY YOU FEEL LIKE ... GOING ON A SPREE ...
WELL HERE I AM ... SO WHAT ABOUT ME.
    I THINK YOU ARE ... AS PRETTY AS CAN BE ...
SO LET ME KNOW SOMETHIN' ... WHAT ABOUT ME.

VERSE ONE:
    IF YOU WANT SOMEONE ... THAT IS SINGLE AND FREE ...
DON'T LOOK NO FURTHER ... WHAT ABOUT ME.
    IF YOU THINK I'LL DO ...GET ME WHILE YOU CAN ...
CAUSE I DON'T LIKE BEING... A SECOND HAND MAN.

VERSE TWO:
    WHAT ABOUT ME ... WHAT DO YOU THINK ...
WE CAN GO OUT ... AND REALLY HAVE A FLING.
    PUT YOUR RED DRESS ON ... AND LET YOUR HAIR DOWN ...
WE'LL HAVE A BLAST ... WHILE WE PAINT THE TOWN.

VERSE THREE:
    WHAT ABOUT ME ... WE'LL DO WHATEVER YOU WANT TO ...
YOU'LL FIND OUT I CAN DO ... ANYTHING THAT HE CAN DO.
    YOU BETTER HOP IN THE CAR ... BEFORE I TURN THE KEY ...
YOU WON'T HAVE TO WORRY ... AS LONG AS YOU'RE WITH ME.

VERSE FOUR:
    BUT DON'T KEEP ME WAITIN' ... I WON'T WAIT LONG ...
I MIGHT BE HERE NOW ... BUT I'LL SOON BE GONE.
    IF YOU WANT TO GO OUT ... AND DRAG THE STREETS ...
YOU BETTER ASK YOURSELF ... WHAT ABOUT ME.

WHAT AM I DOING WRONG

VERSE ONE:

    HAVE YOU EVER WONDERED ... WHAT AM I DOING WRONG ...
OR DID YOU EVER FIND YOURSELF ... SOMEWHERE YOU DID'NT BELONG.
    IT SEEMS THAT BAD LUCK ... JUST KEEPS GOING ON AND ON ...
AND YOU KEEP ASKING YOURSELF ... WHAT AM I DOING WRONG.

CHORUS:

    WHAT AM I DOING WRONG ... OH WHAT AM I DOING WRONG ...
I DON'T KNOW HOW MUCH LONGER ... THAT I CAN KEEP GOING ON.
    I'VE GOT TO FIND A WAY ... TO EASE SOME OF THIS PAIN ...
AND NEVER HAVE TO ASK ... WHAT AM I DOING WRONG AGAIN.

VERSE TWO:

    YOU THINK THE THINGS YOU DO ... WILL BE ALRIGHT BUT STILL ...
THEY DON'T TURN OUT RIGHT ... AND IT SEEMS THEY NEVER WILL.
    YOU KEEP SAYING TO YOURSELF ... AND ASKING ALL DAY LONG ...
I KEEP DOING THE SAME OLD THING ... WHAT AM I DOING WRONG.

CHORUS:

    WHAT AM I DOING WRONG ... OH WHAT AM I DOING WRONG ...
I DON'T KNOW HOW MUCH LONGER ... THAT I CAN KEEP GOING ON.
    I'VE GOT TO FIND A WAY ... TO EASE SOME OF THIS PAIN ...
AND NEVER HAVE TO ASK ... WHAT AM I DOING WRONG AGAIN.

VERSE THREE:

    SOMETIMES I FEEL MISGUIDED ... BUT IT DON'T LAST TOO
LONG ...
I TELL MYSELF IT'LL BE ALRIGHT ... AND THAT I'M NOT ALL ALONE.
    I GUESS THAT I GO TO PLACES ... WHERE I DON'T BELONG ...
BUT THAT DON'T TELL ME NOTHING ... WHAT AM I DOING WRONG.

CHORUS:

    WHAT AM I DOING WRONG ... OH WHAT AM I DOING WRONG ...
I DON'T KNOW HOW MUCH LONGER ... THAT I CAN KEEP GOING ON.
    I'VE GOT TO FIND A WAY ... TO EASE SOME OF THIS PAIN ...
AND NEVER HAVE TO ASK ... WHAT AM I DOING WRONG AGAIN.

WHAT ARE YOU GOING TO DO NOW

VERSE ONE:
WHAT IF YOU WERE LAYING ... ON THE DEATH BED DYING ...
HAVE YOU EVER WONDERED ... WHAT WOULD YOU LEAVE BEHIND.
DID YOU EVER HELP SOMEONE ... THAT WAS IN NEED ...
OR DID YOU TURN THEM AWAY ... IGNORING THEIR PLEAD.

VERSE TWO:
DID YOU FEEL LIKE ALL YOU HAVE ... YOU MADE FOR YOURSELF...
YOU SURE AIN'T GOING TO GIVE IT ... TO SOMEONE ELSE.
BUT WHO'S GONNA GET IT NOW ...YOU CAN'T TAKE IT WITH
YOU ...
YOU'LL HAVE TO LEAVE IT BEHIND ... THERE'S NOTHING YOU
CAN DO.

VERSE THREE:
SO MANY TIMES ... YOU SHOULD HAVE DONE A GOOD DEED ...
AND TOO MANY TIMES ... YOU SAW PEOPLE IN NEED.
BUT EVERYTHING YOU HAVE ... IS NO GOOD TO YOU NOW ...
IT'S LIKE BREAKING UP A FIELD ... WITHOUT A PLOW.

VERSE FOUR:
YOUR LIFE HAS COME TO AN END ... SOON YOU WILL BE GONE ...
AND THE THINGS YOU DID IN LIFE ... WAS ONLY FOR YOUR OWN.
IT SURE IS A SHAME ... TO HAVE TO LEAVE THAT WAY ...
WHAT ARE YOU GOING TO DO ... ON YOUR JUDGEMENT DAY.

VERSE FIVE:
ALL OF A SUDDEN YOU WAKE UP ... ON A HOSPITAL BED ...
YOU THINK ABOUT ALL ... OF THOSE THOUGHTS IN YOUR HEAD.
YOU CLOSE YOUR EYES ... AND YOU BEGIN TO PRAY ...
PLEASE LORD THERE'S SOME PEOPLE ... I NEED TO HELP TODAY.

WHAT CHANGED YOUR MIND

VERSE ONE:
> I NEVER DID HURT YOU ... LIKE YOU HAVE HURT ME ...
WHEN YOU LEFT ME HERE ALONE ... AND IN AGONY.
> YOU JUST WALKED OUT ... AND WOULD'NT LISTEN TO MY PLEA ...
BUT WHAT CHANGED YOUR MIND ... ABOUT LOVING ME.

VERSE TWO:
> YOU TOLD ME YOU LOVED ME ... AND WOULD NEVER SET ME FREE ...
THAT THINGS WOULD ALWAYS BE THE SAME ... BETWEEN YOU AND ME.
> BUT SOMETHING SURELY HAPPENED ... TO CAUSE THIS MISERY ...
SO TELL ME WHAT CHANGED YOUR MIND ... ABOUT LOVING ME.

CHORUS:
> WHAT CHANGED YOUR MIND ... ABOUT LOVING ME ...
I'M STILL THE VERY SAME MAN ... THAT I USED TO BE.
> I HAVE'NT CHANGED ANYTHING ... I'M SURE YOU CAN SEE ...
BUT WHAT CHANGED YOUR MIND ... ABOUT LOVING ME.

VERSE THREE:
> I HEARD A SAD SONG SUNG ... ABOUT MISERY LOVES COMPANY ...
BUT I NEVER DID THINK SOMEDAY ... THIS WOULD HAPPEN TO ME.
> WHEN YOU SAID THAT YOU LOVED ME ... I REALLY DID BELIEVE ...
BUT WHAT CHANGED YOU MIND ... ABOUT LOVING ME.

VERSE FOUR:
> SOMEDAY YOU WILL HAVE TO PAY FOR ... ALL THIS MYSTERY ...
WHEN YOU STOP AND THINK ABOUT ... THOSE LOVING MEMORIES.
> YOU'LL COME CRAWLING BACK AGAIN ... WANTING MY SIMPOTHY ...
THEN I'LL ASK AGAIN WHAT CHANGED YOUR MIND ... ABOUT LOVING ME.

CHORUS:
    WHAT CHANGED YOUR MIND ... ABOUT LOVING ME ...
I'M STILL THE VERY SAME MAN ... THAT I USED TO BE.
    I HAVE'NT CHANGED ANYTHING ... I'M SURE YOU CAN SEE ...
BUT WHAT CHANGED YOUR MIND ... ABOUT LOVING ME.

WHAT WOULD IT BE LIKE

VERSE ONE:
> I ALWAYS FELT NORMAL ... I NEVER GAVE IT ANY THOUGHT ..
OF WHAT IT WOULD BE LIKE ... TO REALLY BE BAD OFF.
> UNTIL ONE DAY I VISITED ... AN OLD AGE NURSING HOME ...
AND THE THINGS THAT I SAW ... CUT ME TO THE BONE.

VERSE TWO:
> THERE WAS PEOPLE BED RIDDEN ... JUST LYING EVERYWHERE ...
AND PEOPLE THAT COULD'NT WALK ... SITTING IN WHEEL CHAIRS.
> PEOPLE WAS HURTING ... THEY WAS SCREAMING FOR HELP ...
NO ONE SEEMED TO CARE ... THEY ONLY THOUGHT OF THEMSELVES.

VERSE THREE:
> WHAT WOULD IT BE LIKE ... TO BE IN THEIR SHOES ...
AND NOT ABLE TO DO NOTHING ... THAT YOU WANTED TO DO.
> THEY COULD'NT GET UP ... TO GO TO THE BATHROOM ...
THEY COULD ONLY HOPE THAT DEATH ... WOULD COME SOON.

VERSE FOUR:
> WHAT WOULD IT BE LIKE ... IF THAT'S WHAT YOU WENT THRU ...
AND YOU HAD NO ONE AROUND ... TO CARE FOR YOU.
> THESE PEOPLE NEED SOMEONE ... TO JUST SPEAK TO THEM ...
OR MAYBE JUST A SMILE ... WOULD CHANGE THE DARK TO DIM.

CHORUS:
> IT'S SAD TO SEE SOMEONE ... THAT IS IN BAD HEALTH ...
ANDALL YOU CAN DO IS ... BE GLAD IT'S NOT YOURSELF.
> JUST OFFER UP A PRAYER ... MAYBE IT WILL SHED SOME LIGHT ...
AND JUST ASK YOURSELF ... WHAT WOULD IT BE LIKE.

WHAT'S THE GOVERNMENT FOR?

VERSE ONE:
I WAS SITTIN' AT A TABLE ... IN A REAL NICE DINER ...
WHEN A STRANGER SAID ... WHAT YOU SAY OLD TIMER.
HE CAME AND SAT DOWN ... AT THE TABLE NEXT TO ME ...
AND SOME OF THE THINGS I HEARD ... I COULD'NT BELIEVE.

VERSE TWO:
THE OTHER MAN AT THE TABLE ... HAD TO BE A DEMOCRAT ...
BECAUSE A REPUBLICAN ... WOULD'NT SAY NOTHING LIKE THAT.
HE SAID IF THINGS DON'T CHANGE ...THERE'LL BE A RECESSION...
HE SAID HE DID'NT KNOW WHY ... BUT HE WAS JUST A'GUESSIN'.

VERSE THREE:
HE SAID ONE PART OF CONGRESS ... VOTES ONE WAY ...
WHILE THE OTHER PART ... DON'T HAVE NOTHING TO SAY.
AND WHAT THEY DO SAY ... IS NOT WORTH LISTENING TO ...
BECAUSE IT ONLY HELPS THEM ... IT DON'T CONCERN ME AND YOU.

VERSE FOUR:
WHY CAN'T THE GOVERNMENT ... GET THINGS WORKED OUT ...
INSTEAD OF SITTING AROUND SAYING ...WHAT THIS ALL ABOUT.
THEY NEED TO WORK TOGETHER ... NOT FIGHT ONE ANOTHER ...
THEN THEY COULD GET IT DONE ... IF THEY WORKED TOGETHER

CHORUS:
IF WE'RE TO BE FREE ... WHAT IS THE GOVERNMENT FOR ...
TELLING US THAT WE CAN'T LIVE ... THE WAY WE DID BEFORE.
MAKING NEW LAWS ... TO MAKE IT TOUGHER THAN BEFORE ...
IF YOU CAN PLEASE TELL ME ... WHAT IS THE GOVERNMENT FOR.

WHAT'S WRONG

VERSE ONE:
    SOMETIMES I WONDER ... WHAT CAN IT BE ...
TO MAKE PEOPLE WONDER ... WHAT'S WRONG WITH ME.
    I'VE NEVER DONE NOTHING ... TO HURT ANYONE ...
\SO IT CAN'T BE ANYTHING ... THAT I HAVE DONE.

VERSE TWO:
    EVEN IN A CROWD ... I FEEL SO ALL ALONE ...
WHY CAN'T THEY SEE ... WHAT THEY HAVE DONE.
    I HAVE TO SIT ALONE ... IN SOME DARK SPOT ...
BECAUSE OF THE FRIENDS ... THAT I AIN'T GOT.

VERSE THREE:
    WOULD THEY SEE THINGS ... A LITTLE DIFFERENTLY...
IF IT WAS THEM ... INSTEAD OF ME.
    I CAN'T GO OUT ... AND HAVE ANY FUN ...
CAUSE THEY MAKE ME FEEL LIKE ... I'M JUST NO ONE.

VERSE FOUR:
    I MUST BE THE LONLINEST ... PERSON IN TOWN ...
BECAUSE NO ONE WANTS ME ... TO COME AROUND.
    WHY CAN'T THEY SAY ... WHAT'S WRONG WITH ME ...
AND HELP ME TO GET OVER ... ALL THIS MISERY.

CHORUS:
    HAVE YOU EVER FELT LIKE ... YOU HAD NO FRIENDS ...
AND WONDER WHERE ... DID IT ALL BEGIN.
    IF YOU COULD GO BACK ... AND START OVER AGAIN ...
WOULD IT BE ANY DIFFERENT...THAN IT WAS BACK THEN.

WHEN DEATH HITS HOME

WHEN DEATH HITS HOME ... IT MAKES YOU FEEL SO ALONE ...
WHEN A FAMILY MEMBER DIES ... YOU KNOW THEY ARE GONE.
YOU KNOW THEY WON'T BE HERE ... TO SHARE LIFE WITH YOU ...
BUT YOU WILL NEVER FORGET ... THINGS THAT YOU USED TO DO.

WHEN DEATH HITS HOME ... THERE'S EMPTINESS IN YOUR
HEART ...
THAT YOU WILL ALWAYS MISS ... BECAUSE THEY PLAYED A BIG PART.
BUT ALL OF THOSE MEMORIES ... WILL ALWAYS BE THERE ...
BECAUSE OF THE LOVE ... AND JOY THAT YOU SHARED.

WHEN DEATH HITS HOME ... IT TAKES SOMETHING AWAY ...
LIKE A LOT OF HAPPINESS ... THAT CANNOT BE REPLACED.
YOU WILL ALWAYS MISS THE ONE ... THAT HAD TO LEAVE ...
BUT MAYBE THEY ARE BETTER OFF ... JUST TRY TO BELIEVE.

WHEN DEATH HITS HOME ... YOU CAN'T HELP BUT TO CRY ...
AND SOMETIMES YOU MAY EVEN ... FEEL LIKE YOU WANT TO DIE.
BUT THERE WAS A REASON ...THEY HAD TO LEAVE THIS LIFE ...
PERHAPS TO GET AWAY ... FROM SO MUCH TROUBLE AND STRIFE.

NOW YOU HAVE GOT TO TRY ... TO KEEP PUSHING ON ...
YOU CAN'T CARRY MISERY ... LIKE A DOG CARRYS A BONE.
YOU'VE GOT TO REALIZE ... THAT YOUR LIFE STILL GOES ON ...
AND YOU'VE GOT TO PUT IT BEHIND YOU... WHEN DEATH HITS
HOME.

WHEN I WAS YOUNG

VERSE ONE:
 IT USED TO BE ... WHEN I WAS YOUNG ...
I WAS'NT AFRAID OF ... THINGS THAT I HAD DONE.
 IT SEEMED I ONLY LIEVED ... TO HAVE MY FUN ...
AND BELIEVE ME BOYS ... I REALLY HAD SOME.

VERSE TWO:
 I'D GO OUT AT NIGHT ... AND GET PRETTY TIGHT ...
I'D WIND UP IN JAIL ... BECAUSE I LOVED TO FIGHT.
 I WOULD CHASE THE GIRLS ... FROM DARK TO DAWN ...
THAT'S THE WAY I LIVED ... WHEN I WAS YOUNG.

CHORUS:
 WHEN I WAS YOUNG ... I WAS SO FULL OF PEP ...
AND I DID'NT NEED ... ANYBODY'S HELP.
 I DID IT ALL ON MY OWN ... I DID'NT NEED NO ONE ...
BUT THAT WAS THEN ... WHEN I WAS YOUNG.

VERSE THREE:
 DRINKING FIGHTING AND WOMEN ... I HAD PLENTY TO DO ...
IT'S A WONDER I WAS'NT KILLED .. BEFORE I GOT THRU.
 AS I GOT OLDER ... I SLOWED DOWN SOME ...
BUT THAT'S HOW IT WAS ... WHEN I WAS YOUNG.

VERSE FOUR;
    NOW LIFE IS WORTH LIVING ... AND I APPRECIATE MORE ...
AND I DON'T DO THE THINGS ... THAT I DID BEFORE.
    AS I LOOK BACK ... I'M ASHAMED OF WHAT I HAD DONE ...
BUT THAT'S THE WAY IT WAS ... WHEN I WAS YOUNG.

CHORUS:
    WHEN I WAS YOUNG ... I WAS SO FULL OF PEP ...
AND I DID'NT NEED ... ANYBODY'S HELP.
    I DID IT ALL ON MY OWN ... I DID'NT NEED NO ONE ...
BUT THAT WAS THEN ... WHEN I WAS YOUNG.

WHEN THE BLUE BIRD SINGS

VERSE ONE:

    I ALWAYS WORK HARD ... EVERYDAY THAT I WORK ...
BUT WHEN I HAVE TO MISS A DAY ... IT REALLY DOES HURT.
    MY BILLS STILL COME DUE ... WHETHER I HAVE IT OR NOT ...
AND HOW CAN I PAY ... WHAT I AIN'T GOT.

VERSE TWO:

    I DON'T MAKE ENOUGH MONEY ... THE WAY IT GOES ...
AND IF I GET BEHIND ... EVERYBODY SEEMS TO KNOW.
    BUT IF I'M NOT CAREFUL ... I'LL LOSE EVERYTHING ...
THEN I'LL HAVE TO LISTEN ... TO THE BLUE BIRDS SING.

CHORUS:

    WHEN THE BLUE BIRD SINGS ... SOMETIMES IT'S SAD ...
WHEN HE CALLS FOR HIS MATE ... THAT HE ONCE HAD.
    THE TUNE CAN SOUND SWEET ... BUT STILL HE MOANS ...
WHEN HE MISSES SOMETHING ... THAT NOW IS GONE.

VERSE THREE:

    WHEN THE BLUE BIRD SINGS ... HE SINGS A SAD TUNE ...
AND I MAY BE SINGING WITH HIM ... SOON AND VERY SO9ON.
    MY WORKING DAYS ARE ALMOST OVER ... I'M GETTING TOO
OLD ...
AND I CAN HEAR THE SAD SONGS ... BEGINNING TO UNFOLD.

VERSE FOUR:

    I MISS THE YEARS ... THAT HAS COME AND GONE ...
AND SOME OF MY FRIENDS ... AND THINGS WE HAVE DONE.
    BUT LIKE THE BLUE BIRD ... WHEN HE IS ALL ALONE ...
I CAN FEEL SO SAD ... WHEN THE BLUE BIRD SINGS HIS SONG.

CHORUS:

    WHEN THE BLUE BIRD SINGS ... SOMETIMES IT'S SAD ...
WHEN HE CALLS FOR HIS MATE ... THAT HE ONCE HAD.
    THE TUNE CAN SOUND SWEET ... BUT STILL HE MOANS ...
WHEN HE MISSES SOMETHING ... THAT NOW IS GONE.

WHEN THE RAIN FALLS

VERSE ONE:
    THESE ARE NOT RAIN DROPS ... IN MY EYES ...
THEY'RE REAL TEAR DROPS ... THAT I CRY.
    I'VE CRIED THEM SO LONG ... OVER AND OR' ...
IF IT DID'NT EVER RAIN ... I WOULD'NT CRY NO MORE.

VERSE TWO:
    WHEN THE WEATHER MAN CALLS ... FOR RAIN TODAY ...
I KNEW THAT MY TEARDROPS ... WERE ON THE WAY.
    I CAN'T HIDE MY TEARS ... BEHIND THESE WALLS ...
IT HAPPENS EVERYTIME ... WHEN THE RAIN FALLS.

CHORUS:
    WHEN THE RAIN FALLS ... MY BROKEN HEART CALLS ...
IT'S BEEN SO LONG ... SINCE YOU BEEN GONE.
    THE RAIN CAN'T WASH ... ALL MY TEARS AWAY ...
SO I SURE DO HOPE ... IT DON'T RAIN AGAIN TODAY.

VERSE THREE:
    THROUGH YOUR EYES ... I MIGHT SEEM SMALL ...
BUT MY TEARS ARE HUGE ... WHEN THE RAIN FALLS.
    WHEN THE RAIN IS A FALLING ... ON THE ROOF OUTSIDE ...
IT STARTS THE TEARDROPS TO FLOWING ... FROM MY EYES.

VERSE FOUR:
    IF RAIN DROPS AND TEAR DROPS ... WOULD GO AWAY ...
MAYBE THEN I COULD HAVE ME ... A SUNNY DAY.
    IT WAS RAINING ON THE DAY ... THAT YOU LEFT ME ...
SO WHEN THE RAIN FALLS ... IT BRINGS BACK THE MEMORY.

CHORUS:
    WHEN THE RAIN FALLS ... MY BROKEN HEART CALLS ...
IT'S BEEN SO LONG ... SINCE YOU BEEN GONE.
    THE RAIN CAN'T WASH ... ALL MY TEARS AWAY ...
SO I SURE DO HOPE ... IT DON'T RAIN AGAIN TODAY.

WHEN YOUR LIFE ON EARTH IS DONE

VERSE ONE :

MY MOTHER ALWAYS SAID ... SON YOU MUST ALWAYS DO GOOD ...
AND TRY TO TREAT OTHERS ... THE WAY THAT YOU SHOULD.
ALWAYS SHOW RESPECT ... TO YOUR FRIENDS AND EVERYONE ...
AND YOU WILL BE REMEMBERED ... WHEN YOUR LIFE ON EARTH IS DONE.

VERSE TWO :

SOMETIME LIFE GETS ROUGH ... AND YOU DON'T KNOW WHAT TO DO ...
BUT ALWAYS DO YOUR BEST ... UNTIL YOUR LIFE ON EARTH IS THROUGH.
IF YOU HAVE NO ENEMIES ... THEN THE BATTLE HAS BEEN WON ...
NO ONE WILL SAY NOTHING BAD .. WHEN YOUR LIFE ON EARTH IS DONE..

CHORUS :

WHEN YOUR LIFE ON EARTH IS DONE ... AND LIFE SHALL BE NO MORE ...
AND YOU'RE READY TO DEPART ... OVER TO THE OTHER SHORE.
YOU WILL SEE A LOT OF FRIENDS ... THAT HAS GONE ON BEFORE ...
THERE'S A BETTER PLACE A'WAITING ... WHEN YOU GET YOUR REWARD.

VERSE THREE :

DON'T GO WHERE THERE'S TROUBLE ... OR DRINKING OF ALCOHOL ...
JUST BE PREPARED TO GO ... WHEN THE DEATH ANGEL CALLS.
DON'T EVER CHEAT LIE OR STEAL ... OR SPEAK VULGAR OF ANYONE ...
YOU WILL LEAVE A GOOD MEMORY ... WHEN YOUR LIFE ON EARTH IS DONE.

CHORUS :

    WHEN YOUR LIFE ON EARTH IS DONE ... AND LIFE SHALL BE
    NO MORE ...

AND YOU'RE READY TO DEPART ... OVER TO THE OTHER SHORE.

    YOU'LL SEE A LOT OF FRIENDS ... THAT HAS GONE ON BEFORE ...

THERE'S A BETTER PLACE A'WAITING ... WHEN YOU RECIEVE YOUR
REWARD.

WHERE HAS ALL THE LAUGHTER GONE

VERSE ONE:

WE WOULD ALWAYS LAUGH ... AROUND THE OLD HOME ...
BUT IT SEEMED ALL THE LAUGHTER ... LEFT AS TIME WENT ON.
WHEN EACH OF US MOVED OUT ... AS WE BECAME GROWN ...
NOW WE JUST ASK ... WHERE HAS ALL THE LAUGHTER GONE.

VERSE TWO:

NONE OF US KNEW WHAT ... OUR PARENTS WENT THROUGH ...
TAKING CARE OF EVERYTHING ... AND TRYING TO RAISE US TOO.
WE THOUGHT LIFE WAS EASY ... WE LAUGHED ALL DAY LONG ...
BUT NOW WE WONDER WHERE ... HAS ALL THE LAUGHTER GONE.

VERSE THREE:

WE HAD TO TAKE RESPONSIBILTY ... FOR OUR OWN MISTAKES ...
WE COULD'NT JUST LET IT GO ... WHEN OUR LIVES WAS AT STAKE.
WE COULD'NT GO THRU LIFE ... BEGGING LIKE A DOG FOR A
BONE...
BUT WE CAN STILL ASK WHERE ... HAS ALL THE LAUGHTER GONE.

VERSE FOUR:

AND NOW THE ECONOMY ... IS NOT LIKE IT USED TO BE ...
WHEN WE WOULD GO FOR A SUNDAY RIDE ... OUT IN THE COUNTRY.
OUR PAYCHECKS WAS'NT MUCH ... BUT GAS WAS'NT SO HIGH ...
WHERE HAS ALL THE LAUGHTER GONE ... FROM DAYS GONE BY.

CHORUS:

NOW THINGS ARE NOT AS FUNNY ... AS THEY WERE BACK
THEN ...
AND IT'S HARD TO LAUGH ... WHEN YOU CAN'T EVEN GRIN.
BUT LIFE IS WHAT YOU MAKE OF IT ... SO KEEP MOVING ON ...
AND SMILE AND DON'T ASK ... WHERE HAS ALL THE LAUGHTER
GONE.

WHERE THE TASTE TELLS THE TALE

VERSE ONE:
  THIS IS WHERE ... THE TASTE TELLS THE TALE ...
THAT WHAT YOU EAT ... IS HOW YOU FEEL.
  YOU WILL LEAVE HAPPY ... THERE IS NO DOUBT ...
CAUSE THIS MESSAGE IS WHAT ... IT'S ALL ABOUT.

VERSE TWO:
  NOW THIS IS WHERE ... THE TASTE TELLS THE TALE ...
SO USE THE COUPONS ... THAT YOU GET IN THE MAIL.
  YOU CAN GO TO TOWN ... LOOKING AROUND ...
AND STILL NOT BE HAPPY... AT WHAT YOU HAVE FOUND.

VERSE THREE:
  WHEN YOU EAT HERE ...YOU'LL WANT TO SHOUT ...
THE MEALS ARE SO GOOD ... LIKE RIDING ON A CLOUD.
  THIS IS WHERE ... THE TASTE TELLS THE TALE ...
AND YOU WILL KNOW ... THAT YOUR MEAL WAS SWELL.

CHORUS:
  IF YOU WANT TO GO OUT ... AND HAVE A GOOD MEAL ...
COME ON BY ... YOU'LL FIND OUR SERVICE IS REAL.
  YOU WILL FIND OUT ... WE'RE NOT HERE JUST FOR THE SALE...
BECAUSE THIS IS WHERE ... THE TASTE TELLS THE TALE.

WHEREVER YOU GO

VERSE ONE:

     I WISH I WAS STILL ... AS YOUNG AS I USED TO BE ...
WHEN EVERYONE RESPECTED... AND LOOKED UP TO ME.
     BUT SOMEDAY YOU'LL FEEL ... DOWN AND LOW ...
WHEN THEY LOOK DOWN ON YOU ... WHEREVER YOU GO.

VERSE TWO:

     WHEN I WAS VERY YOUNG ... AND IN MY PRIME ...
I HAD A LOT OF ENERGY ... ALMOST ALL OF THE TIME.
     BUT NOW THAT I AM OLD ... I WALK REAL SLOW ...
TO KEEP FROM STUMBLING ... WHEREVER I GO.

VERSE THREE:

     NOW YOU CAN LAUGH ... AS MUCH AS YOU WANT TO ...
BUT YOU WON'T LAUGH ... WHEN IT HAPPENS TO YOU.
     SO GO AHEAD ... AND GET ON THE FRONT ROW ...
SOMEDAY THEY'LL LAUGH AT YOU ... WHEREVER YOU GO.

VERSE FOUR:

     JUST STOP AND THINK ... YOU SHOULD RESPECT THE OLD ...
SOMEDAY YOU'LL WALK IN THEIR SHOES ... SO WALK REAL SLOW.
     DON'T LAUGH AT THEM ... LIKE YOU DID SOME TIME AGO ...
JUST RESPECT YOUR ELDERS ... WHEREVER YOU GO.

CHORUS:

     I'VE LEARNED TO RESPECT ... THE YOUNG AND THE OLD ...
AND I KNOW THAT'S RIGHT ... CAUSE MY MOMMA TOLD ME SO.
     SO GO HAVE YOUR FUN ... LET THE GOOD TIMES ROLL ...
BUT SHOW SOME RESPECT ... WHEREVER YOU GO.

WHO DO YOU THINK I AM?

CHORUS:
>   WHO DO YOU THINK I AM ... YOU MAKE ME FEEL LIKE A
>   CLOWN ...

YOU SAY I SHOULD STAY HERE AT HOME ... WHILE YOU RUN AROUND.
>   WHO DO YOU ... THINK I AM?.

VERSE ONE:
>   I HAVE A LIFE TO LIVE ... JUST LIKE YOU ...

I WANT TO DO THE THINGS ... THAT I WANT TO.
>   YOU THINK I SHOULD STAY ... ALL CLOSED UP LIKE A CLAM ...

WHO DO YOU ... THINK I AM?.

VERSE TWO:
>   YOU HAVE NO FEELINGS ... FOR ME AT ALL ...

YOU CALL YOUR FRIENDS ... AND SAY LET'S HAVE GO A BALL.
>   THEN YOU LEAVE HOME ... WHEN THE SUN GOES DOWN ...

WHO DO YOU ... THINK I AM?.

CHORUS:
>   WHO DO YOU THINK I AM ... YOU MAKE ME FEEL LIKE A
>   CLOWN ...

YOU SAY I SHOULD STAY HERE AT HOME ... WHILE YOU RUN AROUND.
>   WHO DO YOU ... THINK I AM?.

VERSE THREE:
>   IF I HAD ANY SENSE ... I WOULD DROP YOU ...

BUT MY HEART SAYS NO ... THAT AIN'T THE THING TO DO.
>   WAIT A LITTLE LONGER ... MAYBE SHE'LL COME AROUND ...

BUT WHO DO YOU ... THINK I AM?.

VERSE FOUR:
>   I'VE WAITED TOO LONG ... FOR YOU TO COME HOME ...

WHEN YOU COME IN THIS TIME ... YOU'RE FIND ME GONE.
>   I CAN'T TAKE IT ANYMORE ... I AIN'T HANGING AROUND ...

WHO DO YOU THINK ... I AM?.

WHY! OH WHY?

VERSE ONE:

 WHY! OH WHY?... DID THIS HAVE TO HAPPEN TO ME ...
WHY! OH WHY? ... COULD'NT I OPEN MY EYES AND SEE.
 I WAS HEADED THE WRONG WAY ... ON A ONE WAY STREET...
BUT WHY! OH WHY? ... DID IT HAVE TO HAPPEN TO ME?

VERSE TWO:

 I THOUGHT I WAS SMARTER ... THAN THE OTHER GUYS ...
I SAID I CAN HANDLE IT ... WHEN YOU JUST PASSED ME BY.
 I SAID THERE'S NO ROOM ... IN MY LIFE FOR JEALOUSY ...
WHY! OH WHY?... DID THIS HAVE TO HAPPEN TO ME.

VERSE THREE:

 WHEN I SAW YOU A' WALKING ... A' COMING MY WAY ...
SOMETHING HAPPENED TO MY HEART ... IT EXPLODED THAT DAY.
 IT WILL NEVER BE THE SAME ... AS IT USED TO BE ...
WHY! OH WHY? ... DID IT HAVE TO HAPPEN TO ME.

VERSE FOUR:

 I USED TO BE SO HAPPY ... SO FULL AND SO FREE ...
UNTIL YOU WALKED BY ... AND INTRODUCED ME TO MISERY.
 I WISH THINGS WERE STILL ... LIKE THEY USED TO BE ...
WHY! OH WHY?... DID THIS HAVE TO HAPPEN TO ME.

CHORUS:

 I KNOW YOU ARE MARRIED ... OUR LOVE COULD NEVER BE ...
BUT LET'S STEAL AWAY ... AND MAKE A NEW MEMORY.
 NO ONE WILL EVER KNOW ... WE'LL PRETEND IT'S FANTASY ...
OH WHY! OH WHY?... DID THIS HAVE TO HAPPEN TO ME.

WHY ASK WHY

VERSE ONE:
  WHY DOES THE BLUE SKIES ... SOMETIMES TURN GRAY ...
AND WHY DOES IT HAVE TO BECOME ... A RAINY DAY.
  WHY DOES BRIGHT WHITE CLOUDS... HAVE TO TURN DARK ...
AND THEN WHY DOES THE RAIN ... HAVE TO START.

VERSE TWO:
  WHY IS THE WORLD ROUND ... AND WE WALK ON THE GROUND...
WHY DON'T WE FALL OFF... AS THE WORLD GOES AROUND.
  WHY DOES OUR BODIES WEAR OUT ... LIKE AUTOMOBILES DO...
AND WHY DOES SO MANY DIE ... WHEN THEY CATCH THE FLU.

VERSE THREE:
  WHY DOES A REAL GOOD DAY ... ALWAYS HAVE TO END ...
AND THEN WHY DOES A BAD DAY ... EVER HAVE TO BEGIN.
  WHY DOES AN AVERAGE PERSON ... HAVE TO BE POOR ...
AND WHY DOES THE WEALTHY ... ALWAYS WANT MORE.

VERSE FOUR:
  WHY DOES A DOG BARK ... FOR NO REASON AT ALL ...
AND WHY DO WE TEACH THEM ... TO CHASE AFTER A BALL.
  WHY DO WE GET SICK ... AND HAVE TO LAY DOWN ...
WHY DID WE GO OUT ... AND HAVE A NIGHT ON THE TOWN.

VERSE FIVE:
  WHY DO WE LIVE IN A WORLD ... OF JUST HURT AND PAIN ...
WHY DOES INTELLIGENT PEOPLE ... SOMETIMES GO INSANE.
  WHY DO WE DREAD DEATH ...WHEN WE KNOW WE HAVE TO
  DIE ...
THERE IS A MILLION WHY'S ... AND YET YOU ASK WHY ASK WHY.

WHY CAN'T THEY SEE

CHORUS:
>IF IT WAS'NT FOR ... WHO I AM ...
I WOULD'NT BE ... WHERE I AM.
>I COULD'NT BE ... SOMEONE ELSE ...
AND STILL BE ... MY OWNSELF.

VERSE ONE:
>THINGS DON'T GO ... THE WAY I PLAN ...
BUT I HAVE TO BE ... MY OWN MAN.
>NOW I DON'T BLAME ... SOMEONE ELSE ...
FOR THINGS I DO ... MY OWNSELF.

VERSE TWO:
>WHY CAN'T THEY SEE ... I'M JUST ME ...
AND I'M NOT ... WHO THEY WANT ME TO BE.
>I'M GONNA DO ... WHATEVER I WANT TO ...
AND LET THEM DO ... THE SAME THING TOO.

VERSE THREE:
>NOW EVEN THOUGH ... NO ONE WILL HELP...
I'M GLAD TO BE ... MY OWNSELF.
>SO TURN ME LOOSE ... AND LET ME BE ...
SO I CAN RUN ... WILD AND FREE.
>..... SING CHORUS AGAIN ......

WHY DOES IT ALWAYS

VERSE ONE:

     WHY DOES IT ALWAYS ... HAVE TO HAPPEN TO ME ...
WHY CAN'T IT STOP ... AND JUST LET ME BE.
     WHY DOES BAD LUCK ... CAUSE SO MUCH MISERY ...
WHY DOES IT ALWAYS ... HAVE TO HAPPEN TO ME.

VERSE TWO:

     I DID'NT ASK FOR THINGS ... TO HAPPEN TO ME ...
BUT IT DID'NT COST NOTHING ... CAUSE BAD LUCK IS FREE.
     I THINK I DESERVE ... A LITTLE BIT OF APOLOGY ...
WHY DOES IT ALWAYS ... HAVE TO HAPPEN TO ME.

CHORUS:

     SOMETIMES I WISH ... THAT I WAS LIVING IN FANTASY ...
AND I COULD GET AWAY ... FROM ALL THIS STUPIDITY.
     IT SEEMS LIKE BAD TIMES ... JUST COMES NATUALY ...
BUT WHY DOES IT ALWAYS ... HAVE TO HAPPEN TO ME.

VERSE THREE:

     EVERYTHING I DO ... SEEMS TO BRING ON JUST AGONY ...
AND I'M NOT ASKING ... FOR YOUR SYMPHOTHY ...
     I SURE DON'T GO OUT ... AND GET THEM WILLINGLY ...
SO WHY DOES IT ALWAYS ... HAVE TO HAPPEN TO ME.

CHORUS:

     SOMETIMES I WISH ... THAT I WAS LIVING IN FANTASY ...
AND I COULD GET AWAY ... FROM ALL THIS STUPIDITY.
     IT SEEMS LIKE BAD TIMES ... JUST COMES NATUALY ...
BUT WHY DOES IT ALWAYS ... HAVE TO HAPPEN TO ME.

WICKED WOMAN

CHORUS:

THAT WICKED WOMAN TOOK MY HEART ... AND TORE IT ALL APART ...
I TRIED TO PLAY HER SILLY GAME ... BUT I DID'NT PLAY IT TOO SMART.
I DID EVERYTHING I COULD ... TO HELP HER TO END HER MISERY ...
BUT SHE TOOK IT ALL FOR GRANTED ... AND WALKED ALL OVER ME.

VERSE ONE:

I MET HER ON THE STREET ... AND SHE LOOKED SO SWEET ...
WHEN I HEARD HER TALK ... MY HEART FELL AT HER FEET.
SHE HAD JUST GOT IN TOWN ... AND DID'NT HAVE NO WHERE TO GO ...
SHE WAS A WICKED WOMAN ... BUT AT FIRST I DID'NT KNOW.

VERSE TWO:

I ASKED HER TO COME WITH ME ... I INVITED HER TO MY HOME ...
BUT WHEN WE GOT THERE ... I WISHED I HAD CAME ALONE.
SHE FLOPPED DOWN ON MY SOFA ... WITH A CIGARET IN HER HAND ...
AND I KNEW RIGHT AWAY ... THAT WICKED WOMAN HAD A PLAN.

CHORUS:

THAT WICKED WOMAN TOOK MY HEART ... AND TORE IT ALL APART ...
I TRIED TO PLAY HER SILLY GAME ... BUT I DID'NT PLAY IT TOO SMART.
I DID EVERYTHING I COULD ... TO HELP HER TO END HER MISERY ...
BUT SHE TOOK IT ALL FOR GRANTED ... AND WALKED ALL OVER ME.

VERSE THREE:

I ASK HER WHERE SHE WANTED TO GO ... AND SHE SAID NO WHERE ...

I WANT TO STAY WITH YOU ... THAT IS IF YOU DON'T CARE.
    I SAID YOU CAN'T DO THAT ... I'M EXPECTIG SOME FRIENDS ...
AND I NEVER WANTED TO SEE ... THAT WICKED WOMAN AGAIN.

CHORUS:
    THAT WICKED WOMAN TOOK MY HEART ... AND TORE IT ALL
    APART ...
I TRIED TO PLAY HER SILLY GAME ... BUT I DID'NT PLAY IT TOO
SMART.
    I DID EVERYTHING I COULD ... TO HELP HER TO END HER
    MISERY ...
BUT SHE TOOK IT ALL FOR GRANTED ... AND WALKED ALL OVER ME.

WITHOUT GOD

VERSE ONE:

WITHOUT GOD ... IT WOULD BE A DIFFERENT ME ...
AND I WOULD BE THE SAME ... AS I USED TO BE.

WITHOUT GOD ... I WOULD HARDLY EVER SMILE ...
UNTIL ONE DAY ... I WALKED DOWN THE AISLE.

VERSE TWO:

WITHOUT GOD ... I WOULD ALREADY BE DEAD ...
BUT HE GAVE ME ... A NEW LIFE INSTEAD.

WITHOUT GOD ... THERE WOULD BE NO DAY AND NIGHT ...
BUT HE SAID LET THERE BE LIGHT ... AND THERE WAS LIGHT.

VERSE THREE:

WITHOUT GOD ... THERE WOULD BE NO RIGHT OR WRONG ...
AND OUR HOPE FOR THE FUTURE ... WOULD ALL BE GONE.

WITHOUT GOD ... LIFE WOULD NEVER HAVE BEGIN ...
ANDTHERE WOULD BE NO ... BEGINNING OR END.

VERSE FOUR:

WITHOUT GOD ... ALL OUR HOPE WOULD BE GONE ...
AND THERE WOULD BE NO EXISTANCE ... FROM NOW ON.

WITHOUT GOD ... THERE WOULD BE NO PEAS IN THE POD ...
THERE WOULD BE NO MORE TOMORROWS ... WITHOUT GOD.

WORKIN' AND STILL HURTIN'

VERSE ONE:
> I'M SITTIN' HERE WONDERING ... WHAt's GONNA HAPPEN NEXT ...
I DID'NT DRAW ENOGH MONEY ... ON MY PAY CHECK.
> I WORK EVERY DAY ... BUT AT THE END OF THE WEEK ...
I STILL DON'T HAVE ENOUGH ... TO MAKE ENDS MEET.

VERSE TWO:
> SOMETIMES I OFTEN WONDER ... WHY I EVEN WORK ...
WHEN EVERYTHING I BUY ... HAS TO BE CHEAPER THAN DIRT .
> I TRY NOT TO COMPLAIN ... THERE'S OTHERS WORSE THAN ME ...
BUT SOMETIMES LIFE JUST AIN'T ... WHAT IT'S SUPPOSE TO BE.

CHORUS:
> I SHOP ALL THE TIME ... WHERE I CAN SAVE A PENNY ...
BUT WHEN I LOOK FOR MY MONEY ... I CAN'T FIND ANY.
> SO HOW CAN I SAVE ... WHAT I SURELY AIN'T GOT ...
WHILE MY WHOLE LIFE HAS BEEN ... JUST ONE BIG BLOT.

VERSE THREE:
> ANYTHING IS BETTER THAN NOTHING ... AND THAT'S WHAT
> I HAVE ...
AND IT MAKES ME FEEL AS POOR ... AS AN UNFED COW.
> BUT I'LL KEEP ON WORKIN' ... WORKIN' AND STILL HURTIN' ...
HOPING THAT SOMEDAY ... THAT I MIGHT HAVE SOMETHIN'.

VERSE FOUR:
> SO STOP YOUR COMPLAINING ... AND WORK A LITTLE HARDER ...
EVEN IF YOU HAVE TO CHANGE JOBS ... THAT WOULD BE A STARTER.
> NOW JUST BE THANKFUL ... YOU STILL HAVE YOUR HEALTH ...
BECAUSE THAT IS MORE IMPORTANT ... THAN ALL THE WEALTH.

CHORUS:
> I SHOP ALL THE TIME ... WHERE I CAN SAVE A PENNY ...
BUT WHEN I LOOK FOR MY MONEY ... I CAN'T FIND ANY.
> SO HOW CAN I SAVE ... WHAT I SURELY AIN'T GOT ...
WHILE MY WHOLE LIFE HAS BEEN ... JUST ONE BIG BLOT.

WORKIN' FOR NOTHIN'

VERSE ONE:

I'M SITTIN' HERE WONDERING ... WHAt's GONNA HAPPEN NEXT ...
I DID'NT DRAW ENOGH MONEY ... ON MY PAY CHECK.
I WORK EVERY DAY ... BUT AT THE END OF THE WEEK ...
I STILL DON'T HAVE ENOUGH ... TO MAKE ENDS MEET.

VERSE TWO:

SOMETIMES I OFTEN WONDER ... WHY I EVEN WORK ...
WHEN EVERYTHING I BUY ... HAS TO BE CHEAPER THAN DIRT .
I TRY NOT TO COMPLAIN ... THERE'S OTHERS WORSE THAN ME ...
BUT SOMETIMES LIFE JUST AIN'T ... WHAT IT'S SUPPOSE TO BE.

CHORUS:

I SHOP ALL THE TIME ... WHERE I CAN SAVE A PENNY ...
BUT WHEN I LOOK FOR MY MONEY ... I FIND I AIN'T GOT ANY.
SO HOW CAN I SAVE ... WHAT I SURE AIN'T GOT ...
WHEN ALL MY LIFE HAS EVER BEEN ... IS JUST ONE BIG BLOT.

VERSE THREE:

ANYTHING IS BETTER THAN NOTHING ... AND THAT'S WHAT I HAVE ...
AND IT MAKES ME FEEL AS POOR ... AS AN UNFED COW.
BUT I'LL KEEP ON WORKIN' ... WORKIN' FOR NOTHIN' ...
HOPING THAT SOMEDAY ... THAT I MIGHT HAVE SOMETHIN'.

VERSE FOUR:

SO STOP YOUR COMPLAINING ... AND WORK A LITTLE HARDER ...
EVEN IF YOU HAVE TO CHANGE JOBS ... THAT WOULD BE A STARTER.
NOW JUST BE THANKFUL ... YOU STILL HAVE YOUR HEALTH ...
BECAUSE THAT IS MORE IMPORTANT ... THAN ALL THE WEALTH.

CHORUS:
      I SHOP ALL THE TIME ... WHERE I CAN SAVE A PENNY ...
BUT WHEN I LOOK FOR MY MONEY ... I FIND I AIN'T GOT ANY.
      SO HOW CAN I SAVE ... WHAT I SURE AIN'T GOT ...
WHEN ALL MY LIFE HAS EVER BEEN ...IS JUST ONE BIG BLOT.

WORKIN' OVERTIME

CHORUS:

 WELL NOW WORKIN' OVERTIME ... IS GETTING OLD TO ME ...
IT TAKES AWAY MY FREEDOM ... AND I WANT TO BE FREE.
 IT'S GOOD TO HAVE A JOB ... BUT DON'T TAKE IT TOO FAR ...
BECAUSE TOO MUCH OVERTIME ... CAN DRIVE A MAN BAZZAR.

VERSE ONE:

 NOW I LOVE TO WORK ... BUT NOT WHEN IT HURTS ...
AND WORKIN' TOO MUCH OVERTIME ... CAN DRIVE A MAN BAZERK.
 JUST WORKING REGULAR HOURS ... IS GOOD ENOUGH ...
BECAUSE I DON'T NEED OVERTIME ... AND ALL OF THAT STUFF.

VERSE TWO:

 THE BOSS MAN MAY NOT LIKE IT ... BUT I'VE GOT TO GET AWAY ...
AND SAVE SOME OVERTIME ... FOR ANOTHER RAINY DAY.
 BECAUSE THIS WORKIN' OVERTIME ... I CAN'T TAKE ANYMORE ...
SO I'M HANGIN' IT UP ... AND WALKING OUT THE DOOR.

CHORUS:

 WELL NOW WORKIN' OVERTIME ... IS GETTING OLD TO ME ...
IT TAKES AWAY MY FREEDOM ... AND I WANT TO FREE.
 IT'S GOOD TO HAVE A JOB ... BUT DON'T TAKE IT TOO FAR ...
BECAUSE TOO MUCH OVERTIME ... CAN DRIVE A MAN BAZZAR.

VERSE THREE:

 NOW SOME PEOPLE NEEDS A JOB ... THEY CAN'T FIND ANY
 WORK ...
BUT WORKIN' OVERTIME ... IS LIKE A BIG BOULDER IN THE DIRT.
 IT'S TOO MUCH FOR ME ... AND IT'S A HEAVY OVERLOAD ...
SO I'M QUITTING THIS JOB ... AND I'M HITTING THE ROAD.

CHORUS:

 WELL NOW WORKIN' OVERTIME ... IS GETTING OLD TO ME ...
IT TAKES AWAY MY FREEDOM ... AND I WANT TO FREE.
 IT'S GOOD TO HAVE A JOB ... BUT DON'T TAKE IT TOO FAR ...
BECAUSE TOO MUCH OVERTIME ... CAN DRIVE A MAN BAZZAR.

WRITE ME A SONG

MANY TIMES I HAVE THOUGHT ... ABOUT WRITTING A SONG ...
BUT I DID'NT KNOW WHERE TO START ... SO I LEFT IT ALONG.
AND THEN ONE DAY ... THE WORDS CAME ALONG ...
AND I WROTE THEM DOWN ... IN THE WORDS TO THIS SONG.

VERSE TWO:
IT SAID OPEN UP YOUR MIND ... AND TELL ME WHAT YOU
THINK ...
IS IT GOOD OR BAD ... YOU CAN TELL ME ANYTHING.
IT CAN BE ABOUT LOVE ... OR JUST RIDING ON A TRAIN ...
YOU CAN TRUST ME ... SO TELL ME SOMETHING.

CHORUS:
WRITE ME A SONG ... THAT YOU CAN SING ...
WRITE ME A SONG ... ABOUT ANYTHING.
WRITE ME A SONG ... ABOUT THINGS THAT ARE GONE ...
WRITE ABOUT ANYTHING ... BUT JUST WRITE ME A SONG.

VERSE THREE:
MAYBE ABOUT RUNNING AROUND ... WITH SOMEONE ELSE'S
WIFE ...
OR ABOUT THE NIGHT ... YOU ALMOST GOT INTO A FIGHT.
WRITE ME A SONG ABOUT ... THINGS THAT ARE TO COME ...
OR SOME OF THE SILLY THINGS ... THAT YOU HAVE DONE.

VERSE FOUR:
WRITE ABOUT THE PARTY ... THE NIGHT YOU GOT DRUNK ...
AND YOU WENT TO SLEEP ... IN SOMEONE ELSE'S BUNK.
IT WAS'NT NO FRIEND ... AND HE GOT MAD WHEN HE CAME IN ...
SO WRITE ME A SONG ... ABOUT WHAT HAPPENED THEN.

CHORUS:
WRITE ME A SONG ... THAT YOU CAN SING ...
WRITE ME A SONG ... ABOUT ANYTHING.
WRITE ME A SONG ... ABOUT THINGS THAT ARE GONE ...
WRITE ABOUT ANYTHING ... BUT JUST WRITE ME A SONG.

YOU KNOW I DO

CHORUS:
> I LOVE YOU ... YOU KNOW I DO ...
WHY MUST YOU DO ... THE THINGS YOU DO?
> THERE IS NO OTHER ... ONE BUT YOU ...
I SAID I LOVE YOU ... YOU KNOW I DO.

VERSE ONE:
> GONE ARE THE TIMES ... THAT WE ONCE KNEW ...
THE GOOD AND THE BAD ... THAT WE'VE BEEN THRU.
> MY LOVE NEVER DIED ... I STILL THINK OF YOU ...
AND I STILL LOVE YOU ... YOU KNOW I DO.

CHORUS:
> I LOVE YOU ... YOU KNOW I DO ...
WHY MUST YOU DO ... THE THINGS YOU DO?
> THERE IS NO OTHER ... ONE BUT YOU ...
I SAID I LOVE YOU ... YOU KNOW I DO.
\
VERSE TWO;
> I LOVE YOU... PLEASE LOVE ME TOO ...
YOU'LL NEVER KNOW ... WHAT I'VE BEEN THRU.
> THINGS HAVE CHANGED ... BUT I'VE BEEN TRUE ...
BECAUSE I LOVE YOU ... YOU KNOW I DO.

CHORUS:
> I LOVE YOU ... YOU KNOW I DO ...
WHY MUST YOU DO ... THE THINGS YOU DO?
> THERE IS NO OTHER ... ONE BUT YOU ...
I SAID I LOVE YOU ... YOU KNOW I DO.

YOU NEVER KNOW

VERSE ONE:

NOW YOU NEVER KNOW ... WHAT TOMORROW HOLDS ...
SOMEDAYS IT'S HOT ... AND SOMEDAYS IT'S COLD.
SOMETIMES YOU PLAN ... WHERE YOU WANT TO GO ...
BUT YOU MAY GET RAINED OUT ... YOU NEVER KNOW.

VERSE TWO:

SOMEDAYS MAY BRING HAPPINESS ... OR MAYBE SORROW ...
JUST LIVE FOR TODAY ... DON'T WORRY ABOUT TOMORROW.
YOU MAY THINK YOU'RE SMART ... BUT TAKE IT SLOW ...
ANYTHING CAN HAPPEN ... YOU NEVER KNOW.

VERSE THREE:

THEY MIGHT CALL FOR RAIN ... BUT IT COULD SNOW ...
SO BE PREPARED FOR THE WEATHER ... YOU NEVER KNOW.
WHAT WOULD HAPPEN ... IF YOU'RE NOT ABLE TO GO ...
UNTIL IT REALLY HAPPENS ... YOU NEVER KNOW.

VERSE FOUR:

LET'S JUST SAY THAT ... YOU CARRY YOUR PLANS THRU ...
THEN SOMETHING BAD HAPPENS ... WHAT WOULD YOU DO.
COULD YOU CARRY THE BURDEN ... WHEN YOU FEEL LOW ...
UNTIL IT ACTUALLY HAPPENS ... YOU NEVER KNOW.

YOU THINK YOU HAVE TROUBLES

VERSE ONE:

    IF YOU THINK YOU HAVE TROUBLES ... LISTEN TO MINE ...
I DON'T COUNT MY TROUBLES ... I'M HAPPY TO BE ALIVE.
    I LOST ALL MY TEETH ... THEY MADE ME A FALSE SET ...
THEN I LOST ALL MY HAIR ... I WEAR A HAT ON MY HEAD.

VERSE TWO:

    I'VE HAD BROKEN BONES ... MY BODY IS FULL OF PINS ...
AND NOBODY KNOWS ... THE TERRIBLE SHAPE I'M IN.
    I'VE GOT A ARTIFICIAL HIP ... AND TWO FLAT FEET ...
AND A HEART THAT SOMETIMES ... SKIPS A BEAT.

CHORUS:

    I'LL PUT MY FALSE TEETH IN ... AND MY NEW HAT ON ...
BECAUSE TONIGHT ... I DON'T INTEND TO STAY HOME.
    I'LL BE LIKE A DOG ... WITH A BRAND NEW BONE ...
BUT FIRST I'VE GOT TO PUT ... MY NEW BIFOCALS ON.

VERSE THREE:

    I HAVE A HEARING AID ... AND ONE GLASS EYE ...
AND I SHED ARTIFICIAL TEARS ... WHEN I CRY.
    IF IT WERE'NT FOR SURGEONS ... I WOULD BE WITHOUT ...
AND PEOPLE WONDERS WHY ... I STAY IN THE HOUSE.

CHORUS:

    I'LL PUT MY FALSE TEETH IN ... AND MY NEW WIG ON ...
BECAUSE TONIGHT ... I DON'T INTEND TO STAY HOME.
    I'LL BE LIKE A DOG ... WITH A BRAND NEW BONE ...
BUT FIRST I'VE GOT TO PUT ... MY NEW BIFOCALS ON.

YOUR WIFE YOUR DOG OR FRIEND

VERSE ONE:

    I NEVER TELL MY WIFE ... SHE KNOWS IT JUST THE SAME ...
SHE CAN TELL BY THE WAY ... THAT I WHISPER HER NAME.
    I DON'T HUG AND KISS HER ... THE WAY I USED TO DO ...
BUT SHE KNOWS THE LOVE I HAVE ... WILL ALWAYS BE TRUE.

VERSE TWO:

    I'M NOT A SPRING ROOSTER ... BUT I CAN CROW A TIME OR TWO ...
AND SHE KNOWS THAT I LOVE HER ... BY THE SIMPLE THINGS I DO.
    I'M NOT A GREAT LOVER ... BUT I LOVE HER JUST THE SAME ...
SHE PUTS FIRE IN MY HEART ... WITH A RED HOT BURNING FLAME.

VERSE THREE:

    MY DOGS NAME IS RED ... SHE WENT WHERE EVER I LED ...
I KEPT HER PLENTY OF WATER ... AND I ALWAYS KEPT HER FED.
    ANYTIME THAT I CALLED HER ... SHE ALWAYS KNEW HER NAME ...
I DID'NT PET HER TOO MUCH ... BUT I LOVED HER JUST THE SAME.

VERSE FOUR:

    SHE WAS MORE THAN JUST A DOG ... SHE WAS MY BEST FRIEND.
AND IF I HAD IT ALL TO DO OVER ... I WOULD DO IT ALL AGAIN.
    SHE KNOWS THAT I LOVE HER ... BY THE TONE OF MY VOICE ...
SHE WOULD ALWAYS WAG HER TAIL ... AS SHE WOULD REJOICE.

CHORUS:

    NOW LOVE IS LOVE BUT EVERYONE ... DON'T LOVE THE SAME ...
LOVE IS WHEN YOUR HEART ... CAN ALWAYS SHARE THE PAIN.
    WHETHER IT'S LOVE FOR YOUR WIFE ... YOUR DOG OR A
FRIEND ...
LOVE CAN CONQUER ALL ... FROM THE BEGINNING TO THE END.